DATE DUE

Using Interne   *ach Critical*
Thinking Skill

Using Internet Primary Sources to Teach Critical Thinking Skills in World Literature

Roxanne M. Kent-Drury, Ph.D.

Libraries Unlimited Professional Guides in School Librarianship

Harriet Selverstone, Series Adviser

LIBRARIES
UNLIMITED
A Member of the Greenwood Publishing Group

Westport, Connecticut ● London

Library of Congress Cataloging-in-Publication Data

Kent-Drury, Roxanne M.
  Using internet primary sources to teach critical thinking skills in world literature / by Roxanne
M. Kent-Drury.
    p. cm. – (Libraries Unlimited professional guides in school librarianship, ISSN 1074-150X)
  Includes bibliographical references and index.
  ISBN 0-313-32009-8 (pbk. : alk. paper)
  1. Literature—Computer network resources. I. Title. II. Series.
PN43.7.K46 2005
025.06'8—dc22   2004063834

British Library Cataloguing in Publication Data is available.

Library of Congress Catalog Card Number: 2004063834
ISBN: 0-313-32009-8
ISSN: 1074-150X

First published in 2005

Libraries Unlimited, 88 Post Road West, Westport, CT 06881
A Member of the Greenwood Publishing Group, Inc.
www.lu.com

Printed in the United States of America

The paper used in this book complies with the
Permanent Paper Standard issued by the National
Information Standards Organization (Z39.48–1984).

10   9   8   7   6   5   4   3   2   1

For my children, Kathryn, Joey, and Jamie Drury

Contents

Acknowledgments

A book of this breadth would not have been possible were it not for the generosity of my colleagues in the Literature & Language Department of Northern Kentucky University. In particular, I would like to thank Barbara Klaw, Katherine Kurk, Hilary Landwehr, Chen-Liang Sheng, Tamara O'Callaghan, and Lydia Coyle for their assistance in areas specific to their academic disciplines.

I would also like to thank my student, Michelle Baxter, who spent a summer helping me check and recheck ephemeral URLs and links on the Internet.

The Faculty Senate and the College of Arts & Sciences of Northern Kentucky University provided critical support for this project through the Summer Research Fellowship program and by granting reassigned time from teaching.

I am also grateful to the Greenwood and Libraries Unlimited editors, especially Sharon Coatney and Sharon DeJohn, whose careful reading and patience throughout this process resulted in a much better book.

Finally, I would like to thank my husband, Joe Drury, for his understanding, patience, and love, without which I could not have accomplished all I have.

CHAPTER 1

Introduction

Purpose

Intended Audience

This volume of the Greenwood Publishing Group's series, Using Internet Primary Sources to Teach Critical Thinking Skills, focuses on providing literature educators, library media specialists, and students with access to some of the best Internet resources available on the topic of world literature. Although this book does not include most Web sites that focus on British and American materials, some sites on these topics of importance to the general study of world literature have been included.

Defining Primary Sources

Primary sources are essentially the source materials that researchers in a particular field study when they generate scholarship. When scholars write about primary sources, reporting their interpretations and findings, the texts they publish are referred to as *secondary sources*. Different fields define *primary sources* in different ways. In historical studies, for instance, journals, diaries, correspondence, legal records, and parish registers would all be considered *primary sources*. In literary studies, *primary sources* have traditionally included creative poetic, dramatic, and fictional works, whereas the critical interpretations of such primary sources have been construed as *secondary sources*. Today, however, the line between primary and secondary sources is not always clear. Contemporary literary scholars also use literary and rhetorical analysis to study texts formerly viewed as based upon "facts," such as diaries, journals, histories, autobiographical works, and scientific reports. In some contexts of literary studies, then, a work may be viewed as a primary source, whereas in others it may be viewed as a secondary source. In addition, in an increasingly interdisciplinary academic environment, researchers today cross traditional boundaries, borrowing one another's methodologies and source materials.

Because of this blurring of disciplinary concerns, tools, and methodologies, in this volume the term *primary sources* has been construed broadly. Consequently, although many of the sites described in this book will include or be linked to primary sources as defined in the traditional literary sense (i.e., e-texts of plays, poems, novels, etc), most of the sites also include extensive materials that provide cultural context, background, and, in some cases, critical theory to permit readers the fullest possible set of resources.

Defining Critical Thinking

One purpose of this book is to provide resources that will assist educators in their goal of helping their students to develop critical thinking skills. Critical thinking, as defined by the *Foundation for Critical Thinking,* is the intellectually disciplined process of actively and skillfully conceptualizing, applying, analyzing, synthesizing, and/or evaluating information gathered from, or generated by, observation, experience, reflection, reasoning, or communication, as a guide to belief and action. (http://www.criticalthinking.org/University/univclass/Defining.html)

Educators who are dedicated to developing their students' ability to think critically generally share the conviction that students' success as learners, as public and private citizens, and as professionals depends on their ability to gather information, assess it critically, and apply it appropriately to new situations, as opposed to memorizing and regurgitating learned facts.

The ability to perform critical analysis in literary studies is multifaceted and complex. At one level, students must learn to recognize formal textual elements, such as rhetorical devices used at the word, sentence, and whole-text levels, as well as formal characteristics that define (or fail to define) a work as belonging to a particular genre. At another level, students must learn to assess the social occasion that produces a literary work by considering the communication that passes from writer to reader through a publisher, or, in the case of drama, from writer to audience via the director, the set and costume designers, and the actors. At yet another level, students must learn, through studies of influence, history, and contemporary events, identities, and actions, to assess the cultural and historical contexts that gave rise to a particular literary work. Finally, students must learn to identify to what extent they and their own beliefs influence their interpretations of a given text, as well as to position those interpretations within a range of critical categories of meta-commentary generally referred to as schools of literary criticism.

Developing such a complex understanding of literature, however, requires resources from which to gather information through research. To some educators who have received one too many papers based on poor information gleaned from Internet resources, however, the term Internet research is an oxymoron. One frequently employed solution is simply to ban or limit the use of Internet resources for school assignments. To adopt this solution, however, is to lose two opportunities. First, the body of reliable research material available on the Web is expanding too rapidly not to take advantage of good information. Second, students are fascinated by Internet technology and increasingly turn to the Internet first to locate information. Although it remains important to develop student research skills to encourage their use of the physical (and increasingly electronic) resources of the library, teaching students to evaluate the other materials that are freely available on the Internet can also encourage them to think critically about all research materials. Chapter 2 provides basic resources intended to teach students how to separate good research materials from poor ones. In addition, Chapter 3 provides access to online materials that address various aspects of traditional and contemporary cultural and critical literary analysis. The remainder of the chapters in this book address specific cultural materials and literary periods, genres, movements, and works, divided geographically and chronologically.

Site Selection Criteria

In keeping with contemporary perspectives on literary scholarship, scholars continually redefine the materials believed important for study, and any attempt to define a new canon is met with skepticism. Consequently, a book such as this should aim to be as inclusive and far reaching as possible, attempting to cover all world literatures, eras, and genres equally. Accordingly, this book was begun with an ambitious and inclusive list of topics, genres, works, and authors. Because only some of the potential topics are actually represented on the Web, however, this book necessarily reflects the Internet's fine coverage in some areas and inadequate or nonexistent coverage in others.

One issue is the nature of the Internet itself. First of all, unlike the world of book publishing, the Internet is in its infancy. More often than not, an outstanding site results, not from institutional backing, market research, government studies, or vetted research, but rather from one person's passion for a topic, willingness to spend time (usually without pay) to bring it to the public, and coincidental knowledge of and interest in Web technologies. Many outstanding Web sites are the product of scholarly or pedagogical efforts at universities, but others result from strong personal interest by individuals who are not specialists in literary fields. Not all are unbiased, accurate, and well-designed, and because Web sites are ephemeral and interconnected, unlike library books, the site is rare that does not have at least some broken links. As any teacher knows, the Internet is immense, its resources are not refereed and are of variable quality, and its materials are not indexed, except by search engines and online directories whose agendas vary widely (see Chapter 2 for sites that track search engines and their search criteria).

Other challenges are involved in writing a book on such an immense topic—most of the literature of the world as recorded through most of human history. An English-speaking audience is assumed for this book. Yet many of the best Web resources for teaching and studying non-English literatures are not posted in English, and these, unfortunately, cannot be included in this book.

In addition, despite its designation as the "World Wide Web," the Internet is still largely a Western phenomenon. Many world literatures are underrepresented on the Internet because the works were written in places without state-of-the-art technological infrastructures and equipment to support Web technologies. Consequently, readers will find many gaps in this book, and the current list of sites will appear skewed toward literatures of the technologically developed world, whereas African, Latin American, and Near Eastern literatures will appear underrepresented. This should not be construed as reflecting an editorial choice or as meaning that a particular literature or author was considered unimportant, but rather that other authors or literatures were better represented on the Web in English.

Readers will also find this book skewed toward earlier literatures, with less coverage of contemporary authors and works. The reasons for this are many. English-speaking scholars of the ancient, classical, and medieval West, in particular, have taken to Web technologies and have created outstanding examples that scholars in other fields might follow. In addition, in this book, freely available resources were preferred over resources that require a fee, and publishing many twentieth-century texts and materials on the Web in a freely accessible format is complicated by copyright issues that vary internationally despite treaties. Internet copyright law is a relatively new field that is in flux, and many Internet publishers of free resources are unwilling to make available materials that are not well beyond copyright protection (see http://eldred.cc for the documents surrounding an important recent case). Such cases make it virtually impossible for materials published after 1925 to appear on the Internet or even in the public domain.

Given these constraints, this book attempts to meet the following goals:

1. To describe some of the ways in which students can acquire critical thinking skills through the study and analysis of literary texts;

2. To identify sites on the Internet that offer major world literary resources, excluding most British and American literature;

3. To identify a tentative set of geographical demarcations that would be recognizable to and usable by most scholars, teachers, and librarians in the field of world and comparative literary studies, and to describe within those categories the major Internet resources available;

4. To construct within each geographical demarcation a comprehensive list of links to as many available, reliable resources for the study of world literary works as possible; and

5. To facilitate alternative approaches to using the available works to teach critical thinking skills by including or providing links to exercises, potential assignments, and additional resources.

The resulting Web site resources were selected, not based upon a predetermined canon of literature, but taking into account several constraints imposed by the nature of the Internet itself. Not all Web sites addressing world literature are reliable as primary sources of information. Unlike traditional publishing, the Internet is in its infancy and not subject to the same standards of review. Consequently, available Internet resources rely for their existence upon the interests of a diverse and dispersed population of Web designers with variable expertise in the field of literary studies.

In addition, Internet sites can be ephemeral, their addresses (uniform reference locators, or URLs) can change without warning, and in the presently volatile e-commerce sector many Internet service providers (ISPs) and users enter and leave the Internet or change their terms of use frequently. Consequently, the following measures were taken to ensure a list of sites that are as stable as possible:

1. Whenever possible, the sites selected were stable over a long period of time and resided on established Internet providers.

2. Stable educational sites were preferred to pages maintained by individual users.

3. When a site maintained by an individual user is included, the stability and reliability of the site were assessed by determining the nature of the user's credentials and affiliation with the Internet service provider housing the site. (For instance, sites maintained by professorial faculty and staff with permanent connections to a university would be considered more stable than sites maintained by graduate students with transitory relationships to the university.)

4. Frequently, the individual maintaining a site was contacted to determine the likelihood that a site would remain stable, as well as to assess his or her credentials.

Another issue encountered in selecting the sites was the need to locate reliable sites and works published in English translation. Availability of materials in translation was constrained by the following concerns:

1. Whether the individual publishing the materials possessed expertise in languages other than English, had adequate knowledge of the texts and the field, and had access and expertise to make good use of Web technologies;

2. Whether an interested Web site designer had sufficient understanding of and interest in good editing practices; and

3. For contemporary authors of literary works, whether they were interested in having their works made available on the Web and in translation. For some modern authors, translation of their work into English defeats its value as an expression of cultural or nationalistic values. For others, publishing on the Web would violate copyright agreements with publishers or would negate the potential for income from royalties. Consequently, many contemporary authors remain unrepresented on the Internet except through links to booksellers.

Where materials were available on the Internet, each site had to be evaluated to ensure its usefulness. Because no individual possesses all of the linguistic skills necessary to evaluate materials relating to all world languages, several criteria were used to evaluate the included sites:

1. Where possible, selected sites feature materials that were originally published in translation by reputable, refereed presses in book or journal article form.

2. Sites maintained by translators, scholars, or institutions with established reputations were preferred.

3. Where attribution was sketchy or a translator's qualifications were not explicit, I occasionally relied on the judgment and advice of several of my colleagues in the Literature and Language Department at Northern Kentucky University. I am especially grateful to Dr. Tamara O'Callaghan, Dr. Hilary Landwehr, and Dr. Katherine Kurk for their generosity.

A final issue was the need for a book adaptable enough to fit the range of approaches adopted by teachers of literature today. Unlike many other fields, literature is taught at the secondary and undergraduate levels from a number of interdisciplinary perspectives, depending on whether a teacher wishes to connect a work to its historical, cultural, national, movement- or genre-specific, sociopolitical, ethnic, or gendered contexts. Sites were selected to provide resources applicable to as many approaches as possible.

Organization

This chapter has provided an overview section that describes the critical thinking skills valued in higher education by defining the term and then explaining how literary analysis and Internet research can both make use of and improve the critical thinking skills of students. Chapters 2 through 10 identify and analyze a number of Web sites that include primary literary, historical, and cultural resources for the study of world literature authors and texts. Chapter 2 addresses how to find quality on the Internet, whereas Chapter 3 describes tools used in literary analysis.

Assuming that most teachers and librarians will seek ideas for lesson units and then information on specific authors and texts, Chapters 4 and 5 address broad categories that cross geographical and historical boundaries. Chapter 4 covers major primary sources of interest to teachers and librarians in all areas of literary study. These resources include significant, major Internet resources for the study of literature that does not fall into a particular geopolitically or culturally coherent region. Chapter 5 discusses a number of sites that address the topics of religion and folklore, religion as a topic that underlies much of world literature, and folklore as an increasingly important topic in K–12 classrooms. Each subsequent chapter addresses a particular geographical region or literary period.

Chapters 6 through 10 cover specific literary periods and places and in general progress from general to specific within widely recognized geographical demarcations, including the ancient world, classical Greece and Rome, Western Europe, the Near East (sometimes called the *Middle East*), South Asia (including the Indian subcontinent), Africa, Asia (including China and Japan), and Latin America. Chapter 6 provides resources for the study of the ancient world. Chapter 7 covers the literature of classical Greece and Rome. Chapter 8 addresses Western European literature before print, whereas Chapter 9 addresses Western European literature from the early modern period forward to the end of the nineteenth century. Chapter 10 provides resources for the study of the literatures of Africa, Latin America, and Asia.

Sections within each chapter include major Internet resources associated with particular regions and periods of literary study and resources for the study of key individual genres, works, and authors, where these are available. The description of each key Internet resource includes at least the following:

1. The name of the site,

2. Its Internet address (URL),

3. A description and assessment of what the site provides,

4. An explanation of how to navigate the site,

5. Possible assignments/exercises that can be used with the site or references to online lesson plans and teaching materials, and

6. URLs of related sites that provide additional opportunities to explore the same topic.

Legend

Within entries, the following conventions were followed to make the book as usable as possible:

1. Formal names of Web sites, book titles, and titles of long works are italicized.

2. Titles of articles, titles of shorter works, and informal categories appear in quotation marks.

3. Formal names of distinct Web pages within a Web site appear in boldface type.

4. Formally named links appear in boldface, italic type.

5. When given, dates are standardized as BCE and CE (i.e., before the common era and of the common era) in keeping with the most common usage among historians today.

CHAPTER 2

Locating and Evaluating Internet Resources

Information Literacy Education

Although not exhaustive, the entries in this chapter provide a few Web sites that can be used as a starting point for teachers and library media specialists interested in developing materials to promote Internet literacy, as well as for students seeking guidelines for how to choose excellent information on the Internet.

CORE: Comprehensive Online Research Education
http://core.lib.purdue.edu/

Site Summary. This Web site provides an outstanding interactive tutorial created by the library at Purdue University to meet the information literacy needs of its student population. Although some of the resources on the site are specific to Purdue, many others are useful for any user attempting to extract information from the digital databases of an academic university. The site provides a comprehensive tour of the library, a glossary, a search engine, a preliminary assessment form, and post-use knowledge quizzes. For the logged-in user, the site tracks quiz results.

Navigating the Site. The main page provides a graphic with clickable rollover tabs. To choose a topic, position your mouse over the desired topic and click when it changes color. A navigation bar to other areas of the site will appear on the left, whereas the topic selected appears on the right. Once within the tutorial, the reader can page through the entire sequence by choosing "Next" or jump to another section by clicking on another topic on the navigation bar. Clicking on cross-linked words produces detailed definitions in popup menus.

Discussion Questions and Activities

    1.   If you are a student, step through the tutorial. How is information in the library organized? In what ways is this different from the ways information is organized on the Internet?

    2.   Using this site as a model, create (or have created) a similar site for your library.

Evaluating Online Resources

Finding Information on the Internet: A Tutorial
http://www.lib.berkeley.edu/TeachingLib/Guides/Internet/

> *Site Summary.* Created by librarians at the University of California at Berkeley, this Web site combines information on Internet research and site evaluation that is available elsewhere only in part. The site provides links to two resources. The first resource is an online tutorial that describes Web browser use and capabilities, the nature of the Web, how search engines work, a procedure for devising a search strategy, links to online directories, detailed criteria for evaluating Web sites, and an extensive glossary of terms associated with the Internet. The tutorial also includes links to evaluation exercises that direct students to analyze several Web sites on the same topic, a thorough analysis of each Web site, and an online PowerPoint presentation that pages through search strategies and provides links to illustrative sites. The second resource provides direct access on one page to specific search engines, required syntax for composing search queries, and the means by which the engines find results.

> *Navigating the Site.* The site is easy to navigate. From the main page listed above, choose one of the two main links.

> *Discussion Questions and Activities*

> 1. Using the materials on this site, construct assignments that teach students how to evaluate Internet sites. Begin with a unit that uses resources in the tutorial entitled "Finding Information on the Internet Site." For example, a four-session learning unit might be constructed as follows:
>
>   a. Begin with worksheets that lead students through the pages that introduce the Internet and explain how search engines work. How do search engines differ? What criteria should be used to select one or more search engines that will locate the best resources on the Internet?
>
>   b. During the next session, have students analyze Web sites for their usefulness as research sites on a particular topic. Construct a list of specific Web sites that address a particular topic; for suggested sites, see http://www.lib.berkeley.edu/TeachingLib/Guides/Internet/EvaluateWhy.html.
>
>   c. A third session might be used to help students locate research materials on the Internet. Give students specific topics and ask them to locate several potential resources using the principles listed on the "Recommended Search Strategy" pages. A sample checksheet for students is located on this Web site at http://www.lib.berkeley.edu/TeachingLib/Guides/Internet/EvalForm.pdf. Ask students to defend their choices.
>
>   d. A final session might address topic selection and search strategies in preparation for a writing assignment. This Web site provides suggestions for narrowing topics at http://www.lib.berkeley.edu/TeachingLib/Guides/Internet/Strategies.html. At this point, students should be prepared to locate high-quality resources on the Internet.
>
> 2. Many sites that publish satire or are satiric appear on the Internet, most without any indication that they are suspect. Based on the criteria provided in the Internet evaluation

worksheets, begin compiling a list of satiric Web sites for use in Internet evaluation assignments for students. Begin with the Scambusters and Urban Legends sites below. You might also run a search on the keywords "Internet Analysis Assignment" to see what other assignments are being used at schools across the United States (http://www. google.com and http://www.vivisimo.com should both yield good results).

Similar/Related Sites

1. Evaluation criteria. The following Web sites offer alternative means of locating high-quality information on the Internet:

   a. *Elizabeth Kirk—Evaluating Internet Information*—http://www.library.jhu.edu/ researchhelp/general/evaluating/index.html—In addition to excellent discussions of five criteria for evaluating Web sites (authorship, publishing body, bias, references to other sources, verifiability), this Web site provides a particularly useful discussion of the primary search criteria of the most popular search engines. New features include articles on bias and propaganda.

   b. *Virtual Salt—Evaluating Internet Research Sources*—http://www.virtualsalt.com/ evalu8it.htm—See entry in Chapter 3.

   c. *Evaluation of Information Resources (Purdue University)*—http://www.lib.purdue. edu/ugrl/inst/evaluationchart.pdf

2. Web site evaluation forms. The following sites provide possible checklists for use by students:

   a. *Critical Evaluation Surveys for K-12*—http://school.discovery.com/schrockguide/ eval.html

   b. *Criteria for Evaluating Internet Resources—University of British Columbia*— http://www.library.ubc.ca/home/evaluating/

   c. *Evaluating Web Resources*—http://www2.widener.edu/Wolfgram-Memorial-Library/webevaluation/webeval.htm—Created by Jan Alexander and Marsha Ann Tate at Widener University, this site is useful for its classification of Web site types: Advocacy, Business/Marketing, News, Informational, and Personal. The site also provides links to Web evaluation sites.

   d. *UCLA College Libraries: Thinking Critically About WWW Resources (Esther Grassian)*—http://www.library.ucla.edu/libraries/college/help/critical/index.htm

3. Hoaxes, urban legends, and satire on the Internet

   a. *Hoaxbusters*—http://hoaxbusters.ciac.org/—This site is sponsored by the U.S. Department of Energy's Computer Incident Advisory Center and is a good resource for current hoaxes on the Internet.

   b. *Urban Legends Reference Page*—http://www.snopes.com/

Choosing a Search Engine

Search Engine Watch

http://www.searchenginewatch.com/

Site Summary. Created and maintained by Danny Sullivan, this outstanding Web site analyzes effectiveness of search engines, as well as the relevance of their search results. The site explores such issues as the "hidden Web" and how to gain access to it, as well as a practice increasingly widespread since the year 2000: prominent placement in search results for site owners who pay fees to the search engine company. *Search Engine Watch* also offers additional resources for improving search results; for instance, tools that can assess the popularity of a particular Web site and relatively new or unknown search engines that can return outstanding, relevant results without the annoying flashing ads.

Navigating the Site. The primary drawback to navigating this site is that its information is so extensive and fascinating that it is easy to get sidetracked. The site, however, is easy to navigate and well designed. The main page provides a three-column layout: on the left are "Departments," regularly updated topics; in the center are relatively new articles; and on the right are offers and solicitations. First-time visitors should spend time browsing the left-hand column.

Discussion Questions and Activities

1. How do you find information when you search the Web (most Internet users have a favorite search engine)? Do you know how that search engine finds resources? Locate the "Search Engine Listings" in the center column of the main page. How does your favorite search engine work?

2. Choose a topic you know well and have "surfed" before. Run a search on your topic using at least three different search engines (from the main page, click on "Search Engine Listings," located in the center column), then assess the relevance of the results. Try running the same search using a mega-search engine (one that searches several search engines at once). How did your results compare, and why?

Similar/Related Sites

1. *Search Engine Showdown*—http://www.searchengineshowdown.com

CHAPTER 3

Tools of Literary Analysis

Literary Guides

Poems, Plays, and Prose: A Guide to the Theory of Literary Genres

http://www.uni-koeln.de/~ame02/ppp.htm

Site Summary. Created by Professor Manfred Jahn of the University of Cologne, this project provides extensive guides to poetry, drama, and narrative, including a guide to the narrative analysis of film. According to Dr. Jahn, the most accessible of these guides is his *Guide to the Theory of Poetry;* however, experienced users will find all of the guides useful to review the precise terminology shared by scholars to discuss the form and structure of literary texts. Although many of Dr. Jahn's examples are derived from English literature, his *Guide to the Theory of Drama* in particular makes reference to traditions in the theater from Greek drama forward. His brief coverage of modern European theater is particularly useful. His *Guide to the Theory of Poetry* also discusses non-Western forms; in addition, his discussion of various figures of speech is particularly useful.

Navigating the Site. The site is easy to navigate. From the main page, select the link to the desired guide, or select the link to the comprehensive index. For clarity, each major guide is uniquely paginated and section-numbered: *P* is used for the poetry guide, *D* for drama, *N* for narrative, and *F* for film.

Discussion Questions and Activities

1. Boccaccio's *Decameron* is a set of stories embedded in a framing tale about ten young people who decide to tell stories to pass the time after they flee the plague-infested city for a country estate. Read sections N.2.3 on *Narrative Communication* and N.2.4 on *Narrative Levels.* Use "Chinese boxes" to diagram the narrative levels implied in *The Decameron*, then write a brief description using the appropriate terminology.

2. Read Section D.7 of the *Guide to the Theory of Drama.* Using the example in section D.7.3, diagram the events in Sophocles's play *Oedipus Tyrannus* or *Antigone*, then create a timeline depicting the actual chronology in which the events themselves occurred. How do the play's events differ from the chronology? Why might Sophocles have presented the play in this order?

University of Toronto Poetic Terms

http://eir.library.utoronto.ca/rpo/display/index.cfm

Site Summary. Created and maintained by Paul Brians as part of the University of Toronto's *Representative Poetry Online* project, this no-frills Web site provides the most complete, technical, and accurate definitions of poetic terms of any site surveyed. The definitions are cross-linked with illustrative poetry from the collection, mostly classical, English, and American. The site is particularly strong from a rhetorical and literary historical perspective.

Navigating the Site. The site is easy to navigate. Within the bulleted list that appears on the main page, click on the word "glossary." Then scroll down the alphabetical listing on the page, and click on the link pertaining to the desired term.

Discussion Questions and Activities

1. Using the *Glossary*, look up the word *epic*, then compare the definition with those given by the authors of the sites listed below under "Similar/Related Sites."

2. Teachers might assign selected terms to students and have them present the terms to the class, with examples.

Similar/Related Sites

1. *Bedford St. Martin's Glossary of Literary Terms*—http://www.bedfordstmartins.com/literature/bedlit/glossary_a.htm—This glossary of literary terms is a free resource provided by one of the largest publishers of educational books. The definitions tend to be Western in focus; for instance, *haiku* is identified, not as an important Japanese form, but rather as a form borrowed from the Japanese. Less familiar forms, such as tanka poetry, are not in this guide. This guide does discuss, in their historical context, terms that originated in Greek and Roman classical literature.

2. *GaleGroup Glossary of Literary Terms*—http://www.galegroup.com/free_resources/glossary/index.htm —This *Glossary of Literary Terms* is a free online resource provided by the Gale Group, a well-known publisher of educational reference materials. Regardless of their origins and historical use, most of the terms appear to refer to literature written in the seventeenth to twentieth centuries, omitting their historical relevance. The guide does, however, reference emerging literary terms in ethnic literatures. The site is also linked to a brief guide to writing a term paper.

3. *A Glossary of Rhetorical Terms and Examples*—http://www.uky.edu/ArtsSciences/Classics/rhetoric.html—A project of the University of Kentucky Classics Department, this guide provides classical contemporary definitions, illustrations, and references that illustrate key rhetorical figures.

4. *Peíthô's Web*—http://classicpersuasion.org/—Although most of this site's pages include a disclaimer, its author, Robin Boyes (aka Agathon), formerly a graduate student at the University of Washington, has devoted considerable time and effort to providing accurate e-texts and resources of classical Greek and Roman rhetoric. The site provides access to a number of out-of-print translations of classical rhetoricians; it also provides the best page on the Web addressing the work, life, and criticism of seventh-century B.C.E. poet Sappho. The Web site includes transcriptions of a variety of translations, Greek texts, biographical materials, and audio files.

5. *Logical Fallacies*—http://www.intrepidsoftware.com/fallacy/toc.htm—This excellent site provides definitions of logical fallacies, cross-linked to excellent illustrations.

Genre Theory

Media and Communications Studies Site
http://www.aber.ac.uk/media/index.html

Site Summary. This site, designed to accompany Web-enhanced courses, provides myriad links to essays that express important theoretical ideas pertaining to British media studies. Established in 1995 by Dr. Daniel Chandler of the University of Wales, Aberystwyth, the site attempts to be comprehensive and useful to cultural studies and social science researchers. The site is also extensively cross-linked with full-text articles. The site provides links to articles written on the following topics:

Active interpretation	Gender and ethnicity	IT and telecommunicationss
Advertising	General issues	Media education
Film studies	General reference	Media influence

Navigating the Site. Materials on the site are accessible from the page listed above. Simply choose the area of interest, then click on the desired paper title. The search engine feature appears to be usable only using the Internet Explorer browser.

Discussion Questions and Activities

1. Terms and Concepts for Film Studies. Viewers often approach films passively, not taking into account the intervening roles of the director, editor, and camera operators. The **Film Studies** page of this Web site provides excellent introductions to film analysis, particularly Dr. Chandler's essay, "An Introduction to Genre Theory," located at http://www.aber.ac.uk/media/Documents/intgenre/. The essay "Generic Textual Features of Film and Television" (http://www.aber.ac.uk/media/Documents/intgenre/intgenre7.html) is also useful; it provides terminology and definitions in a concise and accessible format. Read these two essays, then introduce some of the concepts to your class and have students analyze a scene, gradually introducing more complex filmic techniques and scenes.

2. The Visual Image: Cartoons. Having students analyze cartoons is an outstanding way to develop critical thinking about how images are used in the media as most students come to the classroom with an understanding of the genres, whether produced in the United States or in other cultures (e.g., Japanese anime). Particularly useful here are Dr. Chandler's essays on "Visual Perception" (http://www.aber.ac.uk/media/Modules/MC10220/visindex.html). In one 1983 study he describes, Aimée Dorr asked older children what they would say to a younger child having difficulty processing a cartoon image. This idea could be adapted for a critical thinking lesson plan in which students would watch a cartoon, identify elements that might frighten a hypothetical younger child, and then discuss the positive and negative values cartoons portray, as well as elements such as violence.

Similar/Related Sites

1. *Theorizing Satire*—http://www.otus.oakland.edu/english/showcase/satbib.htm—An excellent, comprehensive bibliography of critical materials pertaining to satire.

Literary Theory

Introductory Guide to Literary Theory
http://www.sla.purdue.edu/academic/engl/theory/

> *Site Summary.* This beautiful site is still a work in progress, but even in its present state it provides well-written, lucid commentary for undergraduate students and teachers seeking background and clarification of critical approaches to literature. The site, created by Dino Felluga of Purdue University, also provides examples of how theory can be used to analyze literature. Links to other relevant sites are annotated, terms are cross-linked to definitions, and in-depth coverage is provided for some authors. The site also provides lesson plans and sample applications. Modules are complete for the following areas of critical theory:

Gender and Sex
Michel Foucault
- Gender and sex
- Repressive hypothesis

Judith Butler
- Gender and sex
- Performativity

New Historicism
Michel Foucault
- History
- Panoptic and carceral power
- Power

Stephen Greenblatt
- History

Postmodernism
Linda Hutcheon
- Postmodernity
- Parody

Jean Baudrillard
- Postmodernity
- Simulation

Fredric Jameson
- Postmodernity
- Pastiche

Marxism
Karl Marx
- Stages of development
- Capital
- Commodity fetishism

Louis Althusser
- Ideology
- Ideological state apparatuses

Fredric Jameson
- Ideology
- Late capitalism

Narratology
Peter Brooks
- Plot
- Narrative desire
- Transference

Roland Barthes
- Plotting
- The five codes

Algirdas Greimas
- Plotting
- Semiotic square

Psychoanalysis
Sigmund Freud
- Psychosexual development
- The unconscious
- Repression
- Neuroses
- Transference and trauma

Jacques Lacan
- Psychosexual development
- Structure of the psyche
- Desire
- Gaze

Julia Kristeva
- Psychosexual development
- The abject

The site can be viewed in multiple browsers; see the "Guide" for detailed parameters.

Navigating the Site. The site is exceptionally well designed. The main page provides links to pages on **Gender & Sex**, **Narratology**, **Postmodernism**, **Marxism**, **New Historicism**, and **Psychoanalysis**.

Discussion Questions and Activities

1. Although being exposed to literary theory for the first time can be daunting to high school and undergraduate students, most find learning about contemporary approaches to literature liberating. For younger students, bring theoretical methodology into the classroom without the nomenclature. See the "Narratology" lesson plans for examples of how to apply narratological concepts to film, but instead of introducing terms like "analepsis" and "prolepsis," construct a timeline of the story, and then talk about how the events are related to convey the ideas of nonlinearity, flashback and prophecy, and digression.

2. See also the "Gender & Sex" lesson plan for Spenser's "Amoretti." Although a lesson plan for older students may include terminology such as "constructed," "gendered," and "other," the concepts can still be conveyed to younger students through questioning; for instance, "What do we find out about the men in this story? What do we find out about women? How does the story suggest people are supposed to behave? Are boys and girls in the story supposed to act the same way? Why or why not? How do the characters feel about it?"

Similar/Related Sites

1. *The LitCrit Web*—http://cc.cumberlandcollege.edu/acad/english/litcritweb/—An excellent site for an introductory literary theory course, this Web site was created in 1999 by Dr. Tom Fish at Cumberland College under a grant from the Appalachian College Association. The site provides lucid and well-written introductions to sociohistorical, Marxist, New Historicist, structuralist, reader-response, feminist, and psychoanalytic criticism. Each introduction is extensively cross-linked to a glossary of helpful key term definitions. The site also provides a "Writer's Workshop" feature that provides self-scoring online quizzes along with instantaneous feedback on answers.

2. *Virtual Salt*—http://www.virtualsalt.com/index.htm—This eclectic set of links, created by teacher Robert Harris, provides information useful to literature students and teachers, some theory based. Among the topics are Internet research (directories, guides, hoaxes, search engines), literature (terms, definitions, theory), and essays that provide advice to students and teachers.

3. *Marxists Internet Archive*—http://www.marxists.org/—This Web site, dedicated to Marxist theory, provides online access to key writings and biographies of major Marxist theoreticians, as well as accessible student introductions to theory and history.

4. *Glossary of Literary Theory*—http://www.library.utoronto.ca/utel/glossary/headerindex.html—This site provides a hypertext edition of Greig E. Henderson and Christopher Brown's glossary of theoretical terms.

Alibris Episteme Links

http://www.epistemelinks.com/Main/MainPers.asp

Site Summary. Founded by Thomas Stone, a graduate of the University of Rochester, *Episteme Links* is a gateway to materials relating to the study of philosophy, providing an index to texts, biographical materials, journals, lesson plans, etc., pertaining to fifty prominent philosophers from ancient times to the present. On this site, philosophy is defined broadly as "issues from metaphysics, epistemology, logic, ethics, politics, aesthetics, and any consideration of the foundations of other fields of study or institutions."

Navigating the Site. The site is easy to navigate. Materials are sorted alphabetically by name, chronologically by period, and by topic, as linked from the center column of the site's main page. Links to lesson plans and lecture notes are also linked to the page; see the navigation bar on the left.

Discussion Questions and Activities

1. Scholars of Voltaire's *Candide* have long noted that the novel offers a stark contrast between Candide's horrific adventures and the unmitigated optimism of the philosopher Pangloss, who believes that the world in which such horrors occur is "the best of all possible worlds."

    a. Some scholars have identified this irony as an implicit criticism of Gottfried Wilhelm Leibniz's *Monadology*. Use Episteme.Links to locate key terms from *Candide* that are defined in Leibniz's *Monadology*. From the main page, locate the "Listing of 50 Common Philosophers," then choose **Leibniz** and then the **Glossary for the Monadology**. Click on terms used by Pangloss in *Candide*, such as *necessary truth* and *sufficient reason*. Then read from paragraph 32 to paragraph 60 to discover why, in Leibniz's philosophy, "things cannot be otherwise than as they are," one of Pangloss's key ideas.

    b. From the main page, choose **Voltaire** from the "Listing of 50 Common Philosophers." Choose **Links to Electronic Texts**, then the link to **The Philosophical Dictionary** on the *Hanover Historical Texts Project*. Choose the link to the entry on **Power, Omnipotence**. What does this entry suggest to you about Voltaire's attitude toward Pangloss's philosophy? What about the entry defining the term **Theist**? Read the entry on **Love**. Does this entry suggest a way to read Voltaire's description of Candide's love for Cunegonde?

Similar/Related Sites

1. *Contemporary Philosophy, Critical Theory, and Postmodern Thought Resource Page*—http://carbon.cudenver.edu/~mryder/itc_data/postmodern.html—For more advanced students, interested in resources pertaining to the most recently influential postmodern theorists, this Web site provides useful overviews and primary texts associated with a number of important theorists.

Major Resources of General Interdisciplinary Interest

The Web sites described in Chapter 4 are of broadly interdisciplinary use to librarians, teachers, and students of world literature. Many sites, such as portals and projects, are constantly updated with new resources and should be consulted regularly.

Portals

Portals are Web sites designed primarily to link users to other resources. Some are special purpose sites that address a limited topic or field; others attempt to address all of the needs of a particular group of users. Often, portals themselves do not provide original material; however, they may provide access to the "hidden Web": Web sites not registered with or reported by major search engines. Sites that provide original material in addition to links to other sites are described elsewhere in this book as *projects*. Portal or gateway sites vary widely in their usefulness and currency. The best are those created and regularly updated by experts in a given field; however, the Internet is not systematic in its coverage, and even the best sites include links that have since gone dead. Portals particularly worth checking on a regular basis include the following.

Humbul Humanities Hub

http://www.humbul.ac.uk/

Site Summary. This Web site is a searchable, annotated portal to Web research projects throughout the world that are identified by Oxford University librarians as useful to teachers and students in particular fields. New projects are indexed weekly, classified by subject and discipline. The Humbul entries cover Internet projects hosted throughout the world. Other site features include detailed Internet research tutorials for teachers and students, as well as presentation materials that teachers can download for use in their own courses. In addition, teachers and researchers can register to use *My Humbul Include*, a database service that allows the user to incorporate Humbul sites and annotations into lists of customized resources for course Web sites. The site is hosted by the University of Oxford and is a service of the Resource Discovery Network, which is funded by the Joint Information Systems Committee and the Arts and Humanities Research Board in the United Kingdom. Broad disciplinary areas include the following:

American studies	Museum/library/archive	Hispanic studies
Archaeology	Philosophy	Italian studies
Classics	Religion and theology	Japanese studies
Comparative literature	Modern languages (general)	Latin American studies
History	African studies	Middle Eastern studies
History and philosophy of science	Celtic studies	Portuguese studies
Humanities computing	Chinese studies	Scandinavian studies
Humanities in general	English studies	Slavonic studies
Linguistics	French studies	Other Asian studies
Manuscript studies	German studies	Other European studies

Navigating the Site. From the main page, explore the site using Internet research tutorials (lower left), a search engine (upper center), or subject areas (lower center). **Subject Area** pages further subdivide the topic Web sites into pages pertaining to **Projects/Organizations**, **Primary Sources**, **Secondary Sources**, and **Bibliographic Sources**, as well as those sites that are **Research Related** or **Teaching/Learning Related**.

Similar/Related Sites

1. *The Librarian's Index to the Internet*—http://www.lii.org/—This annotated, searchable Web site provides links to 10,000+ sites of exceptionally high quality. The Web site also provides a subject index categorized by topic and discipline. Users can also subscribe to a free weekly newsletter. This site is hosted by the University of California at Berkeley and is sponsored by the Library of California and the Institute of Museum and Library Services. From the main page, click on the *Literature* link (under "Arts and Humanities") . Choose among the categories listed. To select works in a specific geographic region, choose the *Authors* link, then choose among the countries listed.

2. *Directory Mozilla (DMOZ) Open Directory*—http://dmoz.org/Arts/Literature—The DMOZ Web site is a no-frills, searchable directory to Web sites classified by subject. Largely a volunteer initiative, DMOZ seeks to categorize Web sites in a free, open access, noncommercial database; its stated goal is to remain free in perpetuity. The site's voluminous listings (6,383 in world literature alone, at this writing) make up for its lack of annotations. From the Literature page, click on the *World Literature* link. Click on the link pertaining to your country or region of interest. As an alternative, follow this path to English translations of world literature: *Arts: Literature: Poetry: In Translation*.

3. *Voice of the Shuttle (VOS)*—http://vos.ucsb.edu—One of the most cited humanities portals on the Web, VOS was created in 1994 by Alan Liu at the University of California, Santa Barbara. The site was recently upgraded from static Web pages to a database system designed to permit users to locate and link to dynamic datasets. Users can also contribute and compile links by signing up for a "My VOS" account. Eventually, users will be able to create subsidiary sets of links for groups of users, such as courses and professional meetings. VOS deserves its reputation as one of the earliest and best humanities portals. In addition, a large number of frustrating dead links have been updated on this site in the last six months.

4. *The Online Books Page*—http://digital.library.upenn.edu/books/—Established in 1993 by John Mark Ockerbloom at the University of Pennsylvania, this site is primarily a portal to a wide variety of primary and secondary materials, which he categorizes by subject according to Library of Congress prefixes. The site also features some e-texts. The links are largely functional and lead to relatively high-quality versions of 19,000 e-texts in a wide variety of fields. In addition, the site features a page of links to *Prize Winners Online*, which provides access to e-texts of Newbery, Nobel, and Pulitzer Prize–winning works. A subset of the materials written by women is also linked to this site, but the works are maintained on a separate site, *A Celebration of Women Writers*, described later in this chapter under "Projects." The *Online Books Page* indexes many important full-text sites.

E-Text Sites

E-text sites are Web sites whose primary goal is to provide users with online access to texts. The e-text sites described in this section were selected with several considerations in mind. Some e-text sites are created, maintained, and/or monitored by scholars in the field; others are not. Users doing scholarly work, and even those doing rudimentary textual analysis, should still use a recognized standard critical edition of an author's works in hard copy form to verify that the e-texts are accurate. Even users doing advanced research, however, may find online e-texts useful for keyword and phrase searches, although findings should always be checked for accuracy against the critical edition.

One other consideration for evaluating online translations of world literature is the origin of most e-texts. Because of copyright restrictions, most e-text sites feature texts that were written, edited, translated, and published before 1930. Although many of these texts are outstanding, other previously published, out-of-copyright translations reflect the time and place in which they were created and may be written in a style that is inaccessible to contemporary readers. Sites that feature new, previously unpublished translations should be used with caution and only after the translator's credentials are carefully verified. Some sites have obtained permission to provide to the general public e-texts that are not in the public domain. Even if such texts are available online, their use is often subject to certain restrictions. Site users should always spend a few minutes reviewing the "conditions of use" posted on most e-text sites and should then comply with the site owner's policies.

Another concern in working with world literature on the Internet is that many of the best sites are written entirely in languages other than English. Users performing advanced research on non-English texts would be expected to consult the texts in the original language; however, other users may not have the advanced language skills necessary to use non-English sites. Although Web translation utilities such as *BabelFish* (http://babel.altavista.com/) may be useful to translate some individual words or to provide a general idea about what a passage means, translation results are usually marginally useful and even ludicrous. To demonstrate, try this experiment on *BabelFish*, a translation utility offered by the company that sponsors the search engine AltaVista:

1. Enter three or four lines of text into the *BabelFish* translation utility and select a translation option of your choice (e.g., English to French).

2. Take the resulting non-English passage and use *BabelFish* again to translate the text back into English.

3. Compare the resulting "English" with the original text you translated.

Because this book is intended primarily for an English-speaking audience, the sites selected feature a large number of English translations. Before assigning a text, however, teachers should also consult a reputable print copy of the work in translation.

A final consideration in selecting e-text sites for inclusion in this section is the recent availability of special "e-text readers." Publishers and libraries have begun experimenting with electronic publishing as an alternative to hard-copy publication of some books. This technology is still in its infancy, and e-book readers are not necessarily published in formats compatible with those of other manufacturers or publishers. Also, to prevent their further dissemination, many copyrighted e-books cannot be printed in hard copy, a drawback for readers who find it inconvenient to read from a digital display.

Based on these concerns, the e-text sites described in this chapter meet the following criteria:

1. A substantial number of the texts on the selected sites can be viewed or downloaded without special equipment (e.g., a special text reader) or software, other than Web browsers, such as Internet Explorer, Netscape Navigator, Mozilla, or Opera (a browser used widely in Europe).

2. The site owners appear to be reputable.

3. Where the original texts are not written in English, the texts are translated into English.

4. A substantial portion of the site can be used free of charge.

International Children's Digital Library
http://www.icdlbooks.org/

Site Summary. Created November 20, 2002, and hosted by the Internet Archive, this Web site features outstanding interactivity and high-quality page images of children's books published throughout the world. The library at this writing has 531 books online, digitized by the Library of Congress. The library is funded by a consortium that includes the National Science Foundation, Kahle/Austin Foundation, and the Institute for Museum and Library Services (IMLS). Additional support was provided by the Library of Congress, the Markle Foundation, Adobe Systems Inc., and Octavo. Plans are presently in place to expand the library over a five-year period to 10,000 books representing fifty cultures; some categories are consequently empty at present, although users can gain a sense of the site's future holdings by browsing the categories. Access to the library is free; however, technical requirements for using the site in "Enhanced Mode" are stringent.

Navigating the Site. Spend some time reading the FAQ and viewing the demos before using the site, or move your mouse over *Basic* and *Enhanced* to view popup menus that describe technical requirements for Windows and Macintosh systems. If your system does not have the required technical attributes, choose *Enter the Library* and click *Basic* in the left-hand toolbar. If you are satisfied that your system will operate in *Enhanced* mode, choose *Enter the Library* and click *Enhanced*. The site will then ensure that your computer is properly configured. If you have technical problems, check the Technical FAQ and, if necessary, consult with the site's technical staff. Once on the site, you may choose to search by subject or by region, or to read the instructions for use. From this point forward, the interface is designed for use by children five to thirteen years of age. Within the **Choose Books by Category** page, menus are arranged hierarchically. When a collection of books on a particular subject is located, thumbnail images of the books appear at the top of screen; when selected, the images are magnified. Within the **Choose Books by Region** page, select a region by clicking on the globe; rotate the globe by clicking on the arrow, then find books in North and South America, Asia, Africa, etc. Then follow the hierarchical menu to the desired book. Once a specific book is selected, the reader can page through the book sequentially using a standard reader, a comic strip reader, or a spiral reader. The reader can also choose a one-page or two-page display. Some books also require that the reader use Adobe Acrobat eBook Reader, version 2.2 or higher. This software is freely downloadable from the Internet; click on the icon provided within the ICDL and follow the instructions for installation. A final note about the downloaded books: The files are quite large and eventually will need to be deleted. Because the ICDL creates its own file structures and cache files, however, you cannot delete them by using the "delete files" utility in your browser. To delete the files, locate the file structure using your computer's utility to search for "ICDL" as the search term, move to the appropriate folder, and then delete the files manually.

Discussion Questions and Activities

1. What choices do publishers and writers make when they design a book? Explore book design categories such as "Color" and "Shape" to find out. One particularly playful use of book shape is *The Slant Book*. Or explore the books designed for specific "Age" groups to identify what makes a good book for ages three to five, six to nine, and ten to thirteen.

2. How do people live in other places and times, and what do they believe is important? How do their lives differ from ours, and how are they the same? Choose **Setting—When and Where**, then choose **Places Where**, and then a specific geographical region. For instance, two African selections, *It Takes a Village* and *Hunterman and Crocodile,* stress the importance of community and attitudes toward nature in West African communities. For older readers, *Equiano,* based on one of the first slave narratives published in England and the United States, retells the story of the West Indian slave trade through the eyes of a young boy purportedly kidnapped from his village, sold into slavery, freed through his own industry, and established in a successful career as a merchant. For an interesting cross-cultural comparison of attitudes of tolerance toward animals, compare the West African *Hunterman and Crocodile,* the Estonian *Elinda, Who Danced in the Sky*, and the Native American story *A Man Called Raven.*

3. What rules govern specific genres, and how do writers in different cultures and times use them? Choose the **Genres** category, then choose **Poetry/Rhyming Books/Songs**. Choose the book *Carib Breeze*. What themes present in this book's poetry are specific to its Caribbean origin? With what aspects of nature is the author preoccupied? The book is illustrated by Caribbean children. What scenery do they depict? How does it differ from the scenery children might create in your community or school? A good companion book is *Laughing Tomatoes*, a book of poetry written by the respected author Francisco Alarcón.

Oxford Text Archive
http://ota.ahds.ac.uk

Site Summary. Founded by Lou Burnard in 1976, the *Oxford Text Archive (OTA)* provides "high quality, well documented texts for the academic community"; at present, the site offers 25,000 resources in more than twenty-five languages. Texts deposited with the OTA are subject to stringent standards and review, as set forth in the archive's online "Collections Policy." Although some of its several thousand texts can only be disseminated with the permission of the original depositor, most may be downloaded immediately from the site, and all are free of charge. Users can also download the entire OTA catalog in PDF format.

Navigating the Site. Texts can be browsed by author, language, or title. Once a text has been located, the user can search, download, or read more about the text (a good idea as many world literature texts in the archive are in the original language). Downloadable versions are available in many formats, most as zip files. Before downloading each file, users are asked to agree to the OTA's licensing agreements. If viewing a text requires special permission, the user is notified, and the OTA provides the appropriate form for a mail request. If permission is granted, the user is provided a password that permits access to the text. At this writing, one irritating glitch is that only about one-third of the entries on the **Author** and **Title** browsing pages are functional; consequently, the user must browse for the appropriate author, and then use the "Search" function to locate the author's works. Once the "Search" results appear, another glitch is that the link to the author's name rarely works; however, the options to "Search text," "Get text," and get "More Info," which appear under the author's name, do function.

Discussion Questions and Activities

1. Online texts can provide the opportunity to search key terms, effectively operating as a concordance. For instance, common to most Norse sagas are references to the gatherings attended by men and women to settle disputes and to create and enact laws, called *þings* (pronounced *things*). Search several of the sagas, archived online as part of the *Online Medieval and Classical Library* (http://sunsite.berkeley.edu/OMACL/), for the word *thing*,

then read about the kinds of actions and decisions that typified these gatherings. For what purposes were the gatherings called? What kinds of decisions were rendered? With what consequences? Who could participate in them? Under what conditions? (Other productive search terms in the Norse sagas include the words *berserk*, *marriage*, and *murder*.)

2. Use the search engine features on other e-text sites to search on key terms.

Similar/Related Sites

1. *The English Server*—http://eserver.org/—*The English Server* began as a graduate student project at Carnegie Mellon University and has grown into a large publishing community hosted by the University of Washington. Projects and e-texts are created by five tiers of volunteers, who receive varying levels of site privileges in return for their services and leadership. Unfortunately, the sites are unevenly maintained and edited, although some projects of significance to world literature are available, as follows:

   a. *Books.* This project includes full-text editions of a handful of authors, including Aeschylus, Aristotle, Apuleius, Dostoevsky, Homer, and Freud. Most include complete bibliographic detail.

   b. *E-server Drama Collection.* This project is edited by Geoffrey Sauer, *E-Server* director and University of Washington faculty member. The site provides translations to several classical plays, including several comedies by Aristophanes as well as the more frequently anthologized Greek tragedies. The link to Goethe's *Faust* at the Virginia Tech gopher site is dead; however, searching for it using Google may turn up a cached copy.

   c. *The Eighteenth Century.* This project, edited by Geoffrey Sauer, addresses European eighteenth-century studies from a cultural perspective and provides several translations of eighteenth-century philosophical texts by Rousseau, Leibniz, and others.

   d. *Poetry.* This site includes Samuel Butler's translation of Homer's *Iliad* and *Odyssey*. *The Aeneid*, however, has no attribution, but appears to be the translation by seventeenth-century poet John Dryden.

2. *Eldritch Press*—http://www.eldritchpress.org/—Founded by Eric Eldred in 1995, *Eldritch Press* offers a small but eclectic set of well-edited and documented texts, many unavailable elsewhere. Particularly strong world literature offerings include works by Anton Chekhov, Rabindranath Tagore, Lu Hsun, and Luigi Pirandello. Equally fascinating is Eldred's work on behalf of Internet publishing, which is linked to the site. Eldred's site has been cited by the National Endowment of the Humanities for its value as a resource for teachers. Note: If Eldred's site is down, use http://www.google.com to search for the author of interest (e.g., Anton Chekhov). Check the search results for the Eldritch Press, then select a link to the **cache** version. Often, Google can find results other search engines cannot through this **cache** feature.

3. *Internet Text Archive*—http://classics.mit.edu/—Despite a recent crash that left the site with some broken images, MIT has reassembled the *Internet Text Archive* so that it is largely intact, with links to 441 classical literary works by fifty-nine different authors. Some of the texts reside on the MIT site, whereas others exist on highly reputable sites such as *Perseus*. Most are Greco-Roman, but some Chinese and Persian texts, all in English translation, are available. All of the works are presented with full bibliographic references, and each includes a message board where users can post and read comments and queries. This site has been in existence since 1994 and is highly regarded.

4. *Online Medieval and Classical Library*—http://sunsite.berkeley.edu/OMACL/—Part of the *SunSITE Digital Collections* at the University of California at Berkeley Library, this site was created by Douglas B. Killings, formerly a graduate student at Berkeley. Although new works are no longer being added, the site provides access to translations of significant world literature resources, including works that can be classified as belonging to the northern European epic, saga, and romance genres. The texts on this site are frequently referenced by reputable scholars in the field of medieval studies. Most of the translations are from books published before 1920.

5. *Bartleby.com*—http://www.bartleby.com—*Bartleby.com* offers free access to its estimated 200,000 pages of text, including the *Harvard Classics* and the *Encyclopedia of World History,* written by Peter N. Stearns (Carnegie Mellon University) et al. The site is unabashedly dedicated to publishing traditional canonical works. *Bartleby.com* was created in 1993 by Steven H. van Leeuwen, then an employee of Columbia University; the company was incorporated in 1999. The Web site's primary source of income consists of relatively unobtrusive online ads. The Web site is frequently listed as an e-text resource on university library Web sites. Although the texts seem well-proofed and faithfully reproduced, the translation information could be more prominently displayed to aid teachers who want to compare editions.

6. *Project Gutenberg*—http://www.gutenberg.org—*Project Gutenberg* is the oldest e-text provider, claiming a start date of 1971, when Michael Hart began by entering the *Declaration of Independence* onto a mainframe at the University of Illinois. The project's administrators do not attempt to create definitive scholarly editions, but rather texts "99.9% accurate" for use by "99%" of the reading public. The text is coded in no-frills ASCII, which produces very plain documents that can be read by virtually any computer. *Project Gutenberg* also features thirty-eight mirror sites (sites that duplicate the contents of the project) on five continents. Texts are transcribed and proofed by volunteers. Work on new titles has been hampered by Congress's recent unconditional extension of copyright protection for twenty years; consequently, most e-texts on *Project Gutenberg* were published before 1923. Users can browse by author or title and then read online or download to a disk or CD. Because anyone can volunteer to proofread as little as a page at a time, this Web site provides an opportunity for students to gain insight into how editions are planned and created.

7. *University of Adelaide Text Archive*—http://etext.library.adelaide.edu.au/index.html —The *Electronic Texts Collection*, a project of The University of Adelaide Library, offers an extensive selection of new HTML editions from the traditional Western canon that have been published previously on the Web in ASCII format as well as newly entered text. Eventually, the library plans to digitize its own materials. In particular, the site features collections of Greek classical literature, Australian exploration materials, and both Western and Eastern philosophy. The site is up to date and well edited.

8. *Humanities Text Initiative*—http://www.hti.umich.edu—Funded by a grant from Sun Microsystems, the *Humanities Text Initiative* at the University of Michigan offers SGML-encoded online texts. Most texts are restricted to University of Michigan patrons; however, available to all are small collections of travel narratives about southeastern Europe and Bosnia, a searchable Koran, and Bible translations, including the Martin Luther and the Rheims 1582 New Testament.

9. *Hanover Historical Texts Project*—http://history.hanover.edu/project.html—Created by students and faculty at Hanover College to provide access to primary texts in history, this growing Web site is worth tracking. Current offerings include excerpts from Petrarch's *Familiar Letters* and Voltaire's *Philosophical Dictionary,* a number of works about early modern witchcraft, and the entire text of *The Interesting Narrative of the Life of Olaudah Equiano* and *The Diary of Lady Sarashina* (eleventh-century Japan).

10. *The Literature Network*—http://www.online-literature.com/—Hosted by Jalic, an Internet Web design and Web hosting company, the *Literature Network* provides access to full-text versions of a number of works unavailable elsewhere. Unfortunately, the site does not give bibliographic or translation information.

11. *A Celebration of Women Writers*—http://digital.library.upenn.edu/women/writers.html —This growing site provides background resources for the study of women writers, links to texts on other sites, and a growing corpus of full-length e-texts, in translation. Edited by Mary Mark Ockerbloom, *A Celebration of Women Writers* is an evolving database of e-texts, biographies, bibliographies, and articles by and about historical and contemporary women writers. The site was begun in 1994; the most recently posted entries are dated the day before this entry was last updated (September 10, 2004). Entries are indexed by author and by category (genre), and texts referenced are part of the *On-line Books Page* at the University of Pennsylvania (see separate entry). Author entries are cross-referenced with additional biographical and bibliographical information, when available. A particularly useful feature for world literature users is the project's search page, which includes date, country, and ethnicity search fields. The main page of the site serves as a navigation page; announcements appear first on the page, followed by links to works by author, century, country of origin, and ethnicity. A search page also provides the ability to search by a combination of attributes. Editions local to (that is, hosted on this site rather than linked to external sites) the *Celebration of Women Writers*, mostly British and American writers, are also listed separately on pages linked to the main page under the heading "What's Local."

Reference Sites

Annenberg/CPB Learner.org
http://www.learner.org/

Site Summary. This outstanding Web site provides a wide range of pedagogically valuable resources for teachers and students at all levels. In addition to viewing broadcast schedules, users can sign up for access to video-on-demand (marked with a distinctive "VoD" logo) broadcasts of some of the organization's distance learning telecasts; particularly useful to teachers of world literature are *Destinos: An Introduction to Spanish, Fokus Deutsch* (German language instruction), *French in Action* (French language instruction), *Out of the Past* (an exploration of ancient civilizations), and *The Western Tradition* (a series exploring the philosophy, art, and literature of Western Europe and the Mediterranean world). Two exhibits of the Annenberg/CPB's "Teacher's Lab," accessible at http://www.learner.org/exhibits/, provide overviews of medieval and Renaissance culture (see Chapter 8 summary).

Navigating the Site. The site is well-designed and easy to navigate, although the opening page changes frequently. To browse efficiently, scan the main page for features, then browse the "Teacher Resources"; explore all of the categories, as world literature teachers and students will find outstanding information on the Social Studies and History sites as well. Try searching for materials using key words, such as "medieval," "Renaissance," and "Middle Ages." Finally, for special exhibits, click on the link in the left-hand column labeled *Learner.org for Students*. The resulting page provides access to special exhibits on such topics as the "Middle Ages" and "The Renaissance."

Discussion Questions and Activities

1. The online video-on-demand broadcasts listed above provide an outstanding starting point for the study of world literature.

2. For questions and activities associated with this site's medieval and Renaissance exhibits, see Chapter 8.

Library of Congress Country Studies
http://lcweb2.loc.gov/frd/cs/cshome.html

Site Summary. These country studies are books created to provide detailed historical and cultural backgrounds for many countries in the world with which the United States maintains diplomatic contact. Consequently, they represent a good starting place for understanding the historical context of many works of world literature.

Navigating the Site. The site is easy to navigate. Depending on the topic of interest, choose either *Search* or *Browse*. Selecting *Search* brings up a search page; type in the topic of interest, then click *Search*. Results are displayed by topic and country. Selecting *Browse* from the main page brings up a list of countries linked to the corresponding country studies.

Discussion Questions and Activities

1. The institution of slavery forms the backdrop for works of world literature, from slave narratives such as *The Interesting Life of Olaudah Equiano,* to modernist narratives of European imperialism, such as Joseph Conrad's *Heart of Darkness*. What aspects of the history and cultures of various nations can provide background to the transatlantic slave trade of the seventeenth through nineteenth centuries? From the main page of the *Library of Congress Country Studies*, choose *Search*, then enter the truncated search terms "slave*" (the * is a wildcard symbol so that variants of the search terms are also selected; e.g., "slaves," "slavery," etc.). Then click the "Search" button. Investigate some of the search results from the set of links that show the two search terms near each other. What information can you find that sheds light on literature written when seventeenth-, eighteenth-, and nineteenth-century slavery existed?

2. A number of Russian novels are written against the backdrop of Czarist Russia and, later, the Bolshevik revolution. What searches might produce useful information explaining some of the events described in Pasternak's *Dr. Zhivago* or the novels of Dostoevsky?

Similar/Related Sites

1. *World Factbook*—http://www.odci.gov/cia/publications/factbook/—Published by the United States government, these fact sheets are available on virtually every country in the world. In general, the materials are constantly updated. Because no one can be an expert on every country, and educators are frequently called upon to teach about literature that

may be outside their areas of expertise, these fact books are a good place to start research on a particular contemporary world culture.

2. *BBC Country Studies*—http://news.bbc.co.uk/1/hi/country_profiles/default.stm —This outstanding site provides profiles of countries worldwide.

Maps

Perry Castañeda Library Map Collection
http://www.lib.utexas.edu/maps/

Site Summary. Students rarely have a strong knowledge of contemporary geography, let alone historical geography. This Web site, sponsored by the University of Texas, provides online access to a comprehensive set of historical and contemporary maps of areas of geographical interest throughout the world. In addition, a set of links to maps pertaining to topical events provides access to such recent additions as maps identifying the debris path of the space shuttle *Columbia*, areas of Iraq disputed among NATO members, and ranges for North Korean missiles. Most of the maps are in the public domain; consult the FAQ for information on how best to view and print the maps. Teachers of world literature may find the blank, topographical, and historical maps of particular value.

Navigating the Site. The main page is arranged in two columns. Navigational links to collections pertaining to major geographical areas are located in the left-hand column. The right-hand column lists online maps of both current and general interest. To locate a particular map, scroll through the links, choose a region, then scroll through the alphabetized links. Be sure to check not only both country names (e.g., Greece, Italy), but also regional names (e.g., Asia Minor) and political formations (e.g., Hellenistic Greece, Rome).

Discussion Questions and Activities

1. The Perry Castañeda site features maps of historical Greece from 700 B.C.E. to the present. From the right-hand side of the main page, select the link to **Maps of Europe**. From the alphabetical list that appears, select **Europe Historical Maps.** Compare the maps of Greece in 700 B.C.E. (roughly fifty years after the Homeric epics are believed to have been composed) and 450 B.C.E. (when the great Greek tragedies were written). How are the maps different? How similar? What do the differences suggest about the different worlds inhabited by classical Greek people and the literary figures in their literature? Now view the map entitled "Italy: The Growth of Roman Power." What was the extent of the Roman empire when Virgil wrote *The Aeneid* around 79 B.C.E.? Why was this a good time to write a national epic for the Roman empire?

2. Although the **Interactive Ancient Mediterranean** is described in greater detail in Chapter 7, maps particularly useful for teachers are located on the site's "Map Room" at http://iam.classics.unc.edu/map/map_room.html. From this page, select **Map Index**.

3. View the **Terrain and Place Names** and **Terrain and Region Names** maps. What is the geography of Greece like? How does the actual distance between cities compare with the apparent distance between them as described in Greek literature? How might geography have influenced the type of political formations and literature that arose in Greece?

4. Print out both the "Outline and Place Names" map and the "Blank Outline" map of Greece. Study the place names. How many cities can you label on the blank map without referring to the labeled map? With how many cities can you associate a literary figure or story?

Similar/Related Sites

1. *Making Sense of Maps*—http://historymatters.gmu.edu/msc/maps/—Although this site is designed primarily to assist students in the study of U.S. history, it provides excellent advice on how to interpret historical maps.

2. *Rare Maps in the Hargrett Library Collection, University of Georgia*—http://www.libs.uga.edu/darchive/hargrett/maps/maps.html—Although this site primarily provides maps of the United States, it also provides an excellent collection of maps associated with European exploration of the Americas from 1544 to 1774 C.E.

3. *OSSHE Historic Atlas*—http://www.uoregon.edu/~atlas/—Maps powered by Shockwave show migration patterns, military movements, and exploratory expeditions for Europe, the Middle East, North Africa, and North America. Captions only are available, and no background commentary is provided; the user must know the history to use the maps. This site provides particularly useful maps for teaching classical and ancient literatures.

4. *Cartographic Images*—http://www.henry-davis.com/MAPS/carto.html—This site has a few broken links, but many of the map images are incredible. Many are accompanied by explanations. The maps would be particularly useful in courses related to the literature of the ancient, classical, medieval, and Renaissance worlds.

5. *14th Century Catalan Atlas*—http://www.bnf.fr/enluminures/manuscrits/aman6.htm —These pages are part of *The Age of Charles V* site, discussed in Chapter 8. See the guided activities listed under *Representing Other Cultures*.

Historic Cities
http://historic-cities.huji.ac.il/

Site Summary. Sponsored by the Historic Cities Center of the Department of Geography, the Hebrew University of Jerusalem, and the Jewish National and University Library, this Web site is dedicated to the mapping and study of historic cities and promises to be an important resource to teachers of world literature. Each map is available in both low and high resolution. Particularly impressive is this site's collection of over 250 historical maps of Jerusalem.

Navigating the Site. The site is easy to navigate. A left-hand navigation bar makes it possible to find maps by alphabetical listing, year, and mapmaker. A bar on the right provides access to recent additions. Some images may require use of a Mr.SID plug-in, freely downloadable from the site.

Discussion Questions and Activities

1. Mapping Today. Gather several examples of maps we use today; for example, a roadmap, a map from an atlas of your state, and a map from a newspaper that illustrates a particular current event. How do these maps differ? How are they the same? To what extent are the evidence of population, geographical formations, and economic concerns depicted on the map? What *is* represented on the map?

2. Historical Maps. Look at some historical maps and answer the same questions you did for maps of your world. Particularly useful maps are those by Coronelli, maker of Louis XIV's cosmological globes and official cosmographer for his government (see his link from the *Mapmaker* link). What aspects of Coronelli's maps of various cities in Greece are similar to the present-day maps you analyzed above? In what ways do they differ? What features are emphasized, and which are diminished? What extraneous images do they include? What do they tell us about how people of Coronelli's time thought about the world (again, think about population, geographical formations, economic concerns, and strategic issues)?

Projects

Internet History Sourcebook Project
http://www.fordham.edu/halsall/

> *Site Summary.* Easily the historical resource most referenced by teachers and scholars on the Internet, this site is simply outstanding. Even its broken links provide a wealth of bibliographic information for locating further primary source material. The site is so comprehensive that it is the ideal starting place for research on virtually any topic in history or literature; moreover, it forms the basic reading for a number of history course syllabi on the Web. The site was created by Professor Paul Halsall, now at the University of Northern Florida, when he was a graduate student at Fordham University. Fordham continues to host the site as a service. The links, e-texts, and other resources provided on this site are classified in several ways: by chronology, region, and occasionally demography. The major categories, accessible from the main page, are as follows:

By Chronology	By Area/Topic
Internet Ancient History Sourcebook • Mesopotamia • Egypt • Persia • Israel • Greece • Hellenistic World • Rome • Late Antiquity • Christian Origins Internet Medieval Sourcebook Internet Modern History Sourcebook	Africa India Jewish History Islamic Lesbian/Gay Women Global Science Byzantium Saints' Lives Ancient and Medieval Law Film

Navigating the Site. The site is easy to navigate. The main page features several navigation bars and is itself a site map. The toolbar at the top links to all of the major categories listed above; the third row of this same navigation bar connects with several of Dr. Halsall's courses in medieval studies, modern history, and Chinese studies, all of which are excellent resources. The navigation bar in the left margin also links to the site's major sections and appears to be the most reliable set of links for navigating the site. Subsequent pages, each dedicated to a specific topic, repeat the main navigation bar across the top of the page. A hierarchical outline of the page topic, which is cross-linked to supporting resources, appears at the bottom of the page. Many resources are labeled using the following key: "2nd" for secondary sources, "WEB" for Web resources, and "MEGA" for comprehensive resources. Each entry is followed by an abbreviation that identifies the origin of the resource.

Discussion Questions and Activities

1. What does freedom of expression mean in a free society? The story of Galileo Galilei and the censorship of his scientific and literary works by the Spanish Inquisition offers an important case with interdisciplinary implications. From the main page, find *Main* in the left-hand column, then select *Modern*. From the left-hand column of the *Internet Modern History Sourcebook*, choose *Sci Revolution*. Read the letters, essays, and treatises that appear under Galileo's name in the right-hand column. What was the nature of Galileo's scientific beliefs? What scientific principles did he discover? On what basis was he censored? Why did he capitulate to the Church authorities despite his convictions?

2. The work that governs the spiritual lives of Islamic people throughout the world, the Koran, is often regarded as a difficult text for Western students. What are the tenets of the main sects of Islam? How are they derived from the Koran, and how do they intersect with the rich tradition of Islamic poetry? From the main page of the *Internet History Sourcebook*, find "Subsidiary Sourcebooks" and select *Islamic*. Explore the texts on this page to gain insight into the fastest-growing religion in today's world.

3. An important medieval genre in itself, saints' lives also are the basis for literary creations written by Dante, Boccaccio, and Chaucer, as well as for more recent spiritual autobiographies dating from the seventeenth century to the present. For a particularly extensive collection of saints' lives, from the left-hand navigation bar on the main page of the *Internet History Sourcebook,* find *Special Resources* in the left-hand column, then select *Saints' Lives*. Read several of the accounts listed on that page. What are the characteristics of this genre? Which of these characteristics appear in contemporary accounts of faith?

4. Films depicting historical events and literature often take liberties with the source material. The film and history pages provide synopses of recent films, often with critiques of how the films are inaccurate. From the main page of the *Internet History Sourcebook*, find *Special Resources* in the left-hand column, then choose the film page pertaining to the period of interest (e.g., ancient, medieval, modern, and saints).

Similar/Related Sites

1. *World Civilizations: An Internet Classroom and Anthology*—http://www.wsu.edu/~dee/ —This well-designed Web site was originally begun in 1994 to support Web-enhanced world civilizations courses at Washington State University; however, over the past three years Richard Hooker and Paul Brians have extended it to provide an online learning environment for a college credit Internet course. Users may encounter broken links, but persistence will yield extensive materials, all offered freely for nonprofit educational use.

Future plans for the site include an expanded anthology of readings edited by Paul Brians (partially in place), textbook materials, learning modules, and a glossary. Navigate the page from the main page by clicking on the **contents** or **resources** link.

2. *World Literature Study Guides*—http://www.wsu.edu:8080/~brians/guides_index.html—Created by Paul Brians, a colleague of Richard Hooker at Washington State University and co-editor of the *World Civilizations* page (see above), these study guides cover a wide variety of historical and artistic periods. Particularly useful to teachers of world literature are his explorations of the interrelationships among the arts. Brians expresses the hope that his pages will be used by teachers and students as starting points for their own exploration of these works. The site is organized to complement the humanities courses Brians teaches at Washington State University. These include world literature surveys and courses in eighteenth- and nineteenth-century European classics, postcolonial and diasporic literature, and a special topics course on love poetry.

3. *History for Kids*—http://www.historyforkids.org/—Created by Dr. Karen Carr of Portland State University, this well-designed site is intended for children in K–12 and includes major sections on the history of Egypt, West Asia, Germany, Greece, Islam, and the Middle Ages, all of which are extensively cross-linked with information on art, economics, environment, government, architecture, games, clothing, literature, war, philosophy, science, food, religion, and people. This site provides an outstanding set of parent/teacher guides that pose general questions and provide guidelines for classroom discussion and activities. Topics include classroom suggestions for teaching philosophy, religion, architecture, science, economics, the environment, and food, as well as scavenger hunts and hands-on projects. Note that the craft projects page must be accessed through the left-hand toolbar; the links to this page from other internal pages appear to be broken.

4. *NM's Creative Impulse: The Artist's View of World History and Western Civilization*—http://history.evansville.net/—This Web site provides an overview comparable to that of a Western civilization course, but with links to artworks that illustrate the period.

5. *The Applied History Research Group Multimedia History Tutorials—University of Calgary*—http://www.ucalgary.ca/applied_history/tutor/—This series of interdisciplinary tutorials in the history of the Western world provides an excellent starting point for students studying the development of the social sciences, humanities, and fine arts in Europe and the Americas. The site offers excellent backgrounds entitled *Old World Contacts* (Eurasian and African history from 330 B.C.E. to 1500 C.E.); *First Europe Tutorial* (the Greek, Germanic, Frankish, and Roman worlds); *The End of Europe's Middle Ages* (fourteenth and fifteenth centuries); *The Islamic World to 1600*; and *Peopling North America: Population Movements and Migration*. Still largely intact, this Web site has not been updated since 2001.

WebChron: World History Chronology
http://campus.northpark.edu/history/WebChron/index.html

Site Summary. This Web site, created by Professor David Koeller of Northpark University, provides regional and cross-cultural timelines from the origins of human development through the present, cross-linked, in turn, to explanatory text and images. Although the text documents were written by students and are not always thorough, the timelines themselves are largely accurate.

Navigating the Site. To view this site, your browser must support frames. The site is easy to navigate. Select the appropriate timeline by clicking on the appropriate geographical or topic button, located in the left-hand navigation bar. Geographic regions can also be selected by clicking on the appropriate location on the globe image. Events may appear in more than one timeline. Second-level pages linked to the main page provide three sets of navigation tools: a linked overview chronology on the left, a detailed chronology in the center, and links to primary and secondary sources on the right.

Discussion Questions and Activities

1. *Rig Veda* and the *Upanishads*. From the main page, select **India and Southern Asia Chronology**, then select the **Rig Veda**. Read about the *Rig Veda*, then click on the link at the bottom of the page to read portions of the primary text. Follow the same procedure for the *Upanishads*. In what ways does the introduction help to explain how the primary texts might be read? What do the *Rig Veda* and the *Upanishads* explain about the beliefs of Hinduism? (See also Chapter 5.)

Eyewitness Accounts
http://www.eyewitnesstohistory.com/

Site Summary. Created by Ibis Communications, a Web site development company specializing in work for museums, historical societies, and educational institutions, this Web site provides brief descriptions of historical events, accompanied by narrative excerpts from eyewitnesses. Included are a number of narratives relevant to classical Greek and Roman literature; medieval topics such as the Crusades, plague, and exploration of the Americas; the French Revolution; and World War II. Although brief, the entries provide concise, incisive illustrations to accompany lesson plans.

Navigating the Site. The easiest way to navigate the site is from the index page, which provides a detailed listing of the pages featured on the site. Links to the pages are also grouped chronologically. To locate materials useful for teaching world literature, use the navigation bar across the top of the main page. Links listed on pages pertaining to the following historical periods are particularly appropriate:

> The ancient world (includes classical Greece and Rome)
>
> Seventeenth, eighteenth, nineteenth, and twentieth centuries
>
> The Middle Ages
>
> The Renaissance
>
> World War I
>
> World War II

Discussion Questions and Activities

1. The Norman Conquest and the Bayeux Tapestry. Read the *EyeWitness Index* account of the "Invasion of England in 1066." What events led up to the invasion of England by William the Conqueror of France? Compare the history provided on this page with the images on the Bayeux Tapestry, which depicts the Norman Conquest in narrative form (see Chapter 8). What events can you identify, based on the *EyeWitness* page?

2. The Crusades. Read the *EyeWitness Index* account of "The Crusaders Capture Jerusalem in 1099." What do the crusaders want to accomplish? From what point of view is the account narrated? How are the Christians described? How are the Saracens described? How do you think the narrator wants you to evaluate each group?

3. Spanish Massacre of the French in 1565. Read the *EyeWitness Index* account of this attempt by French Huguenots to create a colony in Spanish Florida. Why do the French try to create the colony? Why do the Spanish attack them? Compare the references to religion and to the hardships of the colonies to those in the narrative of Alvar Nuñez Cabeza de Vaca (below). What do these two examples say about the preoccupations of Spanish explorers during this time period?

Similar/Related Sites

1. *New Perspectives on the West: Alvar Nuñez Cabeza de Vaca*—http://www.pbs.org/ weta/thewest/people/a_c/cabezadevaca.htm—Part of Ken Burns's series on the exploration and settlement of the American West, this page provides a lengthy portion of Nuñez's harrowing sixteenth-century journey, mostly on foot, from Florida to Mexico City. (See http://users.ev1.net/~theweb/devacatoc.htm for an online version of the complete text.)

The Hypertext History of Theatre and Drama
http://www.emory.edu/ENGLISH/DRAMA/indextemp.html

Site Summary. This site, which was created by Rosslyn Elliott and Elizabeth Brewer to accompany a two-semester *History of Drama* course at Emory University, is incomplete, with some pages reported as "under construction" since 1997. The site nonetheless offers excellent, unparalleled historical coverage of theatrical settings, productions, images, and critical definitions on one Web site. The first linked page (**English 230**) from the main page provides access to particularly good images of Greek, Roman, medieval, and Renaissance theater diagrams (choose the appropriate period, then choose *Art and Architecture*). Coverage of Greek theater is especially good, including a video clip of the opening chorus from a traditional production of Euripides's play *Medea*. The second linked page (**English 231 Part I**) connects to an image map that links in turn to pages covering the theatrical movements *Symbolism, Surrealism, and the Absurd* and *Expressionism and Epic Theatre*. Coverage of other theatrical periods, though once planned, is reportedly under construction. A third linked page (**English 231 Part II**), under construction but substantial, provides a **Hypertext History of Modern Drama**. For best results, find the *Proceed to Map* link in the body of the page and print it out. Then return to the **Hypertext History of Modern Drama** page and use the linked grid of terms to read the map. Some terms are only briefly described, but others, such as *Bauhaus*, *surrealism*, *Dadaism*, *expressionism*, and *futurism,* include extensive images.

Navigating the Site. The site opens with a no-frills page, with links named to correspond with Emory's theater drama and history courses. Click on the link to the appropriate time period to gain access to the materials. See above for the contents of specific pages.

Discussion Questions and Activities

1. Theater History. Think about your last theater experience. What did the stage look like? The set design? The actors? Their costumes? How did the audience behave during the performance? Make some notes about what you remember. Then study some of the images of theater and set design.

a. From early Greek theater, watch the video clip of a dancing chorus from *Medea* and view the images in Greek art of actors in masks and animal costumes. Finally, look at the diagrams of an open air amphitheater. How do your recollections of your own theater experience compare with what you see in these images of Greek theater?

b. Now view images of stage settings from modern theater movements. How do these differ from your theater experience? How do they differ from Greek theater?

2. Some theater movements, such as Bauhaus, surrealism, Dadaism, and futurism, have connections with movements in the other arts. View the images of stage settings from these modern theater movements. Then go to the *World Art Web Kiosk* at http://worldart. sjsu.edu/ (see description below). Locate paintings from the art movements that bear the same names. What features do they have in common with the set designs?

Painting and Poetry Page
http://www.emory.edu/ENGLISH/Paintings&Poems/titlepage.html

Site Summary. Created by Harry Rusche of Emory University, this Web site provides links to forty-five twentieth-century poems that were written as responses to earlier paintings. Although many of the poems were written by British or American poets, most of the paintings are the work of continental European artists.

Navigating the Site. Links on the main page lead to pages that juxtapose each poem with its subject painting. Click on the painting to enlarge the image.

Discussion Questions and Activities

1. Schools often set up courses so that art and literature are studied as separate fields of study, yet these poets used their poetry to "read" paintings. Choose a title that interests you and select the link. Study the painting and read the accompanying poem. What elements of the painting does the poet find important? What words does the poet use? In what ways are the words of the poem visual? In what ways does the painting tell a story?

2. Choose another title and study the painting without reading the poem. Then write down your responses to the poem. Finally, read what the poet said about the painting. What did you see in the painting that the poet did not see? In what ways does the poet's "reading" add to your understanding of the painting?

The Literary Traveler
http://www.literarytraveler.com/

Site Summary. The *Literary Traveler* is an online journal begun in 1998 by Francis and Linda McGovern. Although the site encourages paid subscriptions to its newsletter, the articles are available online with no restrictions. The site focuses on the importance of place in artistic works and encourages submission of articles by travelers whose itineraries take them to places formerly inhabited or frequented by famous writers or artists; the site then publishes these articles alongside photographs. The site supports itself through paid subscriptions, donations, and partnering with Barnes & Noble. Although this site is not scholarly, it provides insight into the lives of such writers as Pablo Neruda, Bertholt Brecht, Federico García Lorca, Ovid, Rousseau, and Kafka.

Navigating the Site. The site is well constructed, with navigational tools in the left column, abstracts of longer columns in the center, and features on the right. The titles of the abstracts link to longer versions of the articles or to other categories. Not all of the articles are indexed well; for instance, the article on Kafka appears on the main site page as a feature, but is not listed on the **European Authors** page. Consequently, it is usually best to navigate from the *Author Index* link, located on the left-hand side of the main page.

Discussion Questions and Activities

1. Franz Kafka. How does a sense of place affect the creative process of a writer? Choose the *Author Index* link, then locate *Franz Kafka* in the center column of the resulting page. Read Kafka's *The Metamorphosis* and *The Trial* alongside the article on *The Writer's Life in Prague*. What similarities do you notice between the article's descriptions of Kafka's life in Prague and the life of Gregor Samsa in *The Metamorphosis*? Of the main character in *The Trial*?

2. Memoir. Create a memoir of a place you have visited where an important event took place. Describe the place completely, tying its features closely to your memoir.

3. Other World Literature Articles. Read these articles alongside the works of the writer to gain insight into his or her world:

   a. Pablo Neruda's Isla Negra—"A Single Drop Lucid and Heavy"

   b. Federico García Lorca—"The Poem of the Deep Song"

   c. Karen Blixen—"The Danish Home of Isaak Dinesen"

   d. Jean-Jacques Rousseau—"Happiness at Les Charmettes"

   e. "Marguerite Duras in Sa Dec, Vietnam"

   f. Ovid—"Ovid in Exile"

   g. Nikos Kazantzakis—"The Peace of Mt. Athos"

   h. Hans Christian Andersen—"The Traveler and Ugly Duckling"

Teaching Resources

Mr. Dowling's Electronic Passport
http://www.mrdowling.com/

Site Summary. Mr. Dowling's Electronic Passport is a Web site created in 1999 and maintained by Mike Dowling, a middle school geography teacher in Florida. The site provides brief historical, geographical, and cultural overviews of major regions and civilizations of the world, as well as downloadable study sheets, tests, pedagogical aids, and links to other significant resources on the Internet. The site is billed as "Safe for Kids." The site is well designed, with engaging clip art and cartoons throughout to encourage students to explore topics.

Navigating the Site. From the main page, select one of the topics by clicking on an icon. Once on a page, it is possible to navigate to all other major topics on the site by selecting a link in the left-hand column. Within a topic, navigate among pages by clicking on embedded links in the text.

Discussion Questions and Activities

1. Go to the page on *Ancient Egypt*, then choose the **Rosetta Stone** link for a look at early Egyptian writing in hieroglyphics. The link from the text **hieroglyphics** connects with a site that provides a hieroglyphics translator. Try translating your name or a phrase of your choice. From the **Cool Links** page, try out the Duke Papyrus Archive for information on the technologies of writing in ancient Egypt.

2. Go to the page on **India**, then choose the **Siddhartha Gautama** link to read about the life of Buddha. Click on the link to **Buddhists** for an outline of the teachings of Buddha. What are some beliefs held by Buddhists?

Similar/Related Sites

1. *The Web English Teacher*—http://www.webenglishteacher.com/—Created in 2000 by teacher Carla Beard, this Web site serves as a space for the exchange of ideas among teachers of English in grades K–12. The site provides a large variety of original lesson plans, in addition to linking to offsite resources. In terms of world literature, the site is particularly strong in its coverage of mythology and folklore materials. Under the topic "Literature," see lesson plans for Achebe's *Things Fall Apart*; Conrad's *Heart of Darkness*; Dante's *Commedia*; *Diary of Anne Frank*; Tolkien's *Lord of the Rings*; and works by H. G. Wells. See also the topic "Mythology, Folklore, and the Hero," and under "Poetry" see the page of lesson plans relating to Homer.

2. *World Wise Schools: Peace Corps Teaching Resources*—http://www.peacecorps.gov/wws/—This outstanding site, which provides lesson plans on understanding cultural differences, would serve as an excellent starting point for any cross-cultural literature-based assignment. The site also provides a page of stories told by Peace Corps volunteers, as well as a page devoted to folktales.

3. *EDSITEMENT*—http://edsitement.neh.gov/websites_all.asp—Maintained by the National Endowment for the Humanities, this site operates as a clearinghouse for links to Web resources pertaining to the teaching of art and culture, literature and language arts, foreign languages, and history and social studies.

4. *Global Schoolhouse*—http://globalschoolhouse.org—This Web site serves as a clearinghouse and facilitator for Internet-based, collaborative learning projects.

Linguistics

Exploratorium: Where Do Languages Come From?
http://www.exploratorium.edu/exploring/language/index.html

Site Summary. This Web site is the companion site to a specific issue of the quarterly magazine *Exploratorium* that focused on the origin of languages. Within just a few pages, this site provides an overview of how linguists identify relationships between languages, how languages evolve, and major concepts surrounding linguistic study.

Navigating the Site. The site is easy to navigate. The main page provides options to visit subtopic pages or to step through the pages sequentially.

Discussion Questions and Activities

1. Translation: Art or Science? Page 2 of the *Exploratorium* site invites users to compare the origins of the word for "hand" in several languages. Page 4 compares different counting words. What other common words share affinities within language families? Using Altavista's BabelFish translator (http://babel.altavista.com), translate other counting words, family words (father, mother, brother, sister, etc.), words for the seasons and weather, words relating to agriculture, etc. What kinds of words are related? Which are not?

2. The History of Words. Choose a word that has evolved greatly in meaning over time and look it up in the *Oxford English Dictionary* (available by online subscription, on CD, or in book form in many libraries). For instance, look up the words "mop" and "sharper." What have these words meant over time? When reading historical literature or even older translations of world literature, what misunderstandings could arise from not knowing the contemporary uses of the words?

Similar/Related Sites

1. *Scientific American—Early History of Indo-European Languages*—http://www.geocities. com/Paris/LeftBank/6507/chronicle120.html—This fascinating article describes information key to the development of many modern languages from a common Indo-European root, including Grimm's Law (concerning sound shift) and the methods by which linguists can reconstruct aspects of life 5,000 years ago by comparing words common to many modern languages.

2. *Languages of the World*—http://www.ethnologue.com/country_index.asp—The Ethnologue Country Index provides a list of languages associated with a particular region of the world. Click on the map to bring up a list describing the languages.

Art

World Art Web Kiosk

http://worldart.sjsu.edu/

Site Summary. This comprehensive Web site, administered by Professor Kathleen Cohen of California State University, San Jose, contains a database of over 20,000 high-resolution images of world art. The site includes resources from the California State University Image Exchange Online (CIELO) system. Art in the database can be searched by collection, artist, object (including historical era, art form, nationality, style, type of object, and city or site), date, or keyword.

Navigating the Site. The entry page layout provides major navigational links on the left, artworks with captions in the center, and detail navigational links on the right. The detail links are arranged so that users can identify artwork by title, date, region, keyword, medium, artist, genre, etc. A search engine is also available on the site. The art pages themselves feature thumbnail images of representative art; additional artworks of the same type are listed in a drop-down menu. Alternatively, a user can select other ways to view all of the art associated with a page by selecting among views that include "thumbnails," "text list," "image & label," and "description." Clicking on a thumbnail produces an enlarged image. The site also offers an on-site search engine.

Discussion Questions and Activities

1. Celtic Interlace. A key element of Celtic design is the use of interlace patterns in costume, book, and jewelry design. In the "Quick Search" field of the *Web Kiosk* site, enter the keyword "interlace," and click "Go." A page of thumbnail images appears. Then click "Belt buckle with interlace design" to view an artifact from the Sutton Hoo burial site. Click the image itself for an enlarged view. Compare the interlace design from the buckle with the page design of the *Book of Kells*, a medieval Latin text of the four gospels, possibly created around 800 C.E. in Ireland (see http://www.snake.net/people/paul/kells/, especially the "bmp" images). In what ways is interlace used in the page designs of these books?

2. Art and Modern Theater. Read about modern drama on the **Hypertext History of Theatre and Drama**. View the images of stage settings associated with *impressionism, expressionism, futurism, Dadaism*, and *surrealism*. Then search the **Art Kiosk** for paintings from parallel movements (search on *expressionist, futurist, Dada, surrealist*). What features do art and stage productions influenced by the same movements have in common?

Similar/Related Sites

1. *Art History Resources on the Web*—http://witcombe.sbc.edu/ARTHLinks.html—This incredibly comprehensive art history Web site provides timelines for the development of art from prehistory through the twenty-first century, across specific geographic regions, and in specific media. The site is extensively cross-linked with definitions of terms, important museums, online art images, and additional research links. Also included are images of the art described, although these are sometimes too small to facilitate close study. The site was created and is maintained by Professor Chris Whitcombe, an art history professor at Sweet Briar College.

2. *The Mother of All Art History Sites*—http://www.art-design.umich.edu/mother—Primarily a gateway to other sites, this Web site is sponsored by the University of Michigan School of Art and Design.

3. *Webmuseum*—http://www.ibiblio.org/wm/—Although this site is unaffiliated with any museum or university, it offers descriptions of movements, biographical information on artists, and descriptions of works.

4. *Artserve*—http://rubens.anu.edu.au/—This site provides images of art and architecture, mostly from the Mediterranean basin and Japan.

5. *Metropolitan Museum of Art*—http://www.metmuseum.org/collections/index.asp—This Web site, maintained by the Metropolitan Museum of Art in New York, provides 3,500 images online of art from the museum's collections.

Philosophy

Great Voyages: The History of Western Philosophy Course
http://www.orst.edu/instruct/phl302/

Site Summary. This site, created by Bill Uzgalis at Oregon State University for a 1995 philosophy course, traces the development of Western philosophy, including perceptions of non-Western peoples, from Columbus's landfall in 1492 through initiation of the slave narrative genre.

Connected to this course on philosophy in the age of discovery are e-texts and commentary on the ideas of Machiavelli, Montaigne, Descartes, Pascal, Sir Thomas More, Rousseau, Spinoza, Leibniz, Locke, and others, linked to a page at http://www.orst.edu/instruct/phl302/e-text.html. The bottom of this page links to study guides for most of these works.

Navigating the Site. The site is easy to navigate. Links at the bottom of each page lead to the next segment of the site. Seventeenth- and eighteenth-century e-texts are cross-linked with the syllabus.

Discussion Questions and Activities

1. From the **e-texts** page, read from Leibniz's *Monadology* and Voltaire's satire *Candide*. What aspects of Leibniz's philosophy does Voltaire satirize?

2. Both Sir Thomas More, author of *Utopia*, and Montaigne, author of the *Essays*, were Renaissance humanists, and they wrote about some of the same topics. Compare the discussions of education in *Utopia* and in Montaigne's essay *On the Education of Children*. What do these essays have in common? How do they differ?

Similar/Related Sites

1. *Internet Encyclopedia of Philosophy*—http://www.utm.edu/research/iep/—Created, maintained, and edited by James Fieser, University of Tennessee, with Bradley Dowden of California State University, Sacramento, and an international host of area editors, this comprehensive Web site provides three types of materials: "(1) original contributions by specialized philosophers around the internet, (2) adaptations of material written by the editors for classroom purposes, and (3) adaptations from public domain sources (typically from two or more sources for per article)." Designated "proto-articles" by the editors, types (2) and (3) will eventually be replaced by original articles written by philosophers. All of the articles are well documented and signed by a contributor; however, the site does not provide primary texts on philosophical texts.

2. *Humanistic Texts*—http://www.humanistictexts.org/—Created and maintained by Webmaster Rex Pay, this Web site offers extensive selections of texts from oral and written traditions throughout history and throughout the world, beginning before 1000 B.C.E. and continuing to the present. This eclectic and ambitious site seeks to represent humanistic discourse as broadly as possible.

3. *Philosophy Since the Enlightenment*—http://www.philosopher.org.uk/—Created by Roger Jones, a philosophy instructor in Great Britain, this Web site provides summaries of major Western philosophical ideas beginning with Descartes.

Heroic Literature

HyperEpos

http://www.auburn.edu/~downejm/hyperepos.html

Site Summary. Created by Professor Jeremy Downes of Auburn University, this Web site is dedicated to the study of epic poetry from preclassical through contemporary history. Professor Downes's definition of epic is quite broad; users are cautioned to research the prevailing definitions available in standard dictionaries of literary terms when assessing this site. Nonetheless,

HyperEpos provides useful links to online texts of major epics, background materials, sites dedicated to authors of epics, and bibliographies.

Navigating the Site. The site is easy to navigate. The main page provides navigation links to epics, which are categorized by historical period and authorship. A separate list of general resources helpful in the study of epics is also provided.

Discussion Questions and Activities

1. *The Argonautica*

    a. *The Argonautica* recounts the story of Jason and the Argonauts on their quest to retrieve the Golden Fleece. Read this lesser-known epic and compare it with Homeric epic. What elements does the *Argonautica* share in common with the *Iliad* and the *Odyssey*?

    b. The *Argonautica* also tells the story of how Jason met Medea, the subject of Euripides's play and a section of Ovid's *Metamorphoses*. What details of the *Argonautica* provide background to the play?

2. Homeric Fragments. Read the translations of the Homeric fragments available on this site. What do they add to your understanding of Greek heroic literature? What do they suggest about the quantity and variety of epic literature that must have existed in ancient Greece, in addition to the more frequently studied *Iliad* and *Odyssey*?

CHAPTER 5

Religion and Folklore

Introduction

For thousands of years, religion and religious texts have been studied as and have formed a basis for other literature. Even in the relatively secularized societies of contemporary Western civilization, most literary texts written before 1800 are only partially understandable without some knowledge of major religions, their mythologies, and their philosophical underpinnings. Even literature written after 1800 continues to draw on these earlier traditions. Regardless of the culture under study, contemporary world literature courses frequently begin by comparing myths of origin. This chapter seeks to provide access to some of the best religion, mythology, and folklore Web sites available, based on the extent to which the texts are also studied by literary scholars and teachers. The sites were selected according to whether they reflected the study of religion as conducted using established academic anthropological/folkloristic principles. The inclusion or exclusion of a Web site, however, should not be viewed as the acceptance or rejection of the religious beliefs of any group.

Religion Sites of General Interest

The Internet Sacred Text Archive

http://www.sacred-texts.com/index.htm

Site Summary. In existence since 1999, *Sacred Text Archive* comes closer than any other site to being an all-inclusive, comprehensive site providing primary texts for the study of belief and belief systems. This nonprofit site is administered by J. B. Hare and features free access to e-texts "about religion, mythology, legends and folklore, and occult and esoteric topics." The site's primary aim is to promote religious tolerance through the study of religions and religious ideas. The site also includes many secondary texts, bibliographical information, and translations of many unique texts unavailable elsewhere on the Internet, including "comprehensive translations of Shintô texts, the Kalevala, the Upanishads, and the Rig Veda," as well as African, Native American, and Polynesian texts. Also reproduced here is an extensive collection of sagas and legends, commonly taught Greek and Roman literature, sacred books of Eastern religions, and documents associated with recent religions. The site also provides a page on traditions. Most of the texts are scanned from previously published translations, some with commentary; others are newly contributed. Materials marked with a CD are also available on the site's CD, which is offered for sale. The editor's commentary throughout is sensitive and astute. The site is frequently updated—at least weekly.

Navigating the Site. The site is relatively easy to navigate. Links to major site features appear at the top of the site's main page; links to pages covering major topics and geographical regions appear in a column on the right. Navigational tools are scarce beyond the site's opening page; the user must use the browser's "Back" button for navigation. The site does not offer a search engine.

Discussion Questions and Activities

1. Sacred Texts. What religious texts do the major religions hold sacred? Compare those of Judaism, Christianity, and Islam. Did you find any commonalities?

2. Creation Myths. How do the major religions explain the origins of the world? From the left-hand navigation bar on the main page, follow the paths provided in the table below to identify representative foundational myths. Read a number of such accounts on the *Sacred Text Archive* site and on the sites listed below, comparing their similarities and differences. How closely related are the creation stories of widely dispersed belief systems? What beliefs are held in common?

▶ African

    ▶ Myths and Legends of the Bantu ▶ Chapter II. Where Man Came From

    ▶ West and Central Africa ▶ Myths of Ífè ▶ I. The Beginning

▶ Ancient Near East ▶ The Enuma Elish

▶ Bible

    ▶ Compare translated versions of *Genesis* (KJV & JPS)

▶ Egyptian

    ▶ Legends of the Gods ▶ Summary I, and Creation A and B

▶ Greek/Roman

    ▶ *Bullfinch's Mythology*, Chapter II

    ▶ Ovid's *Metamorphosis*, Book I

▶ Native American

    ▶ Native Californian Religion ▶ Indian Myths of South Central California ▶ The Beginning

    ▶ Cherokee Religion Myths of the Cherokee ▶ 1. How the world was made.

    ▶ Hopi Religion ▶ Traditions of the Hopi Origin Myth

    ▶ *The Popul Vuh*

▶ Sikhism ▶ Shri Guru Granth Sahib ▶ Jup

▶ Taoism ▶ Taoist Teachings Translated from the *Book of Lieh-Tzü* ▶ Cosmogony

---

3. *Jamaican Anansi Stories*—http://www.sacred-texts.com/afr/jas/index.htm—Also available on this site are significant materials useful in the study of folklore, including this page dedicated to Margaret Warren Beckwith's 1924 book that included a number of Jamaican Anansi stories. Read several of the stories about this traditional African trickster figure, as well as the excellent notes that accompany each text. What happens to Anansi in each story? What lessons does he learn, and what cultural values are reinforced?

Similar/Related Sites

1. General information sites

   a. *Ontario Religious Tolerance Consultants*—http://www.religioustolerance.org/—This site offers extensive explanations of contemporary religious beliefs and links to sites addressing historical and contemporary religions.

   b. *The Religious Movements Homepage Project*—http://religiousmovements.lib.virginia.edu/—This site provides descriptions, written by undergraduate sociology students, of religious movements worldwide.

   c. *Your Guide to Religions of the World*—http://www.bbc.co.uk/worldservice/people/features/world_religions/—Sponsored by the British Broadcasting Corporation, this Web site provides an accessible overview of the beliefs underlying major religious groups, including Islam, Hinduism, Christianity, Buddhism, Judaism, and Sikhism.

   d. *From Primitives to Zen—Mircea Eliade*—http://alexm.here.ru:8081/mirrors/www.enteract.com/jwalz/Eliade/—This site is a transcription by J. D. Walz of the famous 1966 sacred text anthology and commentary compiled by Mircea Eliade, then professor of Religious Studies at the University of Chicago. The anthology is arranged thematically rather than systematically, and no index is provided; consequently, the anthology is easiest to follow for those doing comparative studies rather than single-culture studies.

2. Other creation myths

   a. *Altaic Creation Story (Turkey)*—http://web.umr.edu/~gdoty/poems/altaic/creation.html—This Web site provides a poetic adaptation, written by Gene Doty of the University of Missouri, Rolla, of Gülten Yener's prose translation of the Altaic creation myth.

   b. *Japanese Creation Myth*—http://www.wsu.edu:8080/~wldciv/world_civ_reader/world_civ_reader_1/kojiki.html

3. South Asian sacred texts

   a. *Sanskrit Texts and Stotra*—http://sanskrit.bhaarat.com/Dale/—This Web site provides translations of many Sanskrit texts.

   b. *The Vedic Experience*—http://www.himalayanacademy.com/books/vedic_experience/VEIndex.html—The Web site features commentary on sacred Hindu texts.

Encyclopedia Mythica
http://www.pantheon.org/

Site Summary. Created in 1995 and still edited by Micha Lindemanns, *Encyclopedia Mythica* publishes articles written by contributors, in consultation with an editorial board, on mythology, bestiary, folklore, and heroes. The 6,000 entries and images offer a convenient reference resource for mythology topics worldwide.

Navigating the Site. The site is exceptionally well designed and offers both a hierarchical structure for browsing and a search engine for keyword searches. Choosing ***Explore*** from the site's main page leads to second-level pages, with menus of navigational links back to other major topics on the left and to subtopics on the right. The third-level pages, typically addressing a particular region or subtopic, provide an alphabetical index to all articles on the left and the entry associated with the selected subtopic on the right. Each page includes links back to the major site divisions and the main page.

Discussion Questions and Activities

1. Use the search engine to look up articles about the blind soothsayer Tiresias, a character who appears frequently in Greek drama (see *Oedipus Tyrannos* and *Antigone*) and in epics (e.g., *The Odyssey*). Based on what you read about Tiresias, what might a classical theater audience have expected simply because Tiresias had been led onstage?

2. Consult the ***Bestiary*** for definitions of strange creatures that appear in literature, such as the sphinx (*Oedipus Tyrannos*), werewolf (Marie de France's *Bisclavret*), barghest or black dogs (British folklore), and the Nemean lion and hydra (fought by Heracles).

3. Choose the ***Featured Items***, then choose the link to the ***Arabian Nights***. Click on the link to the chapter from ***The Arabian Nights*** and read the story of Sultan Schahriar and his wife Scheherazade. What occasioned the telling of the *Arabian Nights*?

Similar/Related Sites

1. *Digital Librarian's Mythology Links*—http://www.digital-librarian.com/mythology. html—Although this portal provides a number of valuable mythology links, they are not categorized; however, persistence will be rewarded.

2. *Myths and Legends*—http://members.bellatlantic.net/~vze33gpz/myth.html—An extensive set of links compiled by high school and college physics teacher Christopher Siren while a student at MIT, this site offers brief annotations of cited resources, many quite useful.

Myths
http://www.windows.ucar.edu/tour/link=/mythology/mythology.html

Site Summary. Cultures throughout the world have sought through mythology to explain the origin and function of astronomical phenomena. Part of a larger astronomy site sponsored by the University Corporation for Atmospheric Research, the mythology pages of this site are of particular value to K–12 world literature and science educators interested in using a cross-disciplinary, comparative approach to belief systems. Each entry on the site is provided in three versions, for beginning, intermediate, and advanced students. The site offers links to materials that document the various ways cultures have interpreted the solar system. Consequently, this site is particularly useful for cross-disciplinary science and literature units. Also included are links to materials about classical and other world mythologies, including excellent family trees, descriptions of prominent deities, artwork inspired by mythology, and an interactive mythology hangman game for students. The "Links for Educators and Students" all relate to science and math education.

Navigating the Site. The site is best viewed using Internet Explorer. To take advantage of the site's navigational system (a large viewing screen is best), enter through the main page at http://www.windows.ucar.edu/ and choose the ***Frames*** option. This option produces a three-level navigation system: a bar across the top with options for other site features, a bar across the bottom that leads to major site topics, and a bar on the left that allows the user to view all site information on a particular solar system feature. Users who do not use the **Frames** option can still navigate the site, although the browser **Back** button must be used.

Discussion Questions and Activities

1. What did the day and night sky mean to ancient peoples? Read what people thought about the sun, moon, planets, and stars. Compare the stories. What do these stories tell you about how people of different cultures understood their place in the universe? What function did these stories serve in early times and places?

2. Choose the link to **Mythology** for an interactive map of the world. Then click on the area of the map labeled **Aztec**. How did the Aztecs understand and explain the existence of the sun, moon, rain, and Venus? Compare what you learn with Amazonian and Incan ideas about the sun and the moon. How much variation do you find just within South America? How much variation between continents? Are there any common features?

Pre-Christian Religions by Region

Classical Greek and Roman Mythology

Classical Myth Project

http://web.uvic.ca/grs/bowman/myth/

Site Summary. This site, created by Laurel Bowman at the University of Victoria, includes pages linking with historical accounts of Greek/Roman myths as well as helpful timelines and attributes of the gods. Another particularly useful page reveals how images of deities in Greek art are identified using iconography. For students of literature, understanding the symbolic meaning of visual elements will help to explain imagery and figurative language in Greek and Roman works, such as Homer's epics and the plays of Aeschylus, Sophocles, and Euripides.

Navigating the Site. The site is easy to navigate. Begin by visiting the links listed under **Helpful Information**, then go back to the **Classical Myth** section.

Discussion Questions and Activities

1. Read about iconography in Greek art at Laurel Bowman's *Classical Myth Project*. Then read descriptions of the images at the *Mythology Project at Princeton* (below). Compile a list of attributes associated with each god. If possible, visit the Greek artifacts section of a local art museum, or locate reproductions of art in books at your local public library. What figures from Greek mythology can you identify, based on your list?

2. Compare attributes of the gods and heroes with their behavior in a work of Greek or Roman literature. In what ways would their behavior be expected, based on preconceived ideas about their attributes? How do the physicality and behavior of Greek and Roman deities compare with manifestations of deities in other religious traditions?

Similar/Related Sites

1. *Mythology Project at Princeton*—http://web.princeton.edu/sites/classics/mythology/nav.html—Although this site is somewhat cumbersome to use, it provides additional images for analysis, including each image's provenance and an interpretation of its elements. The site also provides helpful family trees and pages addressing several of the Greek gods. Enlarged images are available only to users at Princeton, but the images available on the public pages are somewhat larger than thumbnails.

2. *Bulfinch's Mythology On-line*—http://www.bulfinch.org/—Created by Bob Fisher, this site hosts the online version of Thomas Bulfinch's *Greek and Roman Mythology* (1855), *Age of Chivalry* (including Arthuriana) (1858), and *Age of Charlemagne* (1863). Bulfinch's original goal in writing, to create an accessible mythology that would provide the general reader with the ability to interpret poetic allusions in literature, has made his works popular for nearly 150 years.

3. *Robin Mitchell-Boyask's Mythology Course Materials*—http://www.temple.edu/classics/mythdirectory.html—Created by Professor Robin Mitchell-Boyask at Temple University, this Web site provides extensive study guides, summaries, charts, and background materials for a wide variety of classical literature. The site is frequently updated.

Pre-Christian Norse and Germanic Religion

Norse Mythology

http://www.ugcs.caltech.edu/~cherryne/mythology.html

Site Summary. Created by Nicole Cherry of Cal Tech in 1996, this site defines its scope as covering "Norse mythology, Scandinavian mythology, Viking mythology," all having to do with "the pre-Christian religion of the Norwegian, Swedish, Icelandic, and Danish peoples," as well as some Finnish mythology. The site's pages provide profiles of major deities, synopses of myths, and prose summaries of major writings.

Navigating the Site. The site is easy to navigate. Navigational links in the left-hand frame list all of the pages available. The corresponding pages appear in the right-hand frame.

Discussion Questions and Activities

1. Read the introduction to the *Norse Mythology* Web site. What modern works of Tolkien and Wagner are based on pre-Christian Norse and Germanic religions? Who is the Gandalf to whom Cherry refers?

2. Compare the creation myths present in the *Eddas* with the creation myths you read on the *Sacred Text Archive* site. How did the beliefs of Norse and Germanic peoples compare with those of other pre-Christian people?

3. Read about Norse cosmology, mythic figures, and Ragnarok. How might you describe the world in which the people who held these religious beliefs lived? (Further reading is available on D. Ashliman's site; see "Similar/Related Sites" below.)

4. Read about the Valkyries and Berserker. How did these peoples define bravery, and how important was it?

Similar/Related Sites

1. *D. Ashliman's Germanic Myths, Legends, and Sagas*—http://www.pitt.edu/~dash/mythlinks.html—See the extended entry provided below.

Turkish Folklore

http://sircasaray.turkiye.org/anadolu/giris.html
http://sircasaray.turkiye.org/anadolu/myth/myth.html

Site Summary. This Web site, created by Turkish nationals, provides an eclectic look at Turkish culture and traditional literature. Most of the literature in English is provided on the **Turkish Mythology** page, accessible through a link on the main page and directly through the second URL listed above. Although the first set of texts provided on this page are in Turkish, the set that follows provides translations for seven of twelve legends from *The Book of Dede Korkut*, a heroic epic of the Oghuz (predecessors of the Ottoman and Seljuk Turks). Translation of this text is credited to Faruk Sümer, Ahmet Uysal, and Warren S. Walker. The final set of texts provides accounts of legends and myths associated with locations in modern Turkey that are also described in Greek mythology; unfortunately, no translator or writer is identified. Separate pages linked to the main page discuss Turkish book history through the **Art of Illumination** page; the **Lyric Poems of Yunus Emre**, translated by Kabir Helminski and Refik Algan; and **Sufism**, mystical religious practices followed by the Sunni Islamic Mevlevi sect called dervishes, whose beliefs are described through the poetry of the famous poet Rumi (also see Chapter 10 for a discussion of Sufi poetry). The other pages attached to this main page include excellent photographs and descriptions of Turkish traditional culture. (For added insight into traditional Turkish culture, particularly worth exploring are the English pages on the **The Yörük Nomads; Nymphs of the Bosphorus**, which actually depicts traditional residences along the waterfront; **Women's Headdresses, Turkish Baths, Turkish Belts**, and traditional summer housing called Yaylas.)

Navigating the Site. Navigate among the main pages of this site using links and the browser's ***Back*** button. Most subpages have navigational arrows at the bottom to move within pages pertaining to a particular topic; the last page of a topic usually displays a script *H*, which returns the user to the homepage. Navigation among these other pages is not always systematic; experiment to view all of the site's features. Although navigation may be somewhat frustrating, the photographs provided are stunning.

Discussion Questions and Activities

1. *Book of Dede Korkut.* From the **Turkish Mythology** page, select the *Book of Dede Korkut.* Read several of the stories. What does this epic tell you about the cultural values of the society in which it was created? What do you learn about family life and relationships between men and women? What is the symbolic meaning of colors? How do these compare with your own understanding of what colors signify?

2. *Turkish Myths.* Read several of the myths and compare them with Greek myths pertaining to the same topic. What elements suggest a common origin for many of the stories?

Contemporary Religions and Their Historical Roots

Judaism

Jewish History Center Resource
http://jewishhistory.huji.ac.il/

Site Summary. This comprehensive Web site, sponsored by the Dinur Center for Research in Jewish History at the Hebrew University of Jerusalem, provides basic descriptions of contemporary and historical philosophies, extensive timelines, reading lists, and access to numerous historical texts in English, Hebrew, and many other languages. The site is updated regularly.

Navigating the Site. The site is easy to navigate. The main page offers five drop-down menus—*Timelines*, *Basic Readings*, *Academic World*, *Organizations*, and *Tools*. Items within these menus that are marked with asterisks (*) are provided in English as well as Hebrew. E-texts are provided as part of *Basic Readings*. The site is also searchable.

Discussion Questions and Activities

1. From the main page, click the drop-down menu under *Resources*, then choose the *Texts and Documents* link. Under "Biblical Studies," explore the texts listed under *Ancient Near Eastern Myths*. Do these stories have anything in common with the Old Testament?

2. Return to the **Texts and Documents** page. Under "Second Temple and Talmudic Era," explore the texts listed under *Old Testament Pseudepigrapha* (Alan Humn). How does the story of Adam and Eve from Genesis compare with the *Life of Adam and Eve* (English translations of Armenian, Georgian, Slavonic, Latin, and Greek versions are provided for comparison)? What about the *Cave of Treasures*?

3. Return to the **Texts and Documents** page. Under "Holocaust," read the first-person narratives that begin with quotation marks or with the word *Auschwitz*. Why do the narratives refer to "Special Action" and "Material for Special Treatment" rather than using more specific language? Finally, read the *Eyewitness Account of Einsatz Executions*. Why do the victims behave as they do? What does the narrator do? Why?

The Jewish Roman World of Jesus
http://www.religiousstudies.uncc.edu/JDTABOR/indexb.html

Site Summary. Created by Professor James D. Tabor of the Department of Religious Studies at the University of North Carolina at Charlotte, this outstanding Web site seeks to provide insight into the "political, social, cultural, and religious ideas and realities of the wider Mediterranean context" within which early New Testament events took place. The site is extremely well written, providing extensive overviews, commentaries, and quotations from primary texts in lucid, accessible terms. The site is divided into six main topics: introductions to the *Roman World* and to the *Jewish World of Jesus*, *Hellenistic/Roman Religion and Philosophy*, *Archaeology and the Dead Sea Scrolls*, *Christian Origins and the New Testament*, and *Ancient Judaism*. This Web site is indispensable to world literature and Bible as literature courses. The Web site also provides a page of links and a gallery of images of the Dead Sea Scrolls.

Navigating the Site. The site is easy to navigate. All of the materials are linked to a site map on the main page. A navigation bar at the bottom of the page provides access to a page of links and a gallery of images.

Discussion Questions and Activities

1. *Introduction* and *Hellenistic/Roman Religion & Philosophy.* Read through Professor Tabor's assessment of the system of beliefs commonly held during Jesus's lifetime. What elements of this belief system remain important in modern day Christian religions? Which remain important in Judaism?

2. *Christian Origins and the New Testament.* Read the six pages that describe the differences and affinities among the New Testament gospels Matthew, Mark, and Luke, as well as the "gospel according to Q." How do their contents compare? What explanations does Dr. Tabor offer for these differences?

3. *Ancient Judaism.*

   a. Print out the list of words found on the **Basic Vocabulary** page and look them up. These key terms are important in understanding other references on these pages.

   b. Read the rules for living available on the **Summary of the Torah** page. Which of these do you observe in your everyday life? Which have been inscribed in law? Which would you consider to be matters of belief or individual choice? Why?

Hebrew Bible: Navigating the Bible II: Online Bar/Bat Mitzvah Tutor

http://bible.ort.org/

Site Summary. This excellent Web site is sponsored by WorldORT, a nonprofit organization that operates worldwide to support education, training, and counseling programs, particularly in Jewish schools. The Web site provides parallel Hebrew/English translations of the *Torah*, with commentary, set up as a resource for students preparing for their bar or bat mitzvahs. In addition to useful study tools, the site also provides a discussion board that can be used to clarify questions.

Navigating the Site. From the main page, select the *English* link, then choose among the tool options on the left (*Calendar, Find, Reference, Singing,* or *Genealogy*), or choose from the study options on the right. These include *Translation* (that is, access to the entire Hebrew Bible), *Torah* (the weekly reading, with text provided in English and Hebrew, plus audio files sung by a cantor), the accompanying selections from the *Haftarot* and the *Brachot* (blessings). To listen to the sound files that appear throughout the site, you must have Real Player (freely downloadable from the Internet). The sound files can be played by clicking on the speaker icon that appears near the text. Choosing the *Singing* tool brings up a page that provides the Hebrew text, the music, and a sound file.

Discussion Questions and Activities

1. Begin by visiting Mechon Mamre (see "Similar/Related Links," below); choose the *Torah Basics (Torah 101)* link. Begin by reading the pages labeled *Basic* and work up through *Intermediate* and *Advanced.*

2. Return to the *Bar/Bat Mitzvah Tutor.* Choose a portion of the *Torah* to read and listen to the audio file. How does this presentation of biblical verse compare with that used in Christian or Islamic religious services?

3. Choose a portion of the *Torah* to read. Based upon your reading about Judaism, describe what might be significant about the passage you read.

4. For the same passage, read the accompanying *Haftarot* and *Brachot* passages. Think about how the passages might be connected. Why are these three passages grouped together on the same day? Compare the structure and contents of the readings with those read during the religious services of another major religion.

Similar/Related Sites

1. *Mechon Mamre*—http://www.mechon-mamre.org/index.htm—This Web site provides several online resources for learning the Torah, defined as "God's Laws given all people, whether Jews or Gentiles, through Moses at Sinai." Although much of the site is in Hebrew, the explanation of ***Torah Basics*** (Torah 101) provides an excellent overview of the ideas and beliefs underlying Judaism—necessary to understand fully the significance of the Torah and its study.

2. *On-line Rare Manuscripts—Haggadah Online*—http://www.cn.huc.edu/libraries/haggadah/klau.html—Maintained by Hebrew Union College, this site provides an online exhibit of beautiful illuminated images from fifteenth- through eighteenth-century editions of the Haggadah.

Christianity

Christian Bible Translations: Bible Gateway

http://bible.gospelcom.net/

Site Summary. This site, sponsored by Gospel Communications Incorporated (Muskegon, MI), an evangelical Christian organization, provides a number of biblical translations sponsored by various protestant sects. The site features both simple and advanced searches, permitting comparative studies of translation choices. Translations of the following are provided in nineteen languages: The New American Standard Version (NASV), Amplified Version (AMP) (Lockman Trust—provides multiple translations for of Hebrew/Greek words), New Living Translation (NLT), King James Version (KJV), New King James Version (NKJV), 21st Century New King James Version (KJV21), American Standard Version (ASV), Worldwide English New Testament (WE), Young's Literal Translation (YLT), and the Darby Translation (DARBY). The advanced search tool permits parallel searching by keyword or by chapter/verse in any combination of the Bible translations online. With so many translations available, which one should you consult? There is no definitive answer to this question, but anyone who consults a biblical translation should know something about that specific translation as well as something about translation in general. Although no definitive Web site is available that addresses all translations in English, see http://www.gospelcom.net/ibs/bibles/translations/ for a partial listing. The site correctly identifies translation as classifiable according to whether the translator leaned more toward "word for word" or "sense for sense" (paraphrase) translation. The site also ranks the translations; however, the site clearly advocates purchase of the *New International Version*, implying its position in the middle is somehow "centrist." The brief paragraph descriptions are nonetheless helpful. For access to earlier translations of the Bible, see also the link to ***Version Information*** in the left-hand column at *The Unbound Bible*, located at http://unbound.biola.edu/. (Also, see entry below under "Similar/Related Sites".)

Navigating the Site. The site is easy to navigate. From the main page, two search options are available: *Passage search* and *Keyword search*; an example of how to structure search terms is provided. Enter your search terms, then choose a version of the Bible. Click **Search.** The passage will appear on the screen. For more options, click on ***Use advanced search form***. To use *Passage Lookup*, enter the bible verse(s), then select as many versions as desired. Click ***Go.*** The search results list the translations on the same page. To locate uses of a phrase or to identify the location of a specific verse, enter a phrase in the *Word Search* box, choose the appropriate search criteria, choose the desired bible versions, and click ***Go.*** A range of possibilities will appear on the screen.

Discussion Questions and Activities

1.   The Bible as Translation. One passage that has caused controversy over Bible translations is Isaiah 7:14. From the main page, choose ***Use advanced search form***, enter "Isaiah 7:14" into the *Passage Lookup* search form, then select all of the boxes before clicking the ***Go*** button. Compare the versions. What are the substantial differences among the entries? Can you identify what ambiguity between the original text and the various translations has led to this disagreement?

2.   Historical Literature. Whenever possible, look up passages in the Bible version the author might have used. For instance, try the Geneva Bible for biblical references in British literature of the Renaissance and the King James Version after 1611.

3.   Literary Allusions. This site is extremely useful for tracking down the contexts of literary allusions (brief references in a literary work to something outside the text), when they refer to biblical passages. For instance, in Chaucer's "Miller's Tale," the foolish carpenter believes a clever student's tale that an impending second flood requires that he sleep in a bathtub suspended from the ceiling—clearing the way for the student to sleep with the carpenter's wife. Even assuming this argument could be plausible at a time when religion was central to everyday life, read *Genesis 9* to understand why the carpenter should have known better.

4.   Keyword Searches. Use this site to check the uses of a particular keyword or phrase. For instance, search on the keyword *pastor*. How many different ways is this word used? What are some synonyms for the different uses? (Hint: Think about related words, such as *pasture, pastoral, shepherd*, etc.)

Similar/Related Sites

1.   *The Net Bible*—http://www.bible.org/netbible/index.htm—This site offers a new translation of the Bible with extensive commentary on translation decisions, courtesy of the Biblical Studies Foundation.

2.   *The Unbound Bible*—http://unbound.biola.edu/—Sponsored by Biola University, this site offers several searchable Bibles, including the Douay-Rheims, which it identifies as the basis for most Catholic Bibles in English.

3.   *New Testament Gateway*—http://www.ntgateway.com/—Despite its title, this site, compiled by Dr. Mark Goodacre, Department of Theology, University of Birmingham, provides annotated links to resources for the study of all biblical texts, including the Old Testament, New Testament, and noncanonical texts. Additional links are provided to sites and pages that explain the genesis of historical concerns, such as the canonicity of biblical

writings, backgrounds to the life of Jesus, the "synoptic problem" (resolution of discrepancies among the gospels), and textual analysis and criticism. Special pages are also provided for women's issues and art. Another valuable resource is the "All-In-One Bible Studies Search Page," a mega-search page permitting the user to search a number of resources from a single location.

4. *The Old Testament Gateway*—http://www.otgateway.com/—Created by Roy and Sue Nicholson of Birkland, Queensland, Australia, this site provides a comprehensive set of links for the study of the Old Testament from a variety of perspectives.

5. *The Five Gospels Site*—http://www.utoronto.ca/religion/synopsis/—Edited by John W. Marshall, Department for the Study of Religion at the University of Toronto, this site offers the opportunity for side-by-side study of the New Testament gospels.

6. *Resources for Bible Study*—http://www.torreys.org/bible/—This site was created by Torrey Seland, professor in biblical studies, Volda University College, Volda, Norway, to aid in "serious scholarly studies of early Christian writings and their social world."

Early Christian Writing: Christian Classics Ethereal Library
http://www.ccel.org/

Site Summary. Sponsored by Calvin College (a denominational college of the Christian Reformed Church), this Web site provides five important features.

1. *World Study Bible.* This feature includes an online edition of the *English Standard Version* of the Bible, with chapters and verses cross-linked with encyclopedia entries; other biblical translations; and extensive, previously published commentary, sermons, articles, meditations, treatises, hymns, audiorecordings, poetry, and notes.

2. *Worldwide Encyclopedia of Christianity.* This feature links the *Catholic Encyclopedia*, *Easton's Bible Dictionary*, *Torrey's Topical Textbook*, and Elwell's *Dictionary of Christian Theology*.

3. *Early Church Fathers, v. 2.0.* This feature provides access to thirty-eight of thirty-nine volumes of anti-Nicene, Nicene, and post-Nicene Christian writing, originally published by T. &T. Clark in Edinburgh, Scotland, in the nineteenth century. Most of the files are available in HTML, in zip files, in Microsoft Reader, and in PDF format.

4. *The Library.* This section includes a large number of full-length books in audio as well as a variety of text formats for e-book readers and Internet browsers.

5. *Hymnary.* This section provides text, music, and audio files for a large number of hymns, indexed by title, composer, and tune.

Navigating the Site. The search feature permits author, title, and full-text searches. To gain access to the other resources on this site, select the appropriate link from the left-hand navigation bar and follow the instructions below.

1. *World Study Bible.* From the table, select the link to the appropriate book of the Bible. The resulting page provides access to the hyperlinked chapter number, as well as general resources pertaining to that book. To find specific resources pertaining to a specific chapter or verse, choose the desired chapter number; the resulting page provides a new set of materials pertaining to the passage of interest.

2. *Encyclopedia of Christianity.* Use the search feature on the index page, or follow the alphabetical links.

3. *Early Church Fathers.* Use the search engine on the index page, browse the HTML version by selecting the appropriate volume number, or select the appropriate version for download.

Discussion Questions and Activities

1. Use the search facility on this Web site to identify writing on key people, events, and concepts in religion. For instance, what were the ideas and reasoning behind the belief of some Protestant sects in *predestination* and *election*, concepts that underpin much of early American and early European Protestant writing?

   a. *Encyc Christianity.* Begin with an overview of the terms. From the main page, choose the **Encyc Christianity** link located in the left-hand navigation bar. In the search form, enter *predestination.* Explore what *Easton's Bible Dictionary, The Evangelical Dictionary of Biblical Theology, The Catholic Encyclopedia,* and the *New Schaff-Herzog Encyclopedia of Religious Knowledge* say about this term.

   b. *Church Fathers.* For deeper insight into the doctrine of *predestination,* return to the main page and choose the link to **Church Fathers**. Enter *predestination* in the search block. Choose the link to the work of St. Augustin, St. Thomas Aquinas (*Summa Theologica*), or Calvin's *Commentaries*. The entire work will appear on the screen. To locate the use of the term *predestination,* use the search feature in your browser (in Internet Explorer choose *Edit: Find* and enter the search term; in Netscape Navigator choose *Edit: Find in Page* and enter the search term). How did thinking about this term evolve?

2. Use the search feature to locate commentaries about specific biblical people and events. Only 100 results can be returned; consequently, wherever possible, limit your search by using the Boolean search function. For instance, to find out more about the biblical figure Job, gain an overview from the **Encyc Christianity**. Then explore the ways in which Job was understood by theologians by choosing **Church Fathers** and entering *Job* in the search block. Note that over 700 results are returned. Limit the search by adding a search term; for example, enter *Job and suffering* this time and choose **Boolean** under the *Match* drop-down menu. Note that only about one-third of the results contain both terms. The default *Sort* option is by *Score*; however, explore the other options as needed.

Similar/Related Sites

1. *Center for Reformed Theology and Apologetics*—http://www.reformed.org/—This Web site provides access to a large number of historical documents relating to Calvinism, Presbyterianism, and early church documents (see especially the left-hand column link to **Historic Church Documents**).

2. *Center for Reformation and Renaissance Studies—Electronic Resources page*—http://www. crrs.ca/new/library/webresources/webresources.htm—This Web site is an outstanding gateway to information pertaining to the Protestant Reformation and the Renaissance.

3. *Latin Vulgate with KJV translation*—http://latinitas.org/biblia/—Although this page is written in Latin, it provides access to PDF files of the Latin Vulgate Bible with parallel translations into English, excerpted from the King James Version.

4. *The Ecole Initiative*—http://www2.evansville.edu/ecoleweb/—Created by Anthony Beavers and edited by Karen Rae Keck and Norman Redington, this encyclopedia of early church history is sponsored as a service by the University of Evansville. The Web site provides documents, a glossary, articles, and images. Although the date search function does not work, this site nonetheless is excellent.

Islam and the Islamic World

Islamicity.org (Sunni)
http://www.islamicity.com

Al-Islam.org (Shi'a)
http://www.al-islam.org

Site Summary. These two Web sites provide differing views of Islam: one is Sunni and the other Shi'ite.

1. Sunni Islam. *Islamicity.com* describes Islam from the perspective of Sunni Islam. Sunni Muslims accept that, after Mohammad's death, authority passed legitimately through his followers rather than through his close family members. This Web site provides the following resources from the main page:

    a. The **Quran** page. This page provides parallel translations in several languages; recitations in Arabic by several readers (some accessible only to members); translations in English by Ayub and Hall, Abdul-Bari and Eaton, Sakr, and Pickthal and Shakir; and translations into twenty-one other languages.

    b. The **Sunnah** page. This page provides access to several Hadith pages (i.e., sayings of Mohammed) and to pages and multimedia presentations on the life of Mohammed.

2. Shi'a Islam. *Al-Islam.org* represents Islam from the perspective of Shi'a Islam. Shi'ite Muslims believe that the legitimate succession after Mohammad should have passed through Mohammad's cousin and his descendants. These successors, called *imams*, were believed to possess great authority and even infallibility. This Web site is sponsored by the Ahlul Bayt Digital Islamic Library Project, a nonprofit Shi'a group based in Toronto, whose stated mission is to present high-quality Islamic resources on the Internet. Significant features linked to the main page of this site include the following:

    a. The **Multilingual Qur'an Project** provides comparative translations by Shakir, Abdullah Yusufali, and Pickthal side-by-side with the Arabic Koran; a commentary is also provided.

    b. The **Shi'ite Encyclopedia** attempts to explain the differences between Shi'a and Sunni Islam.

    c. The **Psalms of Islam** (Al-Sahifa Al-Kamilah Al-Sajjadiyya) provides an online text of the oldest Islamic prayer book.

    d. The **Sayings and Traditions** (Hadith) represent the prayers and records of the "sayings" of Muhammed, described as "second pillar after the Quran upon which every Muslim rests his faith" and the "source of the Islamic religious law" (see link on the *hadith* page to *Al-Hadith*).

e.   **The Qur'an** page provides a series of links to documents that explicate the Qur'an. Also available on this page are links to a number of videotapes in MP3 format.

Navigating the Sites. These sites are easily navigated from the links described above, all of which are connected to each site's main page.

Discussion Questions and Activities

1.   Begin by following the online tutorial available on *The Islamic World to 1600* site (described below) to familiarize yourself with Islam, its history, and its diversity.

2.   Choose several elements of Islam to trace in the Qur'an by exploring the online parallel versions (above).

3.   Explore some of the **Hadeth** pages, making a list of Mohammed's behavior and attributes. What elements of his history and sayings influence the beliefs of Muslims today?

Similar/Related Sites

1.   *Koran*—http://www.hti.umich.edu/k/koran/—This site provides another online edition of M. H. Shakir's translation *The Holy Qur'an.*

2.   *Koran Collection*—http://www.ee.bilkent.edu.tr/~history/Ext/Koran.html—This online exhibit of Koran editions owned by Topkapı Palace in Istanbul, Turkey, shows how artistically image and text were integrated in these beautiful illuminated books.

3.   *The Islamic World to 1600*—http://www.ucalgary.ca/applied_history/tutor/islam/—This outstanding site, sponsored by the University of Calgary and created by senior undergraduate honors and graduate students, features an online tutorial dedicated to Islamic world history.

Asian Religions and Belief Systems

Asia for Educators—Religion and Philosophy Pages

http://afe.easia.columbia.edu/

Site Summary. See additional comments on this site in the complete entry for *Asia for Educators* in Chapter 10. Sponsored by Columbia University, the Religion and Philosophy pages provide lesson plans as well as audio- and videorecordings for the following:

China	*Japan*
A Chinese Proverb	Shintô
Confucian Teaching	Guide to "Shintô: Nature, Gods, and Man in Japan" [Teacher's Guide]
The Confucian Tradition	
Confucian Thought	The Legendary Past: The Age of the Gods [Reading]
Taoism and Legalism	The Origins of Buddhism [Reading] Buddhism in Japan [Reading]
The Origins of Buddhism	
Religion in a State Society	Religious Attitudes Today [Reading]
Muslims in China	Confucian Thought [Reading]

Navigating the Site. The site is easy to navigate. From the main page, select the ***Religion and Philosophy*** link. Drop-down menus link to the topics listed above.

Discussion Questions and Activities

1. Confucianism. Learn about Confucianism by reading and viewing the overviews and selections on the *Asia for Educators* site (click the subject area ***Religion and Philosophy,*** then ***Teaching Units*** for China, and scroll to ***Confucianism*** links). For a larger excerpt from the *Analects*, see "Similar/Related Sites" below.

2. Buddhism.

    a. Read the selections on Buddhism on the *Asia for Educators* site (click the subject area ***Religion and Philosophy***, then ***Teaching Units*** for China, and scroll to ***Buddhism*** links).

    b. Read more about *Buddhism* at **BuddhaNet** (see "Similar/Related Links" below), then read Hermann Hesse's *Siddhartha* (an unattributed translation is available online at http://www.online-literature.com/hesse/).What elements of Siddhartha's life appear to reflect a true understanding of Buddhist thought? What elements reflect Hesse's position as a Western European commentator? (For assistance, see a symposium on teaching *Siddhartha*, online at the *Journal of Asian Studies* site at http://www.aasianst.org/.)

3. See also discussion questions and activities in the *Asia for Educators* site entry in Chapter 10.

Similar/Related Sites

1. *Analects*—http://academic.brooklyn.cuny.edu/core9/phalsall/texts/analects.txt

2. *Buddha Net*—http://www.buddhanet.net

3. *Taoism* Information Page—http://www.clas.ufl.edu/users/gthursby/taoism/—English translations of the *Tao The Ching*.

4. *Taoism and the Arts of China*—http://www.artic.edu/taoism/—Based on an exhibit at the Art Institute of Chicago, this site shows the interconnections between Taoism and artistic production in China, including both visual art and literature. The site offers beautiful images and a few rather slight lesson plans.

5. *Lao Tzu's The Art of War*—http://www.clas.ufl.edu/users/gthursby/taoism/suntext.htm

6. *The Religion Depot*—http://www.edepot.com/religion.html—Part of a larger site on major religions (although Islam and Judaism links connect to a Daoist discussion board), this site provides transcriptions of key Daoist texts and translations and overviews of the belief system. Also worth investigating are the pages on Christianity, Buddhism, and Hinduism.

Hinduism

Boloji.com
http://www.boloji.com/hinduism/

Site Summary. Part of a larger site dedicated to the dissemination of information about the origins and beliefs of Hindus, this Web site provides access to a wide range of sacred poetry and narratives, retold in a conversational style. Of particular interest to teachers and students of world literature are the links to sacred texts listed in the following table; these works are accessible from the URL cited above. Also available on this Web site are a few traditional poems (ghazals) by Mirza Ghalib (http://www.boloji.com/ghalib/index.htm) and an article and poetry excerpts of Mevlana Rumi (http://www.boloji.com/literature/00123.htm) (see the entry on Sufi poetry in Chapter 10 for more about Rumi).

MYTHOLOGY

    Hindu Gods, Deities and Spirits

SACRED TEXTS

Bhagavad-Gita

    Essence of the Gita

    Introduction to Gita

    The Gita For the Beginners

Upanishads

    Introduction to Isha Upanishad

    Introduction to Katha Upanishad

    The Principal Upanishads

    The Vedic Quest concerning the Universe, Space and Time

EPIC LITERATURE

Mahabharata

    Love Stories from Mahabharata

    Stories from Mahabharata

Ramayana

    Stories from Ramayana

FABLES

Panchantantra

    Stories from Panchantantra

Navigating the Site. From the main page, click on the desired link text.

Discussion Questions and Activities

1.   Begin by reading about Hindu mythology on the **Hindu Gods, Deities, and Spirits** page.

2. Before reading the *Upanishads* and the *Rig Veda* on the *Sacred Text Archive* site (above), read the introductions to these works on *Boloji.com*. What is the significance of these works to Hindu people? What guidelines do they provide for conducting one's life? What is "literary" about them (think about narrative form, characterization, plot, etc.)

3. Compare the *Ramayana* and the *Mahabharata* with other epics, such as Homer's *Iliad* and *Odyssey*, Virgil's *Aeneid*, and *Beowulf*. Do Rama and Arjuna most resemble Achilles, Odysseus, Aeneas, or Beowulf? In what ways? What do these similarities and differences suggest to you about heroic values in the culture that created these epics?

4. Read some of the "Love Stories from the *Mahabharata*" and compare them with Marie de France's *Lais* (see Chapter 8) and the Cinderella variations on the folklore sites described elsewhere in this chapter. What features do these stories have in common? How do the stories differ?

5. Compare the children's stories from the *Panchatantra* with the fables of Aesop.

Similar/Related Sites

1. See the entries for the *Kalevala*, the *Upanishads*, and the *Rig Veda* on the *Sacred Text Archive* site (above).

2. The following sites provide more stories from the *Panchatantra*:

   a. *India Parenting*—http://www.indiaparenting.com/stories/panchatantra/index.shtml

   b. *Professor Ashliman's Folktext Site*—http://www.pitt.edu/~dash/panchatantra.html

3. See also the *HyperEpos* Web site, described in Chapter 4, for excerpts from the *Mahabharata* and other heroic/epic Asian literature.

4. *Jambudvipa*—http://www.jambudvipa.net/hinduism.htm—This site is a gateway to information pertaining to Hinduism.

Folklore

Folktales from Around the World

D. L. Ashliman's Folklore Pages
See list below.

Site Summary. This page, constructed by Professor D. L. Ashliman for use in his courses at the University of Pittsburgh, provides links to separate pages of folklore and mythology e-texts. These pages will be useful to teachers and students of the mythology of Northern Europe, Japan, and comparative folklore. Particularly interesting on this site are links to pages for several major Norse gods; each in turn links to descriptive sites. Also useful are Professor Ashliman's archives of fairy tales and their analogs.

Navigating the Site. Although this site is an excellent source of material, the organization of the site may be difficult to follow for a beginner in folklore studies. One useful way of approaching some of the materials is to begin from the sources linked to the Germanic Folklore syllabus located at http://www.pitt.edu/~dash/ger1500.html. The link from the Germanic Myths page to

Folklore and Mythology Electronic Texts (http://www.pitt.edu/~dash/folktexts.html) leads to a listing of folktales categorized by motifs, presumably numbered following Stith Thomson's *Folk-Motif Index*; the selected motifs are then alphabetized. The national culture within which each tale was found is also listed, but these are not indexed. Identifying a number of tales from a particular region, then, requires effort. Folklorists adopting a comparative approach may find the page easier to use. Another way to locate a particular subset of folktales is to go to the University of Pittsburgh's search page at http://www.english.pitt.edu/search.htm and do a keyword search on *Ashliman* and any additional search words. Searching on *ashliman trickster*, for instance, resulted in thirty hits, most linking to trickster tales. Another alternative is to visit the specific pages that may link to an archive of interest; specifically named pages include the following:

Germanic Myths, Legends, and Sagas	http://www.pitt.edu/~dash/mythlinks.html
Folklore and Mythology Electronic Texts	http://www.pitt.edu/~dash/folktexts.html
Grimm Brothers Page	http://www.pitt.edu/~dash/grimm.html
Japanese folktales	http://www.pitt.edu/~dash/japan.html
Japanese Legends about Supernatural Sweethearts	http://www.pitt.edu/~dash/japanlove.html

Discussion Questions and Activities

1. Folktale Versions. What fairy tales do you know? How do they compare with the stories others have heard? Write down a version of Cinderella or another fairy tale you have heard and compare it with those versions that others remember. Then compare several versions of folk and fairy tales with common titles or story lines (see the related Web sites listed below). What are the similarities? What are the differences? What do the variations suggest about the concerns of the communities within which each version arose?

2. Folklore and Oral Tradition. Folk and fairy tales originated in oral tradition, where they were embellished or varied by individual storytellers in performance. Many of these stories were committed to writing only recently (beginning primarily in the nineteenth century). What formulas appear in many of the stories (e.g., "Once upon a time")? What characters? How are the structures of different stories similar? How are the structures of different versions of the same story similar? What elements appear to reflect choices made by individual storytellers?

Similar/Related Sites

1. *Brothers Grimm: The National Geographic Brothers Grimm Webpage*—http://www. nationalgeographic.com/grimm/index2.html—This entertaining site conveys a sense of the similarities in structure and motifs among several Grimm stories as it allows the reader to navigate through the stories by making make plot choices.

2. Hans Christian Andersen

   a. *Hans Christian Andersen Fairy Tales and Stories*—http://hca.gilead.org.il/—Created by Zvi Har'El (a senior lecturer in mathematics at Technion, Israel Institute of Technology) in memory of his son, this well-designed site provides full-text editions of several nineteenth-century editions of Andersen's tales, links to images of other Andersen editions, information on the popularity and editions in which each tale appears, and a chronology of Andersen's life.

b. *Hans Christian Andersen*—http://www.pacificnet.net/~johnr/aesop/aesophca.html —Part of a larger *Aesop's Fables* Web site, this page provides links to 127 fairy tales.

3. *International Children's Digital Library*—http://www.icdlbooks.org/—In addition to the information provided in the longer entry for this site in Chapter 4, the English-language folklore books published on the ICDL site are listed here for convenience:

Europe	**Asia/South Asia**
The Aesop for Children (Greece)	*Cordillera Tales* (Philippines)
The Baby's Own Aesop (Greece)	*Handyong* (Philippines)
Celtic Tales (Ireland, Scotland, Wales)	*More Jataka Tales* (India)
Cinderella (Trad. Western European)	*A Southern Cross Fairy Tale* (New Zealand)
Denslow's *Humpty Dumpty*, *Mother Goose*, and *Three Bears* (United Kingdom)	*Treasury of Stories* (Philippines)
Dutch Fairy Tales for Young Folks (Netherlands)	**The Americas**
East o' the Sun and West o' the Moon (Norway)	*The Cat Woman and the Spinning Wheel* (Jamaica)
Elinda who danced in the sky (Estonia)	*Croaking Johnny and Dizzy Lizzy* (Jamaica)
Grimm's Fairy Stories (Germany)	*How did we get here?* (Jamaica)
The Iliad for Boys and Girls (Greece)	*Magic Dogs of the Volanoes* (El Salvador)
Mother Goose Finger Plays (United Kingdom)	*My First Book of Proverbs* (Mexico and United States)
The Pied Piper of Hamelin (Trad. Western European)	*The Snake that Lived in the Santa Cruz Mountains and Other Ohlone Stories* (Monterey Region, California, United States)
Stories from Hans Christian Andersen (Denmark)	*Sweet, Sweet Mango Tree* (Jamaica)
Story of the Three Little Pigs (Trad. European)	**Near East**
Sun Flight (Story of Icarus) (Greece)	*The Arabian Nights* (Trad. Arabic, Turkish, Persian folktales)
Welsh Fairy Tales (Wales)	*Something from Nothing* (Trad. Jewish folktale)
A Wonder Book for Girls and Boys (Greek mythology)	
Africa	
The Hunterman and the Crocodile	

Sur la Lune Fairy Tale Pages
http://www.surlalunefairytales.com/

Site Summary. Created by Heidi Heiner, an information technology specialist, this well-designed Web site provides annotated texts, historical perspective, book history, critical backgrounds, and international versions of a large number of fairy tales. Although the site is not scholarly, it is well-researched and thorough in its approach. The site provides resources on the following tales:

Beauty and the Beast	*Jack and the Beanstalk*
Bluebeard	*Little Red Riding Hood*
The Brave Little Tailor	*Princess and the Pea*
Brother and Sister	*Puss in Boots*
Cinderella	*Rapunzel*
Diamonds and Toads	*Rumpelstiltzkin*
Donkeyskin	*Six Swans*
East of the Sun and West of the Moon	*Sleeping Beauty*
The Frog King	*Snow White and Rose Red*
The Gingerbread Man	*Snow White and the Seven Dwarfs*
Goldilocks and the Three Bears	*The Three Billy Goats Gruff*
The Goose Girl	*The Three Little Pigs*
Hansel and Gretel	*The Twelve Dancing Princesses*

Navigating the Site. The site is easy to navigate. The main page provides the hierarchical structure of the site; "Part 1: Front Matter" provides access to critical statements about the nature of fairy tales and their study. "Part 2: The Annotated Tales" provides access to a separate page for each tale. On pages devoted to a given tale, the tale itself appears in the center column, whereas the navigation bar appears on the left. Material available on each tale includes annotations, history, illustrations, analogs, modern interpretations, a bibliography, and page images of early printed versions.

Discussion Questions and Activities

1. Write down a version you have heard of at least one fairy tale that is on *Sur la Lune.* Then compare the versions of fairy tales that you have heard with those on the site. What similarities and differences do you find?

2. Compare the printed versions of similar tales. How do the illustrations guide your interpretation of the tale? How do the illustrations reflect the time in which they were created?

3. Study the history and annotations associated with a particular tale. What elements of the tale does this information clarify?

Similar/Related Sites

1. *Virtually Virtual Iceland*—http://www.simnet.is/gardarj/folk/folk.htm—This site provides translations of several Icelandic folktales. See also the site's page of Viking Proverbs —*Hávamál*—at http://www.simnet.is/gardarj/havamal.htm

Michael Salda's Fairy Tale Analog Pages

Cinderella—http://www.usm.edu/english/fairytales/cinderella/cinderella.html
Red Riding Hood—http://www.usm.edu/english/fairytales/lrrh/lrrhhome.htm
Jack and the Beanstalk/Jack the Giant Killer—http://www.usm.edu/english/fairytales/jack/jackhome.html

Site Summary. The pages listed above were created based upon the work of Michael Salda at the University of Southern Mississippi and graduate students in his "Bibliography and Methods" course. Although the site has no formal opening page, an introductory page exists for each project—one on Cinderella analogs, one on Red Riding Hood analogs, and one on Jack and the Beanstalk/Jack the Giant-Killer analogs. In addition, although these introductory pages are not user-friendly, the resources linked to them will be invaluable to teachers who wish to introduce students to the concept of folklore through fairy tales.

Navigating the Site. This site is relatively easy to navigate. Read about the projects at the URLs listed above. Then move to the linked stories to compare the versions provided on second- and third-level pages.

Discussion Questions and Activities

1. *Cinderella.* What version of *Cinderella* do you know? Write it down, and then compare it with the online page images and transcriptions of eighteenth-, nineteenth- and twentieth-century Cinderella stories on this site. To view transcriptions, click on the link to ***Archive Inventory*** (located in the fourth paragraph); to view page images, click on the ***Images Only*** link (in the sixth paragraph).

2. *Red Riding Hood.* What version of *Red Riding Hood* have you heard? Compare it with these. To view the transcribed text of a story, go to the second paragraph and click on ***Text and Images***. To compare specific story features among several texts, try the ***Archive Inventory*** feature; its link is located in the fourth paragraph. To view scanned images only of the original books from which the stories were transcribed, choose the ***Images Only*** link in the sixth paragraph.

3. *Jack and the Beanstalk/Jack the Giant-Killer.* Compare your version of *Jack and the Beanstalk* with the versions linked to this page. Navigation links to both transcribed text and actual page images appear in the second paragraph. Also available on this page is a link to text and images from a nineteenth-century board game on the same topic.

Similar/Related Sites

1. *Cinderella Analogs*—http://www.acs.ucalgary.ca/~dkbrown/cinderella.html—This Web site is part of a larger Web site, the *Children's Literature Webguide*. This page provides links to a variety of resources useful in teaching variations of Cinderella. The link to the *Tales of Wonder* site, which provides links to several Cinderella analogs, has been changed to http://www.darsie.net/talesofwonder/ (see "England") .

2. *Cinderella Bibliography*—http://www.lib.rochester.edu/camelot/cinder/cinintr.htm—Created by Russell Peck, this annotated bibliography of *Cinderella* analogs includes *Beauty and the Beast* tales as well as some other folk tales with thematic parallels (e.g., *Sleeping Beauty, Hansel and Gretel, The Goose Girl, Little Red Riding Hood*). The coverage provided by this bibliography is impressive; Professor Peck provides synopses of tales from Africa, Central Asia, Central Europe, China, India, Ireland, Japan, the Middle East, Russia, Scandinavia, Scotland, Siberia, and England, as well as from Native American sources.

3. *Little Red Riding Hood*—http://mld.ursinus.edu/Maerchen/redridinghood.html—This Web site provides links to a brief introduction and versions of the story written down by the Brothers Grimm, Charles Perrault, and Joachim Ringelnatz. The versions on this Web

page may be particularly useful for high school and college students as the site demonstrates the contemporary relevance and flexibility of these familiar stories and the ways in which they can reflect social and political issues.

4. *Snow White*—http://scils.rutgers.edu/~kvander/snowwhite.html—Created by Kay Vandergrift, this scholarly Web site provides teaching resources, illustrations from published versions, versions recorded from oral tradition, information on media representations of the story, excerpted critical analyses, and bibliographic references.

Legends
http://www.legends.dm.net/

Site Summary. Paula Marmor, a Web developer and English Renaissance enthusiast, created and edits this well-designed Web site, which provides resources for the study of legendary figures. Much of the site is dedicated to British and American materials, including the **Robin Hood** pages and pages on **Ballads and Broadsides, Pirates and Privateers,** and **Shakespeare's Stories.** Resources particularly important for the study of world literature include the following pages:

1. **King Arthur & the Matter of Britain**—This page is designed to augment features of the *Camelot Project* (see entry in Chapter 8). This material is important to the study of the continental Arthurian tradition.

2. **Swashbucklers & Fops**—This page refers primarily to British and American works, but it also provides useful links to Dumas and *Cyrano de Bergerac* resources on the Internet.

3. **Erin & Alba**—This page provides links to materials and texts that provide materials for the study of Irish Literature, specifically the *Mythological Cycle* (Tuatha Dé Danaan stories), the *Ulster Cycle* (including stories about King Conchobar and the Cúchullain), the *Fenian Cycle* (the stories of Fin MacCumhaill), and the *Historical Cycle* (pertaining to the kings of Ireland). (See CELT entry in Chapter 8.)

4. **Beowulf**—Use this page with the additional resources provided in Chapter 8 under *Beowulf.*

5. **Sagas & Sea-Kings**—This page provides links to a number of Norse sagas, with especially useful resources for *Sigurd the Volsung* and Viking history.

6. **Paladins & Princes**—This page provides particularly useful coverage of *The Cid* (Spanish) and of *chansons de geste, The Song of Roland,* and *Aucassin and Nicolette* (French).

7. **Poets & Painters**—This page lists excellent links to material on artists whose work was informed by legendary figures, including pages devoted to William Morris (with information on the Pre-Raphaelites) and Howard Pyle.

Navigating the Site. The site is easy to navigate. From the main page, select a link to the genre of interest. Subsequent pages are linked to annotated descriptions of each work.

Discussion Questions and Activities

1. How do stories about legendary figures differ from other folk tales? Read one or two of the legends on this site, and compare their thematic and structural features with those of one or two fairy tales. Then compare their features with the characteristics of *epic* listed on the *HyperEpos* Web site, described in Chapter 8. What features do these legendary tales share with fairy tales? What features are shared with epics?

Similar/Related Sites

1. *The Robin Hood Project*—http://www.lib.rochester.edu/camelot/rh/rhhome.htm—Part of the Camelot Project at the University of Rochester, this site provides a large number of texts from oral tradition and printed books, as well as nineteenth- and early twentieth-century artistic interpretations of Robin Hood tales.

Fables

Aesopica
http://www.aesopica.net

Site Summary. Created as a companion to the recent Oxford Press translation of *Aesop's Fables* by Dr. Laura Gibbs, a classicist at the University of Oklahoma, this Web site provides scholarly Web publication of historical versions of Aesop, including Caxton's *Aesop* (1484), Roger L'Estrange's *Aesop* (1692), George Townsend's *Aesop* (1887), and the author's *Index to the Aesopica*, as well as her own *Aesop's Fables* (2002). Of added interest to high school and college teachers of Latin and Greek, the site also provides access to Latin prose translations (Adamar and Odo of Cheriton), a Latin verse translation (Walter of England), Greek prose versions (Aphthonius, Chambry [1–200 only], and Syntipas), and a Greek verse version (Babrius).

Navigating the Site. The site is easy to navigate. To go to a specific translation from the main page, simply click on the link to that translation. The first fable in the translation will appear on the screen. To page through the same work, click on the red arrow at the upper right-hand side of the screen. To compare translations of the same fable, go back to the main page and click on ***Perry's Index to Aesopica***. Links to all available translations of the first fable will appear. Use the red arrow at the upper right-hand side of the page to page through the index.

Discussion Questions and Activities

1. From the main page, locate the yellow box and click on the link to the ***Perry System.*** Choose a fable by clicking on the link to its ***Perry*** number. For example, choose ***Perry 9,*** the fable of *The Fox and the Goat at the Well*. Read Professor Gibbs's commentary, located in the white box at the top of the page. Then read the versions in English (and other languages if you can). Finally, explore ***Perry 408*** for another version of the same fable. In what ways do the provided "morals" differ?

2. Compare the features of Aesop's fables with fables of other national literatures (e.g., Marie de France's *Lais*, described in Chapter 8, or the fables of the *Panchatranta*, some of which are located at *Boloji.com* and on D. Ashliman's site; both sites are described above). In what ways are the stories similar? How are they different?

3. For a version of Aesop's fables for younger children, see the online book available at the International Children's Digital Library at http://www.icdlbooks.org/ (see entry in Chapter 4).

Similar/Related Sites

1. *Fables*—http://aesop.creighton.edu/jcupub/default.htm—This site provides an extensive annotated bibliography of editions of *Aesop's Fables* in the Carlson Fable Collection at Creighton University. The site also provides excellent photographs of the fables as they appeared in popular and material culture.

2. *Aesop's Fables*—http://www.aesopfables.com/—This site provides access to over 655 fables by Ambrose Bierce, the previously published English translation of *Aesop's Fables* by George Townsend (1887), and a translation from Jean de la Fontaine's French version, published in the late seventeenth century. Although the names of the translators from French are provided, the credentials of these translators are not specified.

3. *Fables*—http://www.hti.umich.edu/cgi/p/pd-modeng/pd-modeng-idx?type=header&id=AesopFable—This site provides another online copy of George Townsend's 1887 translation of *Aesop's Fables*.

4. *MSU Fable Collection*—http://digital.lib.msu.edu/collections/ (click on the link to *Fables*)—This site, sponsored by the Michigan State University Special Collections area of the university library, provides online page images of a translation in English, French, and Latin by Francis Barlow (1687); an 1871 reprint of *Fables,* edited by Oliver Goldsmith and illustrated by the famous English engraver Thomas Bewick (originally published 1776 and 1784); a 1900 translation of la Fontaine, written in verse by Guy Carryl; and Ernest Griset's 1870 edition, based on la Fontaine (1668), L'Estrange (1694), and Croxall (1727). To view a book, go to the Web site listed above and click on *gif*.

5. *Aesop's Fables Traditional and Modern*—http://www.umass.edu/aesop/—Although it is not scholarly, this site, an illustration project for art students at the University of Massachusetts, is thoroughly entertaining. Flash 4 software is required.

Proverbs

http://www.cogweb.ucla.edu/Discourse/Proverbs/index.html

Site Summary. Part of a larger site at UCLA dedicated to the study of cognitive linguistics, this site provides the most comprehensive coverage of proverbial wisdom on the Web.

Navigating the Site. The site is easy to navigate. From the main page, search for proverbs using the search engine at the top, or select from the navigation bar to explore the site.

Discussion Questions and Activities

1. To gain a good understanding of what proverbs are, begin with the **Definitions** page. Next return to the main page, choose the link to *Articles on Line*, and read Hernadi and Steen's article, "The Tropical Landscapes of Proverbia." What is a proverb? Who creates them and why?

2. Explore the proverbs of several cultures. How well does Hernadi and Steen's definition fit the proverbs you have read? In what ways do the proverbs reflect the culture in which they were created? In what ways do they seem strange? In what ways familiar?

3. Read Edip Yuksel's essay "Proverbs and Patriarchy." What is Yuksel's thesis about the power of proverbial language to influence listeners? Re-evaluate some of the proverbs you read earlier. What cultural attitudes do you detect in them? Which do you believe might be viewed positively and which negatively?

Similar/Related Sites

1. General sites

   a. *Phrasefinder Proverbs*—http://phrases.shu.ac.uk/meanings/proverbs.html

   b. *Commonly Used Proverbs*—http://www.manythings.org/proverbs/proverbs1.html

    c.   *DeProverbio*—http://www.utas.edu.au/docs/flonta/—This e-journal for proverb research provides a number of freely accessible online articles on proverb research.

2. Regional sites

    a.   Africa

       i.   *What Is It Like to Live in a Village in Kenya?*—http://fga.freac.fsu.edu/academy/afkenya.htm—Maintained at Florida State University, this Web site describes a multipart lesson plan, including a songs, stories, fables, and a set of proverbs, each with group activities for their use.

      ii.   *African Proverbs, Sayings, and Stories*—http://www.afriprov.org/

    iii.   *Gambian Proverbs*—http://www.africanculture.dk/gambia/Gambia-proverbs.htm

    b.   Near East

       i.   *Turkish Proverbs*—http://www.columbia.edu/~sss31/Turkiye/proverbs.html

      ii.   *Afghanistan Online Proverbs*—http://www.afghan-web.com/culture/proverbs.html

    iii.   *Palestinian Proverbs*—http://www.barghouti.com/folklore/

    c.   *Viking Proverbs—Hávamál*—http://www.simnet.is/gardarj/havamal.htm

Indigenous Australia: Stories of Dreaming: Aboriginal Tales

http://www.dreamtime.net.au/

Site Summary. Sponsored by the Australian Museum, this outstanding Web site provides a glimpse of aboriginal culture in Australia, documenting the history of aboriginal Australians from the time before contact with Europeans through the present. Designed as a teaching site, *Dreamtime* provides information pertaining to the archaeological record (going back 60,000 years) as well as the complex interrelationship among "dreamtime" (the "time before time" of the creation), spirituality, the land, and storytelling, complex phenomena through which aboriginal cultural knowledge has been transmitted and remembered. The Web site includes eighteen stories in text form as well as in audio and video versions, narrated by aboriginal storytellers. Also provided are two commentaries on the importance and functions of the stories in aboriginal life. Finally, the site offers a set of resources for students (a list of frequently asked questions, a set of fact sheets, and a dictionary) and another set for teachers, particularly those located in Australia. The site requires Real Player G2 or above.

Navigating the Site. The site is exceptionally well designed. The main page provides links to major sections in the left-hand column; links to major features appear on the right on this and all other pages of the site.

Discussion Questions and Activities

1. Read several of the "stories of the dreaming," or of creation. How did aboriginal peoples in Australia explain the origins of their landscape? Compare these stories to other creation stories.

CHAPTER 6

The Ancient World

Key Sites of General Interest

ABZU: A Guide to Study of the Ancient Near East on the Web
http://www.etana.org/abzu/

Site Summary. ABZU is an extensive archive of texts and background materials pertinent to the study of the ancient Near East. Created in 1994, the site is edited by Charles Jones, research archivist and bibliographer at The Oriental Institute, University of Chicago. The site was recently upgraded, funded in part by a grant from the Andrew W. Mellon Foundation. In addition to a large number of primary literary texts, the Web site provides access to scholarly archaeological, historical, and cultural essays and Web sites, as well as other extensive primary texts associated with the ancient world. Although the works on this site can be quite technical, others provide excellent resources for those just beginning to explore the ancient Near East.

Navigating the Site. The site is relatively easy to navigate. From the main page, browse by the author's last name or by title, or search on a keyword, author, title, or subject. A link at the bottom of the page leads to a separate page that catalogs the ETANA Core Texts, 135 complete works that are maintained on the site itself. Note that the keyword search returns results only on exact matches but is not case sensitive.

Discussion Questions and Activities

1. Cuneiform. ABZU provides access to turn-of-the-century editions of Sumerian texts written in cuneiform, a writing system that evolved from pictographs to a system of lines and cross-hatching, usually recorded on clay tablets (see below for other sites addressing cuneiform). Although the works provided on ABZU are not all translated, the drawings are excellent. In the keyword or title search block on ABZU, enter *cuneiform* to gain access to dozens of online transcriptions and photographs of ancient Sumerian writing. Included in this collection is an early version of the epic *Gilgamesh*. See the **Mesopotamian Gallery** links at the University of Pennsylvania Museum of Archaeology and Anthropology (below) for a cuneiform generator and an accessible introduction to cuneiform for younger students.

2. Hieroglyphics. ABZU provides online access to E. A. Wallis Budge's 1898 edition of the *Egyptian Book of the Dead*, a compendium of hymns and instructions for the dead in the afterlife that also provides insight into the beliefs and practices of the ancient Egyptians. Budge's book is designed to provide the beginner with insight into the Egyptian system of writing we know as hieroglyphics. For an overview of hieroglyphic interpretation, begin by visiting the online exhibit, *A New Look at Ancient Egypt*, part of the Web site maintained by the University of Pennsylvania Museum of Archaeology and Anthropology (below) (also suitable for younger students). For the more in-depth introduction provided

by Budge, use the author or title search block, or go to the keyword search block on ABZU, then enter "Book of the Dead" to gain access to Budge's two-volume work. Volume 1 provides an overview and complete transcriptions of the extant portions of the *Book of the Dead*; volume 2 is a detailed glossary of hieroglyphics and their translations. More advanced students might try translating one of the hymns.

3. Old Testament Study. ABZU provides a number of resources that could prove useful in a "Bible as Literature" course. To gain access to these critical materials, use search terms such as flood, psalm, or Bible, or enter the name of a specific book in the Bible.

Similar/Related Sites

1. *Egyptian Book of the Dead*—http://www.sas.upenn.edu/African_Studies/Books/Papyrus _ Ani.html

2. *HyperEpos*—http://www.auburn.edu/~downejm/hyperepos.html—This Web site offers international and transcultural coverage of heroic literature. See entry provided in Chapter 4.

Exploring Ancient Cultures on the WWW
http://eawc.evansville.edu/index.htm

Site Summary. Funded through grants by the University of Evansville and edited by Dr. Anthony Beavers, this award-winning, comprehensive site is intended as a supplement to teachers and students of the ancient Near East, India, China, Greece, Rome, the Islamic world, and medieval Europe. The site provides whole and excerpted translations of key texts; excellent, engaging overview essays; extensive timelines; links to external resources; and high-quality images.

Navigating the Site. From the main page, navigation is possible through the clickable images and links at the top; through a navigation bar that appears at the bottom of the page; or by paging through the author's top-level pages, reading each page (beginning with the index page), and clicking "next" at the end of each page. The bottom navigation bar appears on all pages in the site. These subsequent pages also feature left-hand navigation columns that provide topic-specific links to e-texts, essays, teaching tools, etc. The links within the pages are of two types: links in all capital letters lead to the now-defunct Argos search engine, which is no longer available due to the university's loss of funding for Internet initiatives. Links in upper- and lowercase letters connect to ancillary materials and texts.

Discussion Questions and Activities

1. Begin at the index page for the site. According to the site's author, what are the reasons for studying ancient cultures? What does the author mean by terms such as *tradition*, *universality*, *culture*, and *limits of culture*?

2. Read through each of the upper-level pages, consulting the e-texts and taking the self-scoring quizzes that appear along the left-hand margin. What parallels do you see between the cultures described (e.g., beliefs, symbols, significant events, models of heroism)? What differences? How do these cultures compare with our own?

Similar/Related Sites

1. *The Ancient History Sourcebook*—http://www.fordham.edu/halsall/ancient/asbook.html —See Chapter 4, Internet History Sourcebook Project.

Livius—Articles on Ancient Civilization
http://www.livius.org/home.html

Site Summary. Created and maintained by Jona Lendering, this frequently updated Web site provides authoritative and informative articles on ancient Mesopotamia (20), Carthage (3), Egypt (16), Greece (44), Judaism (50), Persia (142), and Rome (71). A resident of Amsterdam, Mr. Lendering studied history at Leiden University and Mediterranean archaeology and history at the Amsterdam Free University, where he taught briefly. Many of the materials on the site are freely downloadable for noncommercial use.

Navigating the Site. The site is organized geographically; choose the region of interest, then click on the appropriate link, located at the top of the main page. A few links to "Popular Articles" are provided on the left-hand side of the main page. Also, although photographic images are cross-linked to geographic descriptions throughout the Web site, a link from the main page to the *Picture archive* provides a separate index. Finally, return visitors to the site can assess changes by visiting the *Plans* link on the main page.

Discussion Questions and Activities

1. Use the articles on the Livius site for background materials to important events and literary works. For instance, read the historical overview provided from the *Germania Inferior* link to gain insight into Tacitus's *Annales.*

2. Use the images available on the site to illustrate key concepts about literary subjects. For instance, compare the photographic images of the following theaters in Asia Minor (specifically in modern day Turkey). How do researchers know that these two theaters are part of the same tradition?

The Odeum at Troy	Anatolia ▶Troy ▶Part III ▶Last image
The Theater at Ephesus	Anatolia ▶Ephesus ▶Last images

Similar/Related Sites

1. See theater links in Chapter 7.

Technology and Iconography of Writing

Scholarship pertaining to the earliest written materials is well documented on the Internet and provides an excellent introduction to such works as the *Epic of Gilgamesh*, early hymns, the *Egyptian Book of the Dead*, and Homer's epics. This section suggests a series of Web sites that can be used to show students how writing evolved from pictographs, how writing was used by ancient civilizations to record their spiritual as well as their temporal activities and concerns, and how modern Indo-European languages share common roots and writing technologies, commonalities that may be invisible at first glance. Consider working through the following Web sites in order.

Evolution of Alphabets
http://www.wam.umd.edu/~rfradkin/alphapage.html

Site Summary. This page, created by Professor R. Fradkin at University of Maryland, provides a video representation of the evolution of several alphabets:

- Cuneiform writing from Sumerian pictures

- Phoenician character set from Proto-Sinaitic glyphs

- Greek character set from Phoenician, and Greek characters that rotated 90 or 180 degrees

- Arabic character set from Phoenician

- Aramaic/Hebrew character set from Phoenician

- Modern Cyrillic character set from Greek

- Latin character set (used in modern English)

Navigating the Site. All of the animations are accessible from the main page. Simply click on the link and view the animated transformation of a given alphabet. To view the animation again, click the "Reload" or "Refresh" button on your browser toolbar.

Discussion Questions and Activities

1. View the "Evolution of Latin Characters" from its origins in the Phoenician character set. What modern English letters share common origins? (See especially C and G; U, V, W, and Y; I and J; P and R; and Z and I.)

2. View the evolution of the Phoenician character set. Compare your observations with the evolution of the Latin alphabet from the Phoenician. What pre-Sinaitic glyph (precursor to the Phoenician alphabet) was a precursor to A, F, and P in the Latin alphabet?

3. Compare the evolution of the Latin alphabet with that of Arabic, and the evolution of the Greek alphabet with that of Cyrillic. What Latin letters share common origins with Arabic script?

Similar/Related Sites

1. *Writing Systems*—http://www.ancientscripts.com/ws.html—Created by Lawrence Lo, a software engineer in the Silicon Valley, this site provides an interesting, if somewhat uneven, survey of how writing systems are defined and classified.

Early Culture Pages at the University of Pennsylvania Museum of Archaeology and Anthropology
http://www.museum.upenn.edu/new/exhibits/online_exhibits/online_exhibits.shtml

Site Summary. All of these witty and engaging online exhibits, written to showcase the exhibits and holdings of the University of Pennsylvania Museum of Archaeology and Anthropology, are worth exploring, but three in particular provide good background for beginners to early cultures as well as an interactive introduction to cuneiform, hieroglyphic, and early Mesoamerican writing.

Navigating the Site. For teachers in search of teaching materials, the best materials are accessible through the main online exhibits page (provided above). Explore both the ***Exhibitions and Virtual Exhibitions*** link and the ***In the Galleries*** link to view exhibits on many other world cultures. To move directly to materials about Mesopotamia and cuneiform, go to the

Mesopotamian Gallery at http://www.museum.upenn.edu/new/exhibits/galleries/mesopotamia.html, which provides an overview of the culture, as well as an interactive cuneiform generator (also directly available at http://www.upennmuseum.com/cuneiform.cgi). To move directly to the materials on Egypt, go to the online exhibit, *A New Look at Ancient Egypt*, which is located at http://www.museum.upenn.edu/new/exhibits/online_exhibits/egypt/egyptintro.shtml; this exhibit is particularly accessible for beginners and for younger students. For information about hieroglyphics and access to the interactive hieroglyphic generator, go directly to http://www.museum.upenn.edu/new/exhibits/galleries/egyptian.html. The hieroglyphics generator itself is located at http://www.upennmuseum.com/hieroglyphsreal.cgi/. To move directly to the Mesoamerican exhibit on *Mayan Hieroglyphic Writing*, go directly to http://www.museum.upenn.edu/new/exhibits/galleries/mesoamerica.html.

Discussion Questions and Activities

1. Hieroglyphics was a pictographic writing system used by the ancient Egyptians.

    a. People everywhere are fascinated by early pictographic writing, and this site provides the opportunity to generate letter for letter representations of names or other words in Egyptian hieroglyphics. Begin with the hieroglyphic generator to create name words. Type your name or another word into the generator. A new screen will appear with the results. What do the individual characters look like?

    b. In addition to standing for a single character, as pictographs hieroglyphic characters can also stand for entire words. To learn more about hieroglyphic characters and what they can mean, consult the scribe by clicking the link at the bottom of the page containing your hieroglyphic name.

    c. As a follow-on project, younger students might next complete art projects in which they reproduce their own hieroglyphic names in marker or paint. More advanced students might move on to more detailed study of hieroglyphics by working on simple translations of stelae or research materials available on other sites. See especially the excellent online hieroglyphic glossary and visual reproductions available on the ABZU site (above).

2. Cuneiform was a writing system used in ancient Mesopotamia. Although it too has pictographic features, the pictures became abstracted as marks and indentations, most recorded on clay tablets that were then fired.

    a. Copying or even translating cuneiform may be more challenging than creating viable hieroglyphics. Instead, have students practice creating cuneiform by making indentations in clay. What are the challenges inherent in using this material to keep permanent records?

    b. More advanced students might go on to the "Cuneiform Tablets" site below to learn more about how cuneiform works as a system of writing and about how to translate easier passages. Although primarily for experts, the cuneiform tablets transcribed on the ABZU site provide evidence that cuneiform was a highly sophisticated writing system.

3. Mesoamerican Culture and Writing. Use this Web site as a starting point for a more advanced study of Mesoamerican glyphs. How does Mayan writing compare with cuneiform writing? With Egyptian hieroglyphics?

Similar/Related Sites

1. *Hieroglyphs!*—http://www.isidore-of-seville.com/hieroglyphs/—This site provides over 100 links to materials pertaining to hieroglyphics.

2. *Cuneiform Tablets at Science Museum of Minnesota*—http://www.smm.org/research/ Anthropology/cuneiform/cuneiform.php—This site provides outstanding, enlargeable images of cuneiform tablets, along with translations (some with rollover images) and detailed transliteration, translations, and discussions of cuneiform symbols on tablets in the museum's collection.

3. See also the USC West Semitic Research Site (below).

Realms of the Sacred in Daily Life: Early Written Records of Mesoamerica
http://www.lib.uci.edu/libraries/exhibits/meso/sacred.html

Site Summary. Sponsored by the University of California at Irvine Library System, this exhibit provides an excellent overview of the purposes, forms, geographical and cultural distribution, and history of Mesoamerican códices. The exhibit was curated by Jacobo Sefamí, professor and chair of UC Irvine's Department of Spanish and Portuguese, and Dawn Anderson, Romance and German literatures librarian, with contributions by Professors Ivette Hernández-Torres and Juan Bruce-Novoa. In addition to an excellent overview of the topic, the site provides online images with detailed descriptions of the history of writing for four regional groups—Aztec, Maya, Mixtec, and Borgia—as well as códices from the post-conquest period (colonial).

Navigating the Site. From the main page, either use the main navigation bar at the top of the page to go directly to the region of interest, or page through the entire exhibit using the links at the bottom of each page.

Discussion Questions and Activities

1. What is the derivation of the word *codex*? For what purposes were códices written? How were they made? Of what materials?

2. What kinds of glyphs were used in the creation of códices? What makes them difficult to read? What kinds of events appear in the códices? For what were they used?

3. What happened to many of the códices? Where are the ones that survive?

4. How do códices from the colonial period (i.e., after European contact) compare with earlier códices?

Similar/Related Sites

1. *Ancient Mesoamerican Writing*—http://pages.prodigy.com/GBonline/ancwrite.html— This site provides additional detail and provenance for the study of the most significant Mesoamerican códices, as well as a description of their symbolism and iconography.

2. *Mesoamerican Art Resources*—http://instructional1.calstatela.edu/bevans/mesoamerican/ webresourcespage.html—This site serves as a gateway to a number of excellent sites providing additional background materials useful in the study of Mesoamerican writing.

Rabbit in the Moon

http://www.halfmoon.org/

Site Summary. This site is widely referenced by researchers in the field as an outstanding resource on Mayan writing. Created and maintained by Nancy McNelly, the site also provides a number of outstanding resources for teachers and students of Mesoamerican cultures.

Navigating the Site. The site is easily navigated from the set of links located on the main page.

Discussion Questions and Activities

1. **Culture, Games, and Resources** Page.

   a. Physical Beauty. Jot down a few notes about how your culture defines beauty, then investigate the Mayan ideal. From the main page, select the **Culture, Games, and Resources** link, then the **Culture, Oddities, and Games** link. Finally, select **Be Attractive the Maya Way.** What did Mayan people find attractive? What techniques did they use to help their children attain this ideal?

   b. Popular Culture. How do later cultures appropriate the beliefs, customs, and art of earlier cultures? From the **Culture, Oddities, and Games** page, select the link labeled **Pop Go the Maya.** According to this page, in what ways has the Mayan resurfaced in our own time? Do some of these seem more acceptable than others? Why?

   c. Games. From the **Culture, Oddities, and Games** page, select the links listed under *Games* to try out "Bul," a Mayan game of chance, and "The Six Tests of Xibalba," a role-playing game.

2. Mayan Language.

   a. Begin from the main page by clicking on the **Mayan Hieroglyphic Writing** link. Click on the link to **A Brief Note on the Mayan Writing System** and read about how Mayans conveyed meaning through their glyphs.

   b. To create your own glyphs, return to the top of the page and select the link **How to Write Your Name in Mayan Glyphs**. Follow the instructions on the resulting page.

3. To hear how the Mayan language sounded, return to the main page and select **Languages, the Talking Syllabary**. To construct words from component sounds, select **The Talking Syllabary**; enter the desired sounds, then click **Done** to see how the sounds are represented in hieroglyphics. Click on the **Syllable Sound** link to listen to how it would be pronounced. To gain insight into the evolution of the Mayan language, return to **Languages, the Talking Syllabary**, then choose **Language chart**. How much diversity existed in the Mayan language? Over how wide an area?

Similar/Related Sites

1. For younger students:

   a. *Secret of the Maya Glyphs*—http://www.nationalgeographic.com/features/97/bureau/index.html—Created by the National Geographic Society, this site provides an interactive role-playing game in which students must decode Mayan glyphs to identify the individual interred in a sarcophagus.

b. *Maya Adventure*—http://www.sci.mus.mn.us/sln/ma/top.html—Created by the Science Museum of Minnesota, this site provides an interactive Web-journey. Language arts activities are available in the form of a travel journal to be completed by students.

2. For more advanced students:

a. *Foundation for the Advancement of Mesoamerican Studies*—http://www.famsi.org/ —This wonderful site provides access to outstanding images of and commentary describing Mixtec códices from the Pohl collection, the John Montgomery dictionary of Mayan glyphs, and excellent regional maps of Mesoamerica.

b. *Mesoamerican Web Resources Index Page*—http://instructional1.calstatela.edu/ bevans/mesoamerican/webresourcespage.html—This page offers an outstanding set of links for further exploration.

Papyrology

Papyrology is the study of manuscripts written on papyrus, paper made from a plant from the Indus Valley. Epigraphy is the study and deciphering of ancient inscriptions. The sites in this section provide opportunities to observe papyrology and epigraphy researchers in these fields at work, to gain insight into the purpose and nature of their work, and to practice the skills they use.

USC West Semitic Research Site
http://www.usc.edu/dept/LAS/wsrp/index.html

Site Summary. Sponsored by the University of Southern California School of Religion and directed by Dr. Bruce Zuckerman, this Web site seeks to provide an educational and scholarly resource that documents the ancient world through high-quality photography. The Web site provides images of ancient texts, commentaries, and archaeological finds that pertain to Bible studies. The **Education** pages also include images and commentary related to early manuscripts, the Leningrad Codex (the earliest Hebrew bible), and the Dead Sea Scrolls, as well as online epigraphy and papyrology projects that allow students to practice epigraphic interpretation and papyrology. This site also offers an inside look at serious researchers at work.

Navigating the Site. The site is easy to navigate. The main page provides opening links to information about the project, educational materials, scholarly materials, and recently added items. Users should begin by clicking on the **Information** link to read about the project. Next, on the main page, click on the **Educational** link. Subsequent pages are listed in a left-hand navigational bar, which provides links that lead to texts and commentary.

Discussion Questions and Activities

All of the discussion questions and activities listed below are accessible from the navigational bar on the left-hand side of the "Educational Site."

1. Research projects. The Dead Sea Scrolls

a. The Copper Scroll. Particularly intriguing are some of the pages pertaining to the discovery and investigation of the Dead Sea Scrolls. Read how the scrolls were discovered, then visit the links. Particularly interesting is the description of the "Copper Scroll," essentially instructions on how to find a cache of buried gold and silver that has never been recovered. Read the instructions. What in particular would make it hard to find the treasure now?

    b.   Qohelet a. Read about this document. Why was the discovery of this document and others like it so important to scholars of the Bible?

2.   Epigraphic reconstruction. The epigraphic reconstruction of "Chicken Little" illustrates how scholars construct texts by extrapolating among the textual elements, located in fragmentary artifacts such as the Dead Sea Scrolls, to approximate whole texts. At the same time, this exercise encourages students to think critically about a familiar narrative. The assignment could be adapted for younger students by substituting a story fragment with fewer significant gaps.

3.   Papyrology project. This project demonstrates how the material nature of the papyrus itself also provides researchers with clues to how fragments relate to one another. This project, which involves piecing together a document using patterns that are apparent on both sides of the paper, could be simplified for lower grades by requiring pattern matches on only one side of the paper.

4.   Making Papyrus. See Encyclopedia Romana, described in Chapter 7, specifically http://itsa.ucsf.edu/~snlrc/encyclopaedia_romana/scroll/scrollcodex.html.

5.   See also the entry on Greek and Roman epigraphy in Chapter 7, Center for the Study of Ancient Documents. Activities listed there along with the activities listed above could form two segments of a lesson plan on "ancient writing."

Similar/Related Sites

1.   *Dead Sea Scrolls Exhibit, Library of Congress*—http://www.ibiblio.org/expo/deadsea.scrolls.exhibit/intro.html—This Web site provides images and translations of texts from the Dead Sea Scrolls.

2.   *Papyrus*—http://www.sas.upenn.edu/African_Studies/Books/Papyrus_Ani.html—This site provides a translation of the *Papyrus of Ani* (*The Egyptian Book of the Dead*), translated by E. A. Wallis Budge.

3.   *Papyrology at UMichigan*—http://images.umdl.umich.edu/a/apis—This site provides high-quality images of papyrus fragments.

4.   *Leuven Homepage of Papyrus Archives Worldwide*—http://lhpc.arts.kuleuven.ac.be/m —This gateway provides links to Web sites of major papyrus research sites.

Key Authors, Genres, and Texts

The Electronic Corpus of Sumerian Literature: ETCSL
http://www-etcsl.orient.ox.ac.uk/

    Site Summary. *The Electronic Text Corpus of Sumerian Literature* is based at the University of Oxford and is intended to provide Internet access to more than 400 Mesopotamian literary works written in Sumerian, classified as follows:

0 = ancient literary catalogs

1 = narrative and mythological compositions

2 = mainly royal praise poetry, and hymns to deities with prayers for rulers

3 = literary letters, letter-prayers, and law codes

4 = hymns and cult songs (mostly hymns addressed to deities)

5 = scribal training literature

6 = proverbs, fables, and riddles

Each text is fully cataloged and coded and is presented in a transcription of the Sumerian text from the original writing system into the Latin alphabet. An English prose translation and bibliographic information are also provided for most compositions. New material and new user facilities are added to the site regularly.

Navigating the Site. Despite the engaging entry page, the site is set up to meet the needs of researchers rather than casual users. Note that translations are available only through the ***Browse by Category*** button. The navigation bar for the site appears at the top of the main page. Click on ***Browse by Category*** for a list of texts sorted by category, then click on either ***Unicode*** or ***ASCII***, then ***Translation***. An alternative classification scheme, primarily for researchers who know what manuscript number they seek, is also accessible from the main page; to use it, click ***Browse by Number***, then click on ***Unicode*** or ***ASCII***, then ***Composite Text***. The untranslated, coded text will appear. For instance, portions of the epic *Gilgamesh* can be located under "0.2.01" because it appears in a manuscript located in Philadelphia, but it also appears under "1.8" as a narrative featuring heroes.

Discussion Questions and Activities

1. *Gilgamesh.* As an ancient text that describes Sumerian heroic values, *Gilgamesh* offers an excellent counterpoint to more recent epics that explore heroic ideals, such as Homer's *Iliad*, Virgil's *Aeneid*, and the anonymous *Beowulf*. Although only fragments of this ancient text remain, *Gilgamesh* also provides interesting commentary on the ongoing human struggles between civilization and the natural world, between industry and idleness, and between authority and freedom. The following questions provide ways of entering these texts:

   a. What events occur in the course of the narrative? What are the central conflicts?

   b. What values appear particularly important in the society described? For whom?

   c. In what ways does Gilgamesh struggle to be a good leader? In what ways does he fail?

   d. Once Enkidu has left the "state of nature" and joined the "civilized" world, what challenges does he face to remain there?

   e. Compare the story about the serpent to the story of the Garden of Eden in *Genesis*. What are the similarities? How do the stories differ?

   f. Compare the flood story on this site to the flood story in *Genesis*.

Similar/Related Sites

1. *Showcase: Ancient Mesopotamia*—http://www.ablemedia.com/ctcweb/showcase/dlottmesopotamia.html—This Web site provides an excellent overview of Mesopotamian culture, along with a page of lesson plans for teaching about the Sumerians.

2. *Hammurabi's Code at the Yale Avalon Project*—http://www.yale.edu/lawweb/avalon/medieval/hammenu.htm—This site provides background and several translations of the Code of Hammurabi, a Babylonian text that represents the first known codification by a ruler of a body of law.

Egyptology Resources

http://www.newton.cam.ac.uk/egypt/

Site Summary. Sponsored by the Isaac Newton Institute for Mathematics at Cambridge University and maintained by Nigel Strudwick, an Egyptologist educated at the University of Chicago, this Web site offers extensive commentary on Egyptology and archaeological digs, videotapes of archaeologists and conservators in action, and links to other resources on Egyptology.

Navigating the Site. The main page provides two sets of links: *Popular Local Resources* and *Main Pages.*

Discussion Questions and Activities

1. Egyptology FAQ. Begin with the excellent **Egyptology FAQ** page for a well-written introduction to the topic, as well as what it is to be (and how difficult it is to become) an Egyptologist. See especially Professor Strudwick's analysis of the mummy film genre.

2. Tomb of Sennefri. What exactly do archaeologists do? Jot down your own list of what you expect to see, then explore the *Tomb of Sennefri* pages. From the main page, select the link to the **Tomb of Sennefri**. Begin by choosing the introductory links to gain an historical overview of the tomb, Sennefri, Egyptian history, and archaeological and conservation practices. Then explore Professor Strudwick's **Dig Diaries**. Finally, watch the *VR Videos* to see the dig and conservation efforts on film (you will need Quicktime software, freely downloadable from the Internet, to watch the videos). What kinds of tasks do archaeologists and conservators perform? How accurate was your first list?

Similar/Related Sites

1. *House of Ptolemy*—http://www.houseofptolemy.org/index.html—This site provides links to further resources in Egyptology, as well as to the study of the Graeco-Roman world.

2. *Akhet Egyptology*—http://www.akhet.co.uk/—This commercial site in the United Kingdom provides an overview of Egyptology, especially mummies and mythology, for younger students.

Daily Life in Ancient Egypt

http://emuseum.mnsu.edu/prehistory/egypt/dailylife/dailylife.html

Site Summary. How did ancient Egyptians spend their time? This Web site, sponsored by Minnesota State University, Mankato, provides an excellent, accessible overview of Egyptian life, hieroglyphics, papyrus making, and games. The site is an excellent resource for students learning about Egyptian life and culture in general.

Navigating the Site. The site's main topics are linked to the exhibit's main page, listed above.

Discussion Questions and Activities

1.   Hieroglyphics. From the main page, choose the ***Hieroglyphics*** link. From the resulting page, follow the links to the site's primary language pages.

     a.   Hieroglyphics Tutor. Try this interactive learning device, which provides an interactive tool for learning the pronunciation and meaning of Egyptian hieroglyphics.

     b.   The Rosetta Stone. Read about the history of the Rosetta Stone. How did this artifact help Egyptologists learn how to interpret Egyptian hieroglyphics? What was the process of this discovery?

Similar/Related Sites

1.   *Middle Egyptian*—http://webperso.iut.univ-paris8.fr/~rosmord/EgyptienE.html—This deceptively simple page offers a downloadable hieroglyphic server/generator, TKSESHWAlpha, for Windows platforms, including 95, 98, 2000, and NT. The generator also works on the Windows XP operating system. Also available on this page is an easy-to-use hieroglyphic name generator, although it is located on a page with French labels.

CHAPTER 7

Classical Greek and Roman Literature

Classics Sites of General Interest

Electronic Links for Classicists
http://www.tlg.uci.edu/~tlg/index/resources.html

Site Summary. Among humanities scholars, those dedicated to the study of the classical world have taken to the Internet in large numbers. This Web site is the best mega-site available on the subject of classical literature. Originally published in the February 1994 issue of the *New England Classics Journal* and regularly updated since then, this comprehensive site is well maintained by Maria Pantelia, a classics professor at the University of California, Irvine. Only a few links are broken, and the rest are well screened and annotated. This Web site is an excellent place to begin any search for resources pertaining to the classical world.

Navigating the Site. The site is organized hierarchically; the left-hand frame lists major categories, which are hyperlinked to second-level pages. Clicking on a link brings up the corresponding page in the right-hand frame. Major categories include *Gateways, Links to Classics Resources, Databases and Web Projects, Home Pages, E-Publications, Publishers and Journals, Bibliographical Indexes, Bibliographies, Images, E-text Archives, Course Materials, Author Specific Sites, Fonts and Software, Software Developers, Professional Organizations, Classics Departments, On-line Seminars, K-12 Resources*, and *Discussion Groups*.

Perseus Project
http://www.perseus.tufts.edu

Site Summary. The *Perseus Project*, an evolving digital repository of extensively hyperlinked primary texts, visual materials, and reference resources, is the premier site for scholars and students of the classical world. The project's holdings are most comprehensive for the classical Greek and Roman world, offering Greek and Latin texts and English translations; Greek and Latin translation tools and lexica; historical overviews from Homer to the death of Alexander; an extensive classical encyclopedia; online scholarly and student essays; online grammars; an interactive color atlas; art and archaeological images; and book-length reference materials. Recent changes in the *Perseus Project* site include expanded coverage of Latin, Renaissance, and even nineteenth-century texts and materials, particularly those frequently taught in high schools. The site features an excellent keyword and phrase search engine that sorts hyperlinked results by category, as well as outstanding navigational tools.

Navigating the Site. The site has many options for navigation. To search all of the project's databases simultaneously, go to the main page and enter your search term in the search form located at the top right-hand side of the page. To search only within one database, go to the main page and select a database from those in the left-hand column. Once within the database, it is only possible to search within that database. To search, locate the search engine at the top right-hand side of the database's main page and enter a search term. Note that each collection's top and left-hand navigation bars are color coded as follows:

Classics—yellow

Renaissance—green

London—tan

Boyle papers—gray

Search engine results for classics are listed by collection. For instance, searching on the term *Odysseus* yields art objects, images, text references, text sections, and source citations. To increase loading speed, only the first three items in each category appear as thumbnails (if art) and as links (if text); click ***More*** to see additional entries for a particular category. If these additional entries and thumbnails are inaccessible and you are using Internet Explorer, ensure that your Javascript settings are enabled, or try Netscape 4.0 or above.

For most full-length works online, the contents appear as a series of clickable links in the left-hand column; the corresponding text appears in the right-hand column. The reader can also navigate through works by clicking on the blue scroll line above the text; the red dot marks the reader's approximate location within the book. Links to the "Table of Contents" provide access to a more detailed contents page. Blue directional arrows at the top and bottom of each screen can also be used to page forward or backward in a work.

Discussion Questions and Activities

1. Greek Art and Epic Values. Greek writers and artists drew upon common myths, legends, and stories when they created their work. An excellent way to identify which stories and characters caught the imaginations of Greek audiences is to analyze their depictions on pottery and in architectural art that has survived to the present day. One frequent subject of Greek artists was Achilles, the epic hero of Homer's *Iliad*. Search the *Perseus* site for the name "Achilles," then scroll to the entry marked "Vases." Finally, click on the blue arrow to get a complete list of available vase images. Find some titles that actually name Achilles as the subject and click on the links to view the images. (If a thumbnail view appears, click on the image; unless the image is restricted, a larger image will appear.) What types of images are depicted? What are the characters doing? What do the images suggest about the concerns and values of people during the "dark age" of Greek history? (For an overview of this historical period, read Thomas Martin's overview on the *Perseus* site.)

2. Precursor Texts and Audience Expectations. When Greek audiences listened to an epic or saw a new play performed, chances are they already knew the story line as well as the other stories associated with the same characters and places. To read about background stories to Greek literature, use the *Perseus* site to search on character and place names, then click on the "Perseus Encyclopedia" links that appear. The entries that appear are cross-linked to primary texts written by classical historians and later scholars. For instance, search the *Perseus* site for the name *Medea* and read what Pausanius, Apollodorus, and Herodotus say about her life before and after she met Jason. What does

understanding the events leading up to the events depicted in *Medea* contribute to your understanding of the play?

3. Greek Literature and Religion. Religion was central to the everyday lives of Greek people. Many serious events, including war, marriage, birth, death, and travel, required strict religious observances, such as sacrifices to honor the gods. Consequently, a central issue in much Greek literature is what the characters must do to observe their religion and understand the will of the gods, as well as the consequences they face when their efforts fail. Search the "Perseus Encyclopedia" for the word "sacrifice" for over 250 references in Pausanius and Apollodorus. Analyze the occasions and descriptions of sacrifice in Homer's *Iliad* alongside these explanations. What evidence of Greek attitudes toward religion can be identified in *The Iliad*? *The Odyssey*?

4. Prophets/seers. Especially in times of adversity, an individual might seek information from an oracle or seer, who was believed to have special insight into the will of the gods. The will of the gods was seen as absolute, capricious, and hidden from most mortals. One important seer who appears repeatedly in Greek and Roman literature is Tiresias. In Homer's *Odyssey*, as Odysseus attempts to return home, he seeks guidance from Tiresias during his journey to the underworld. In Sophocles's *Oedipus the King*, Oedipus sends Creon to consult Apollo's oracle at Delphi but then scorns the advice of Apollo's blind seer Tiresias. Creon also ignores Tiresias' advice in *Antigone*. Tiresias even appears in medieval works, such as Dante's *Commedia*. Use the search engine on the *Perseus* site to find references to the name *Tiresias* and read the entries. What might a Greek have anticipated when Tiresias was led onto the stage? What might such an audience have thought when powerful kings like Oedipus and Creon rejected his advice?

5. Funerary Rituals. Greek religious practice required performance of certain rituals to honor the dead. Improper burial angered the gods and had dire consequences to the living and the dead. To learn about proper funerary practice, go to the essay by Tufts student Jana Shopkorn, " 'Til Death Do Us Part: Marriage and Funeral Rites in Classical Athens," which is now located at http://www.perseus.tufts.edu/classes/JSp.html. (See also the student project on funerary rituals linked to Marilyn Katz's site, below.)

   a. In Homer's *Iliad*, compare the way an enemy's body is treated with Achilles's behavior at the funeral of Patroclus. Also consider how the bodies of Sarpedon, Patroclus, and Hector are treated by the Greeks and the Trojans. Why do the Greek and Trojan warriors exert so much energy protecting the bodies of fallen comrades? What special observances does Achilles lavish on Patroclus?

   b. Considering Shopkorn's essay and the student sites on funerary rituals, analyze the controversy over Polyneices's burial in Sophocles's *Antigone*. How do Antigone's and Creon's positions differ? What is their central conflict, and why does Antigone's position prevail, despite her lack of political authority? What does Shopkorn's essay suggest about the link between marriage and death in *Antigone*?

Similar/Related Sites

1. *Herodotus on the Web*—http://www.isidore-of-seville.com/herodotus/—Dedicated to the Greek historian Herodotus of Halicarnassus, who wrote in the fifth century B.C.E., this Web site provides a wealth of critical materials that provide background materials to assist readers in interpreting the author's extensive commentary on Greek culture and history. Most of the *Perseus* site is cross-linked to Herodotus's commentary on sites and

figures from Greek literature; use this Web site to learn more about the context in which Herodotus wrote.

2. *Roman Sites at University of Kansas*—http://www.ukans.edu/history/index/europe/ancient _rome/E/Roman/RomanSites*/index.html—Although this site was created by a non-specialist (Bill Thayer), it is hosted by the University of Kansas History Department and widely cited as an important mega-resource on the Roman world. The site includes *Lacus Curtius*, a resource offering such pages as the *Roman Gazetteer* (photographs with commentary); portions of William Smith's *Dictionary of Greek and Roman Antiquities*; Samuel Ball Platner's *A Topographical Dictionary of Rome* (rev. 1929 by Thomas Ashby); Rodolfo Lanciani's *Pagan and Christian Rome*; ancient and medieval topological texts; and Thomas Codrington's 1907 *Roman Roads in Britain*, a Roman atlas. Thayer plans future pages devoted to specific regions of Italy.

3. *Encyclopedia Romana*—http://itsa.ucsf.edu/~snlrc/encyclopaedia_romana/—Created by James Grout, director of the Learning Resource Center at the University of California, San Francisco, this Web site provides background articles on topics of interest to students of ancient Rome, including essays on Greek and Roman culture, architecture, and history, as well as pages on Roman Britain. The site is most easily navigated by beginning at the site's main page, above, with the link *SQPR*; choose either the *Site Map* for an overview of the site's organization or the *Index* for a list of topics covered. Also from the main page, the link *Roma* leads to essays about Roman art and architecture; the link *Notae* leads to articles on Roman culture and history; and the link *Nexus* leads to articles on Roman Britain, Spain, and classical and Hellenistic Greece.

The Stoa: A Consortium of Electronic Publication in the Humanities
http://www.stoa.org

Site Summary. Edited by classics professors Anne Mahoney (Tufts University) and Ross Scaife (University of Kentucky), *Stoa* fosters and supports electronic publication of outstanding scholarly projects and research. Most of the resources available on the *Stoa* site are in English; most are significant enough to require separate descriptions. Projects in progress include *Demos: Classical Athenian Democracy* and *The Ancient City of Athens*. Existing projects are described below.

1. Full-text research books

   a. Nicholas Cahill, *Household and City Organization at Olynthus* (Yale UP, 2001) —http://www.stoa.org/olynthus/—This site provides the online text of a book that describes the excavation of a city in northern Greece that was abandoned around 600 B.C.E.—significant to students of Greek literature because this date immediately precedes the period during which the Greek playwrights Aeschylus, Sophocles, and Euripides wrote. The layouts and contents of the houses excavated are described thoroughly, including the pervasiveness of a central courtyard, probable uses of the rooms (including gender-specific activities), and artifacts found (e.g., coins, amphora, loom weights, cooking utensils, etc). The site is easy to navigate. At present, only the book is online; a database will follow later. Within the book, the description of each house is accompanied by the house's complete floor plan, contents, and probable three-dimensional appearance. Most of the images can be viewed in three sizes.

b. Gregory Nagy, *Homeric Questions* (Harvard University Press, 1996)—http://
www.stoa.org/cgi-bin/ptext?doc=Perseus%3Atext%3A2001.06.0002—The first in-
stallment of a project that will publish Harvard's *Homer Project* on the *Stoa* site,
Nagy's book is particularly useful in clarifying what is meant (or should be meant)
when *The Iliad* and *The Odyssey* are described as "oral poetry." This book is not for
the novice, but provides an excellent background for teachers.

c. Martin Mueller, *The Iliad* (Allen & Unwin, 1984)—http://www.stoa.org/cgi-bin/
ptext?doc=2000.01.0002—An accessible, non-specialist analysis of Homer's epic,
Mueller's book seeks to clarify the historical and cultural contexts within which the
Iliad has functioned, both in early heroic and later city-state societies. Users of the
Perseus site will recognize that Mueller's book is formatted similarly to books reproduced on *Perseus*. The contents of the book appear as clickable links in the left-hand
column; the corresponding text appears in the right hand column. Clicking on the
blue scroll line will move the user forward or backward in the text; the red dot marks
the approximate location within the book. The user can also click on the "Table of
Contents" link for a more detailed contents page. Blue directional arrows at the top
and bottom of each screen can be used to page forward or backward.

d. Martin Mueller, *Children of Oedipus* (University of Toronto Press, 1980)—http://
www.stoa.org/cgi-bin/ptext?doc=2000.01.0007—This online version of Mueller's
1980 book is expanded to include more recently published material, including three
essays: "Plutarch's Life of Brutus and the Play of Its Repetitions in Shakespearean
Drama" (*Renaissance Drama* 22 [1991]: 47–94), "*Hamlet* and the World of Ancient
Tragedy" (*Arion* 5 [1997]: 22–45), and "Hofmannsthal's *Elektra* and Its Ancient
Models" (*Modern Drama* 29 [1986]: 71–91). Mueller has also included a chapter on
Mozart's *Idomeneo*, which is accompanied by sound files.

2. Bruce Hartzler's *Metis* project—http://www.stoa.org/metis/—*Metis* is a remarkable series of interactive pages that permit the user to tour Greek archaeological sites. To view
this page, you will need QuickTime, a freely downloadable Apple program (see
http://www.apple.com/quicktime/download/standalone/). The main page features a list
of all of the cities in the database; clicking on a link opens a separate window displaying a
180 degree panoramic view of the city or scene. Clicking on one of these brings up a
QuickTime screen depicting the site. The toolbar across the bottom of the screen provides
the ability to zoom in, zoom out, show "hot spots," and drag a zoomed object. Clicking on
the question mark makes visible the "hot links" underlying the image; these switch between sites, produce overall site maps, or link to *Perseus* commentary on the image. This
is a truly outstanding site.

3. *Suda On Line: Byzantine Lexicography*—http://www.stoa.org/sol/—Initiated in January
1999, *Suda On Line* is an ongoing project to translate a 30,000-entry, tenth-century
Byzantine encyclopedia that provides materials pertaining to ancient literature, history,
and biography. Much of the encyclopedia is already online and is searchable by keyword.
Users must register as a "guest" or "translator" to use the encyclopedia; results are returned free of charge. The site's navigation links appear across the top of the site. From
the site's main page, click "Register." Signing on as a "guest" provides access to the encyclopedia, but not editorial rights. Next, from the main page, click "Help" and read the options for browsing or searching the site. Search results are returned with complete
information about the headword of the article and a coherent segment of text surrounding
the search term, which is highlighted in yellow.

4. *Diotima: Women and Gender in the Ancient World*—http://www.stoa.org/diotima/—Although *Diotima* was recently moved to the *Stoa* site, it has long been recognized as a major Internet resource in its own right. Edited by Ross Scaife since 1995 and sponsored by the University of Kentucky Classics Department, *Diotima's* mission is to provide a forum and publishing medium for the study of gender in the entire ancient Mediterranean world. The site offers extensive course materials; a searchable bibliography; an anthology of primary texts; and a library of articles, books, databases, and images. The site is extremely active; click on the ***What's new?*** link to identify recent changes. Users can also join Anahita-L, a listserv that keeps subscribers up to date on additions to *Diotima*. Although the "Bible Browser" that appears on the **Biblical Studies** page is now defunct, the remainder of the page provides links to resources at other sites. The site is complex, and some browsing is necessary to gain a full sense of what the site has to offer. In addition to ***What's new?***, the site's main page provides links to courses; bibliographies; images; anthologies; biblical studies; *Perseus* (Tufts); and *De Feminis Romanis*, a set of primary text readings, in Latin, with extensive glosses. The main page also provides a table of links to "New Web Resources"; note that this table does not duplicate resources on the "What's New" page.

Navigating the Site. On the main page, select a project from the list on the right.

Discussion Questions and Activities

1. *The Iliad.*

   a. Mueller's *The Iliad* is a good starting point for the non-specialist who wants an accessible overview of *The Iliad*.

   b. Read the introduction to Nagy's *Homeric Questions.* According to Nagy, what is meant by "oral poetry"? What do Homeric scholars say about his epic poetry as written and oral poetry?

   c. Use the *Metis* site to view the remains of Troy (the Troy of the *Iliad,* if historical, is believed to be Troy VIIA). What remains of the city? Troy's position was on a hill overlooking a large, relatively flat plain. Why was its position particularly strategic for the Trojans?

2. *The Odyssey*

   a. Read the introduction to Nagy's *Homeric Questions* for a clarification of what is meant by "oral poetry" and for a summary of disagreements about the orality versus the textuality of Homeric epics.

   b. Read Cahill's book on the excavation of Olynthus, a city whose inhabitants appear to have abandoned it abruptly in the sixth century B.C.E., leaving behind an extraordinary array of household artifacts in the houses. What insight does this book give into Penelope's world? In what other ways was living space gendered? (Despite *The Odyssey's* earlier date, reading descriptions of as few as three houses should shed light on Penelope's preoccupation with weaving and the separation of activities observed in her interactions with the suitors.)

3. Sophocles's *Oedipus Cycle*

   a. Consult *Metis* to view how the "three roads" and "seven gates" of Thebes, the setting of Sophocles's *Oedipus* and *Antigone*, appear today.

    b.   On *Diotima*, read Elise Garrison's essay "Suicide in Classical Mythology" to learn more about the suicides of Eurydice, Antigone, and Haemon in Sophocles's *Antigone*.

  4. *Medea*

    a.   Consult *Diotima's* **Courses** page for insight into Euripides's *Medea*; for instance, follow the link to Laurel Bowman's online resource "Teaching Euripides' *Medea*," which includes texts such as the *Argonautica* (the work that describes Jason's quest for the Golden Fleece) and linked images from *Perseus*. What insights into the plot of *Medea* do these materials provide?

The Classics Pages

http://www.classicspage.com/

Site Summary. Created by Andrew Miller, aka "Loxias," *The Classics Pages* offer a wide variety of interactive learning tools and links. Although Miller does not reveal his identity on the Web site, he claims a M.Phil. from Cambridge and a career teaching and studying classics. His astute commentary seems to bear this out. *Note:* Teachers should screen Miller's pages carefully before using or assigning them to children in grades K–12; some pages include (non-classical) images that depict partial nudity and may not be considered appropriate for all audiences. Pages include the following:

Title (Link)	Contents
Aeschylus	Devoted to discussion of *Agamemnon*
Catullus' Page	Latin love poetry by Horace, Catullus, Propertius, and Sulpicia, translated, glossed, and parsed
Eros	Discusses the identity of Eros; a separate page provides a version of the Cupid and Psyche myth
Euripides	Links to pages that discuss *Medea*, *Helen*, *Phoenissae*, and *Orestes*
Fun with Latin	Games—some pertaining to Latin
Greek Pottery & Greek Sculpture	Fascinating pages describing Greek vase painting, with a brief page about Greek sculpture
Iliad	Devoted to *The Iliad*; includes a link to an interactive *Iliad* game
Iliad **and** *Odyssey*	Devoted to Homer's epics, these pages include links to *Iliad* and *Odyssey* games and to pertinent articles
Lucian	Greek science fiction
Lysistrata	Devoted to a discussion of Aristophanes's play
Medea	Links to a page discussing Euripides's *Medea*, including the interactive "Medea game"

Oedipus	Discusses Sophocles and Greek tragedy; includes links to interactive games dealing with *Antigone* and *Oedipus Tyrannos*, as well as articles on the sphinx, Greek kingship, and Tiresias
Rude Latin	Provides various rude phrases in Latin
Sappho	Spare background on Sappho, with a few lines of poetry, in Greek, including audio files, translations, and grammar analysis
The Oracle	Invites users to submit questions
Virgil's Page	Provides an excerpt from the *Georgics* and a translation of *The Aeneid*, in progress (Books I–IV are online)

Navigating the Site. The site is easy to navigate. From the main page, click on **What's New** to gain access to a log of recent additions to the pages. Click on **Main Menu** to get to the main site links; most are linked to this page. Most pages of the site link back to the main page, a site map, and a search engine.

Discussion Questions and Activities

1. *Iliad, Odyssey, Oedipus Tyrannos, Antigone, Medea, The Aeneid.* How well do you know these works? Take the interactive, thorough online quizzes and play the games available on the site to test yourself.

The Classics Technology Center
http://ablemedia.com/ctcweb/index2.html

Site Summary. Sponsored by Able Media, creator of software for teaching in the classics, this Web site provides extensive teaching materials on classical topics. Whether or not users are interested in using Able Media's software, this site provides an outstanding and comprehensive array of lesson plans for use in teaching classical world literature, Latin and Greek languages, and mythology. Included on this site are background materials (located by clicking on the **Companions** and **Netshots** links). Use the **Showcase** link to locate teaching materials and critical essays submitted by classics teachers, including academic presentations, online exercises and software, riddles, brainteasers, trivia, original artwork and poetry, and free images of Greece and Rome. Also free on this site are downloadable Latin dictionary, texts, and crossword puzzles.

Navigating the Site. The site is easy to navigate. From the URL listed above, choose among the links in the left-hand navigation bar. You will need Acrobat Reader to view the PDF files on this site.

Discussion Questions and Activities

1. Greek Theater.

   a. Begin by selecting the **Companions** link on the left, then locate the **Greek Theatre** link on the right. Use the lesson plans and exercises provided as the basis for classroom assignments on the features of Greek theater.

2. Epic poetry: Homer's *Iliad* and *Odyssey*. Choose the **Teachers Companions** link, then links to **Zeus** and **Homer's Iliad and Odyssey**. Read over the background materials, selecting age-appropriate information to share with students.

    a.   From the *Zeus Teachers Companion*, reproduce the line drawing of a Greek vase and assign younger students the task of creating their own vase design depicting an event from Greek mythology.

    b.   Have older students construct a family tree of the gods, create a timeline of events in the *Iliad* and *Odyssey*, locate formulaic expressions characteristic of oral poetry, and identify images on Greek pottery, as outlined in the *Iliad and Odyssey Teachers Companion*.

3.   Showcase. Select the **Showcase** link from the left-hand column, then investigate the wide range of materials available to teachers on this site.

    a.   Try creating an interactive fable using PowerPoint by following the simplified instructions provided.

    b.   Use the ideas in *The Movie "Gladiator" in Historical Perspective* to plan a unit in which older students research the reigns of Marcus Aurelius and Commodus to assess the historical accuracy of the film in its depiction of historical events.

    c.   Construct and play the games described in the showcase essay on *Roman Board Games* to gain a sense of how some classical Romans passed the time.

    d.   For a crash course on the subjects depicted in Greek pottery, work through the showcase essay and images depicting *The Classic Symposium on Greek Art*. What images can you identify based on your reading of Greek literary texts, such as *Oedipus Tyrannos*, *The Iliad*, and *The Odyssey*?

    e.   Learn about ways to think about Achilles's mother, the goddess Thetis, by reading the essay *Thetis: Protective Mother or Dominated Wife*?

Similar/Related Sites

1.   *Perseus*—http://www.perseus.tufts.edu/—Most of the resources on the Able Media site refer to classroom materials created using its software; however, all of the Webquests described make extensive use of materials from the *Perseus* site at Tufts (see entry above).

The Ancient Olympic Games Virtual Museum
http://minbar.cs.dartmouth.edu/greecom/olympics/

Site Summary. Held every four years from 776 B.C.E. to 393 C.E., the Olympic games were extremely important features of ancient Greek life, especially for men. Links are provided for the history of the games, its victors, anecdotes, scholars, a slide show of Olympic sites, and the story of a fictional competitor. Note that the links to the Panathenaic Vase exhibit do not function.

Navigating the Site. To gain access to many of the features on this site, it is necessary to register (free of charge). On the main page (above), locate the brown *Register* link and follow directions to register. Once logged in, return to the main page. Two navigation tools are available. Use the table of links on the main page, or select *Virtual Olympic Games Museum Lobby* for a visual directory of the links.

Discussion Questions and Activities

1.   *The Iliad.*

    a.   *The Iliad* includes detailed accounts of funeral games held for warriors, including Achilles's friend Patroclus. In fact, the funeral games for Oinomaos are suggested as the possible pretext for the first Olympic games. In what ways are the funeral games in honor of Patroclus similar to the Olympic games as they are described on the *Ancient Olympic Games Virtual Museum* site?

b. *The Iliad* includes graphic descriptions of battles and one-on-one combat between Greek and Trojan warriors. Based on these descriptions and the Web site's discussion of early Olympic events, what is the connection between training for the Olympic games and training for war? How were the games connected with religious practices?

c. What events from the early games remain in today's Olympic games?

Similar/Related Sites

1. *The Real Story of the Ancient Olympic Games*—http://www.museum.upenn.edu/new/research/ Exp_Rese_Disc/Mediterranean/Olympics/olympicintro.shtml—Connected with the Greek page at the University of Pennsylvania Museum site (described below), this page provides additional insight into the games.

Worlds Intertwined: Etruscans, Greeks, and Romans

http://www.museum.upenn.edu/new/worlds_intertwined/main.shtml

Site Summary. This site, a virtual tour accompanying an exhibit at the University of Pennsylvania Museum of Anthropology and Archaeology, includes commentary and a link describing connections among Greek, Etruscan, and Roman cultures. The site is particularly useful for its explanation of elements of Roman culture that were derived from the Greek civilization that preceded it, as well as how Roman culture was influenced by the Etruscan culture it absorbed.

Navigating the Site. The site is easy to navigate. Choose among the hyperlinked images labeled **The Greek World, The Etruscan World**, and **The Roman World**. The *Greek World* site provides a very brief overview of Greek culture. More extensive are the *Etruscan World* and *Roman World* pages, which are similarly designed. Both of these pages are cross-linked to historical timelines and overviews, as well as to images of the museum's collections.

Discussion Questions and Activities

1. Page through each of the three exhibits on this Web site. What elements of Greek culture did Romans claim? What elements of Etruscan culture?

2. In Virgil's *Aeneid*, Aeneas, whose Trojan wife Creusa had been killed during the sack of Troy, is directed by the gods to leave behind Dido, Queen of Carthage, to fulfill his destiny as founder of Rome. Subsequently, Rome and Carthage become bitter enemies, whereas Aeneas later marries Lavinia, an indigenous princess of Italy. How might the information about the Greeks, Etruscans, and Rome on this Web site explain Virgil's decisions as he planned this story line in the *Aeneid*?

Similar/Related Sites

1. *Museum of Antiquities*—http://museums.ncl.ac.uk/archive/index.html—This Web site is particularly accessible to children and describes Hadrian's Wall and Roman Britain.

Epigraphy

Center for the Study of Ancient Documents
http://www.csad.ox.ac.uk/index.html

Site Summary. Sponsored by Oxford University's Faculty of Literae Humaniores and established in 1995, this site provides information on Greek and Latin epigraphy, or the study of inscriptions, including excellent exhibits on early technologies of writing. Images include early writing on papyrus, on wood tablets coated with wax or lead (using a stylus), in stone, and in clay. Although the wax coating on such tablets rarely survives, this site documents how researchers can raise from the wood impressions that were created when the stylus penetrated the thin wax or lead coating.

Navigating the Site. The site is easy to navigate. From the main page, follow one of these paths: 1) click on the ***Imaging Projects*** link to gain an overview of the kinds of materials these researchers study; 2) click directly on the link to the ***Vindolanda Tablets Online***; or 3) to view the researchers' efforts to recover and preserve the written records discovered at Herculaneum, click on the link to the ***Oxyrhynchus Papyri.***

Discussion Questions and Activities

1. Imaging Roman Stilus Tablets. From the main page, choose the link to ***Imaging Projects,*** then ***Imaging Roman Stilus Tablets***. Read about classicists working on the Vindolanda tablets, then use the following set of classroom activities to show how the researchers identified what the tablets said.

    a. Roman "tablets" were created from wooden frames that were filled with melted wax. Create a tablet using a shallow wooden box and melted wax.

    b. How do scholars "raise" old inscriptions from the tablets they find? By mapping the impressions they find in the wax. To demonstrate, begin with a partially used pad of paper that includes deep impressions from earlier writing. Rub the lead of a soft pencil or a graphite block over the top to "raise" the impressions. What was written on the tablet before?

    c. Demonstrate how a similar result might be obtained from a Roman wax tablet. Using a nail as a stylus, mark the "Roman tablet" deeply enough to penetrate the wax as well as the wood. Note that the deepest marks can be raised from the wood, even when the wax is no longer present.

    d. Alternatively, create inscribed "tablets" out of clay, allow them to dry, and then fire them in a kiln. After the tablets are fired, place a thin sheet of paper over the tablets and gently rub graphite over the paper. Were you able to raise an impression?

2. See the entry on the Dead Sea Scrolls and papyrology in Chapter 6, *USC West Semitic Research Site*. Activities listed there along with the activities listed in this entry could form two segments of a lesson plan on "ancient writing."

Similar/Related Sites

1. *USC West Semitic Research Site*—http://www.usc.edu/dept/LAS/wsrp/index.html—See separate entry in Chapter 6.

2. *Philodemus Archive*—http://www.classicspage.com/jact.htm—This page is an account of a project to recover information from papyrus rolls recovered from a villa in Herculaneum, buried by the eruption of Vesuvius.

Mapping

The Interactive Mediterranean Project: On-line Atlas of the Ancient Mediterranean World
http://iam.classics.unc.edu/map/map_room.html

Site Summary. Funded by a University of North Carolina-Chapel Hill Chancellor's Grant, the *IAM Project* has been directed by Dr. Richard Talbert since 1997. Its purpose is to facilitate teaching about the ancient Mediterranean world from the high school through introductory university levels by providing high-quality, online maps. The product of this effort, the *Barrington Atlas of the Greek and Roman World*, has in turn been incorporated into a successor project, the *Ancient World Mapping Center*. The site provides terrain and outline maps, both with and without place and region names, in PDF format. Regions covered include Northern Europe, the British Isles, and the Mediterranean basin. There are detail maps for the Aegean Sea and Greece, Northern Africa, Asia Minor (Turkey), Northern Gaul, the Iberian and the Italian peninsulas, and the Levantine coast.

Navigating the Site. Adobe Acrobat Reader is necessary to view the maps. The site is easy to navigate. From the main page, click on the link to the IAM's *Map Room.* Navigation tools to gain access to the maps appear on the left-hand side of the new screen. For an index to all maps and map formats, click the *Map Index* link. Maps can also be located using clickable large area maps; to gain access to these maps, click on the *Locator Map* link.

Discussion Questions and Activities

1. Ancient Greece. Ancient Greece was composed of separately governed city-states; consequently, in *The Odyssey*, Odysseus travels for years to get from Troy to Ithaca; in *Lysistrata* Athens is at war with Sparta; and in *Oedipus*, Thebes and Corinth are separately ruled. From the main Web site above, click on the *Map Index* link, then choose the first *Terrain and Place Names* map listed under *The Aegean Sea and Greece*. Locate these place names on the map. How far apart are they really? What features of the terrain of Greece and Turkey might influence perceptions of distance in ancient Greece? Why did the ancient Greeks rely more on transportation by sea rather than land?

2. Charting Epic Journeys. Print out several copies of the *Mediterranean Basin* maps. Referring to the detail maps for city and region locations, map the travels of Achilles, Odysseus, and Aeneas.

3. Medea and Greek Civilization. In *Medea*, Medea is repeatedly characterized by Jason as an outsider to Greek culture and society—in terms of her behavior and her region of geographical origin, Colchis. Go to the **Maps of the Ancient Greek World** page (see related links) and select the link to the *Map of the Eastern Mediterranean*. Find Colchis and Corinth on the map. How far apart are they? With what modern day countries are these geographical locations associated?

Similar/Related Sites

1. *Maps of the Ancient Greek World*—http://plato-dialogues.org/tools/mapindex.htm—Part of the *Plato's Dialogues* site (described below), this site provides excellent maps for use in teaching.

2. *The Edges of the Earth in Greek Thought*—http://www.livius.org/ea-eh/edges/edges.html—This site provides an essay on how Greeks thought about both the world and their place in it.

3. *A Cultural Map of Greece*—http://www.culture.gr/2/21/maps/hellas.html—Created by the Hellenic Ministry of Culture, this Web site provides excellent interactive detail maps and images of important Greek cultural sites.

Classical People and Places

Dr. J's Illustrated Guide to the Classical World

http://lilt.ilstu.edu/drjclassics/

Site Summary. Created by Dr. Janice Siegel, Department of Foreign Languages at Illinois State University, this site offers a comprehensive set of photographic images of important sites in Greece. In many cases, the images are accompanied by Dr. Siegel's lecture notes. This site is one of the sites most frequently cited by classical scholars and organizations. Also available on the site are illustrated commentaries on Pericles's *Funeral Oration*, Aeschylus's *Oresteia*, Sophocles's *Oedipus*, and Plato's *Apology*. Other information, such as timelines and photographs of Italy, will be added over time. Also available on this site is an extensive survey of audiovisual aids for teaching about ancient civilizations.

Navigating the Site. The site is easy to navigate. Navigation links are listed at the bottom of the first page. The Greek pages provide thumbnail photographs of important sites that can be enlarged.

Discussion Questions and Activities

1. *Lysistrata.* As part of Aristophanes's plot, the women of Athens take over the Acropolis so that the men will have no money to fight their wars. Study the photographs of the Acropolis on Dr. Siegel's site. Why would this strategic location be easy to defend?

2. Greek Mythology. Read about the features of Mount Olympus, which Dr. Siegel climbed in 1995. What features of the mountain might have made people believe it was the residence of the gods? Especially note the meteorological features Dr. Siegel describes.

Similar/Related Sites

1. *Maecenas—Photos of Greece and Italy*—http://wings.buffalo.edu/AandL/Maecenas/—Created by Leo Curran, professor emeritus of classics at the State University of New York, Buffalo, and assisted by grants from the Classical Association of the Empire State and the Classical Association of the Atlantic States, this site includes more than 2,100 outstanding images of ancient Greece and Rome. Particularly beautiful are Dr. Curran's latest additions, black-and-white photographs, which are still being cataloged and integrated with the color photographs already online. The images may be downloaded and used for any but commercial purposes. The site is easy to navigate. From the main page, click the link provided. The second page lists the place names associated with sets of pictures. Clicking on a place name produces a new listing of links to available images. To

view a photograph, click on a link, or click the "thumbnails" link to view all of the images, then click on the thumbnail to bring up the desired photograph.

2. *Capitolium.org*—http://www.capitolium.org/—This Web site provides the capability to toggle between high-resolution photographs of current Roman archaeological sites and virtual reconstructions. Some virtual video tours are also available, but these prompt to download ActiveX with each viewing. The site also indicates it has live cams mounted on the terrace of Rome's Palazzo Senatori and that these can be operated from the Web site; however, only ten users are permitted on the site at a time.

Corinth Project

http://corinth.sas.upenn.edu/

Site Summary. The *Corinth Project* is a mapping project that uses satellite imagery, low altitude aerial photography, ground surveys, archaeological excavation, and geographic information system (GIS) computing tools to interpret and create virtual fly-bys, photographs, panoramic images, and "interactive actual state plans" over time of Roman Corinth, a city founded by Julius Caesar and built on the site of the earlier Greek Corinth. The Web site demonstrates in fascinating detail how interdisciplinary classical scholars cooperate to increase knowledge of earlier civilizations, as well as how past building practices influence those of the present.

Navigating the Site. The site is easy to navigate. The main navigation bar appears on the left-hand side of the main page. Begin with the "Historical Overview" to learn the history of the site. Other than the main page, most subsequent pages are split into three frames: a static navigation bar on the left and two scrolling frames on the right. Images generally appear at the top; descriptive text appears at the bottom with hyperlinked figure references within the text. Viewing the "interactive actual state plans" requires Whip4, a plug-in GIS program that can be downloaded from the site; the program works only with Netscape Navigator and Internet Explorer. Quicktime 4 or above is needed to view the panoramic images.

Discussion Questions and Activities

1. Archaeological Methods. Study the materials on the **City Plan** and **Methodology** pages. How do contemporary classical scholars reconstruct earlier civilizations? What clues did these researchers read and interpret to learn about and create a complete city plan without excavating the whole site?

2. Roman Culture and Values. Study the kinds of buildings and structures that existed in Roman Corinth. What kinds of buildings are they? Which are the most impressive? What does this tell you about the concerns and activities of classical Roman people?

3. Past and New Civilizations.

   a. Study the "interactive actual state plans" of Roman Corinth. What features of the earlier Greek city remained and influenced the choices made by Roman builders?

   b. Next, click on the navigation bar's *Landscape* link. What features of the Roman city and of Roman land use influenced modern builders?

Similar/Related Sites

1. *Excavations at Troy*—http://www.uni-tuebingen.de/troia/eng/index.html—This site provides summaries of the 1997, 1998, and 1999 digs in Turkey. (*The Iliad* is generally believed to refer to what archaeologists have identified as Troy VIIA. See Mueller's book *The Iliad* on the *Stoa* site.)

2. *Lepcis Magnae: Window on the Roman World in North Africa*—http://www.alnpete.co.uk/lepcis/—This Web site provides plans, excavation records, and photographs of this seventh-century C.E. Roman city on the north coast of Libya. The site also includes a special Kid's Zone, although the virtual museum is not operational at present.

VRoma: A Virtual Community for Teaching and Learning Classics
http://www.vroma.org/

Site Summary. Created in 1997 and funded by a grant from the National Endowment for the Humanities, this site offers a wide range of resources for teaching classical Roman literature and Latin. One important feature is a virtual (MOO) environment that simulates a visit to ancient Rome, where faculty and students can meet and interact by logging in remotely (off-campus) or while in a computer classroom environment. The site allows students and faculty to register as users, adopt Roman identities, and travel through Rome, encountering others who are also visiting the MOO while learning about the culture and history of Rome. Passages from Latin texts are also interspersed throughout the environment; for those who have not studied Latin, translations are provided. Users who do not wish to interact with others in the MOO visit may register as "guests." In addition to MOO-related materials, including sample assignments and instructions on using the VRoma MOO for teaching, the site also provides a large archive of freely downloadable images and teaching resources relating to Latin language instruction, texts and authors, and history and culture. The site also hosts the following additional resources:

1. *Catullus*—http://www.vroma.org/~hwalker/VRomaCatullus/Catullus.html—Created by Professor H. Walker at Bates College, this page provides side-by-side Latin and English translations of Catullus's poetry.

2. *Juvenal—Satire 3*—http://www.vroma.org/~araia/satire3.html—Created by Professor Anne Raia, this page provides a fully annotated edition of the satire in Latin and English.

Navigating the Site. Best results may be obtained by using Internet Explorer to access the VRoma. The site is easy navigate. The main page offers two sets of links: one associated with the Virtual Roma MOO (on the left) and the other associated with Resources (on the right).

1. Virtual Roma. The globe is an image-mapped navigation device. Before entering the MOO, familiarize yourself with the VRoma MOO by clicking on the Eamus VROMAM Tour Guide. A map of Rome, divided into fourteen sections, will appear. Click on all of the links to learn about the choices you will encounter once inside the MOO. Next, sign up for a character by clicking on "Become a VRoman." Fill out the form and send it. Until you receive your VRoma character, you may enter the MOO from the main page by clicking *Log in* and entering as a "Guest." Once inside the MOO, navigate using the right-hand side of the screen by reading about your location in the MOO and clicking on the available links leading to adjacent areas. The left-hand side of the screen includes a gray box at the top that records your movement within the MOO and a small white box at the bottom that provides a space for entering questions, commands, or directions. A row of blue navigation buttons appears at the top of the screen. Click first on *Guide* and print out these basic instructions. The other buttons across the top are as follows: *Help* provides access to help files; *Look* shows your location; *Who* displays a list of other users also logged in; *Options* provides a pop-up form to clarify your online identity; *Request* provides a popup form to request an online identity. To leave the MOO, click on the blue *Quit* button.

2. Resources. From the VRoma main page, click on *Resources* to explore links to the following:

a. Images. This page provides extensive archives of images, searchable by keyword and freely usable

b. Teaching. In this area, suggestions are included for classics in general and for the VRoma MOO in particular. Also useful are templates for creating your own online exercises. Included at http://www.vroma.org/~bmcmanus/slideshows.html are two slide shows that describe VRoma, demonstrate its use, and provide information on how to gain access to the MOO for your courses.

c. Links. This area provides a modest set of links to other excellent classics sources on the Internet.

Discussion Questions and Activities

1. Extensive sample class assignments associated with the VRoma site include the following, described at http://www.vroma.org/course_materials/:

   a. Treasure Hunt Assignments. These include political science, art and architecture, culture, history, and mythology and folklore assignments.

   b. Latin Language Assignments.

   c. Roman Literature Assignments. These assignments include materials for the study of Plautus and Vergil.

Similar/Related Sites

1. *Villa Jvlilla*—http://www.villaivlilla.com/—Although this site appears to have been created by a non-specialist, it is well documented and provides an accessible, eclectic introduction to a few areas of Roman material culture, including personal appearance, clothing, food, housing, and timepieces. Particularly interesting are sections on clothing and makeup.

2. *Forum Romanum*—http://library.thinkquest.org/11402/?tqskip1=1&tqtime=0812—This site is a student project with excellent clickable images that reconstruct the Roman forum.

Feminae Romae: Women of Ancient Rome
http://dominae.fws1.com/Index.html

Site Summary. Created by Suzanne Cross, a paralegal with education and interest in literature and history, this well-designed site provides an accessible and well-researched account of the two primary sources for cultural attitudes toward women in Rome: the relatively restrictive Greek model and the more permissive Etruscan model. The value of this site has been recognized in the BBC Webguide, as has the author's Web site on Julius Caesar (located at http://heraklia.fws1.com/).

Navigating the Site. The site is easy to navigate. Access to the entire site is available from the main page (above) through the left-hand navigation bar.

Discussion Questions and Activities

1. Women in Greece. Choose the *Historical Context* link and read about women in ancient Greece.

a. *The Iliad.* Read about Helen, Hecabe, and Andromache in *The Iliad.* What is the Greek ideal for women? Which characters best fit the Greek ideal for an aristocratic woman? Who least fits the ideal?

b. *The Odyssey.* How well does Penelope fit the description of an ideal Greek woman? Does she deviate from the ideal in any respect?

c. *Antigone.* How does Antigone fit the description of an ideal Greek woman? In what ways does she deviate from that ideal? Creon's description of Antigone strikes the modern reader as blatantly sexist. Based on the description you've read at *Feminae Romae*, what might a Greek audience have thought about Creon? Does knowing about how Greeks might have interpreted Antigone and Creon make Creon's behavior more understandable?

d. *Lysistrata.* Given the description of life for Greek women, how likely is the plot of *Lysistrata*? What does the popularity of the play suggest about how people in Euripides's time felt about the ongoing conflicts between Athens and other city-states? How might they have interpreted the actions of the women?

2. Women in Rome. Read what this Web site has to say about the lives of Etruscan women and then about Roman women.

a. *Aeneid*: Aeneas and Creusa. Many of the characters in *The Aeneid* also appear in *The Iliad*, including Aeneas, who is represented in both epics as one of Troy's greatest warriors. What does *The Iliad* say about Aeneas? *The Aeneid*? Compare the relationships between husbands and wives in *The Iliad* with those in *The Aeneid*.

b. *Aeneid*: Aeneas and Dido. Dido, Hecabe, and Helen are all the wives of rulers, although Dido is a widow when she meets Aeneas. Compare Dido with Hecabe and Helen. How are these women different? What features of Greek and Roman culture might account, in part, for the difference? How do the men in the epics expect them to behave?

Similar/Related Sites

1. *Marilyn Katz's Course Materials*—http://mkatz.web.wesleyan.edu/course_materials/ mkatz_course_materials.html—Resources are linked to syllabi, background materials, and study guides. Working methodically through these materials will pay off. See especially the resource links provided for CCIV 110, "Women in Ancient Greece," Antigone Background Notes, "Funerary Ritual."

I, Claudius Site

http://www.anselm.edu/Internet/classics/I,CLAUDIUS/index.html

Site Summary. This outstanding, student-edited site provides resources for teaching about Roman literature and life using the BBC miniseries *I, Claudius*, considered by many classicists to be among the best films about Rome. The site provides detailed plot summaries; analyses of each episode's adherence both to Robert Graves's novelization of the life of Tiberius Claudius and to the original Roman histories that were Graves's sources; charts that analyze the likelihood that the dramatized elements are factual; and detailed descriptions of each character. The site has been in progress since 1997, with a new board of student editors appointed each academic year.

Navigating the Site. This site is best viewed in Internet Explorer. The site is extremely well designed. The main index page (above) provides access to other materials on the site via drop-down menus that are accessible through the tabs at the top of the page.

Discussion Questions and Activities

1. What classical sources did author Robert Graves use when he created *I, Claudius*, and how likely is the action to have actually happened as Graves describes it? Check out the *Sources* and *Analysis* links to find the answers.

2. What choices did the casting director and the set and costume designers make to ensure that *I, Claudius* was as authentic as possible? Check out the links to *Plot Summaries* and *Personae* to gain insight into this question.

Art and Architecture

The Beasley Archive of Classical Art
http://www.beazley.ox.ac.uk/

Site Summary. Based on the personal archive of Sir John Beazley, a professor of classical archaeology and art, the Beazley Archive (BA) is a research unit maintained at the Ashmolean Museum under the direction of Dr. Donna Kurtz. The collection includes photographs; notes; drawings; books and impressions from engraved gems; and, with subsequent acquisitions, the largest archive of photographs of Athenian vases in the world. The collection has also maintained a pottery database since 1979 and a collection of sculpture casts since 1992. The Web site presents an excellent, accessible overview of the history of Greek vase artistry, scholarship, and collection, in addition to thousands of images with commentary. Also provided is a detailed dictionary, cross-linked with other entries and images, names, technical terms, and vocabulary associated with Greek history, mythology, geography, and art.

Navigating the Site. The site is well designed and easy to navigate. The main page features a tool bar across the bottom. Subsequent pages are set up with three sets of navigation links: across the top for the section, on the left for the page, and at the bottom for the overall site. Clicking on *The Archive* brings up details about the collection; clicking on *Gems* provides resources that describe **Styles & Periods, Uses & Production, History of Collecting,** and **Documents for Study**. Clicking on the *Pottery* link from the main page provides links to an **Overview of Styles & Periods, Production & Distribution, Databases,** and **Beazley Drawings**. The *Sculpture* link from the main page provides links to **Styles & Periods,** a page that shows **How Casts Are Made, History of the Cast Collection,** and a **Catalogue of Casts**. These resources are further organized by subject matter and connected with good photographic images.

Discussion Questions and Activities

1. Vase Painting and Epic Values. The period during which the best classical Greek vase painting was completed coincides with the period that also produced the best classical Greek drama. Compare the subject matter and iconography of the images on vases with

the primary subjects of Greek epic and drama. What do they have in common? Which subjects are treated differently or not at all in one medium? What does this say about the importance of this subject matter in Greek culture?

2. Iconography, Literature, and Decorative Arts. See the *Classical Myth Project*, discussed in Chapter 5, for a description of iconography associated with particular deities, then study the images on a number of vases. Which deities or heroes can be identified based on the iconography associated with them? Can you identify any other figures depicted in the images based on what you have read in narrated stories?

Similar/Related Sites

1. *Art and Architecture, Mainly from the Mediterranean Basin*—http://rubens.anu.edu. au/—This site, sponsored by the Australian National University, provides high-resolution photographs of art and architecture. The site provides little commentary and minimal direction to the novice or non-specialist; however, many of the images are excellent, though sometimes dark.

2. *Images of Troy in Greek Art*—http://www.temple.edu/classics/troyimages.html—This site is linked to images of Troy, most on Greek vases.

Greek Theater

Didaskalia

http://www.didaskalia.net/

Site Summary. Didaskalia, a Web site dedicated to the study of classical Greek and Roman music, drama, and dance in modern performance, is an excellent introduction to theater studies. The site is managed by an editorial board of prominent classics and theater scholars in Great Britain, Canada, and the United States. Key features of the site include an academic journal, lists of classical drama performed worldwide (with opportunities to write reviews), a growing study area, and "The Agora" (forum for discussion). Future plans include imaging of 3-D classical theater models, created at the University of Warwick; at present, only one model of the (Roman) Theatre of Dionysus in Athens appears on the site, although plans are in place to add future drawings that show its evolution over several centuries. The "Study Area" provides introductions to Greek and Roman stagecraft, including definitions, descriptions, photographs, and diagrams. Extensive links to other ancient theater sites are also provided.

Navigating the Site. The site is well designed and easy to navigate. The main page links to major site resources. Subsequent pages have three navigation bars: a bar across the top linked to the main page for the Web site, a second bar below the first linked to major site features, and a bar along the left linked to resources within a given section.

Discussion Questions and Activities

1. Theater Experience. What do you expect when you go to see a play? What does the theater look like? How long does the performance last? What do the actors look like and wear? How does the audience behave? Read about Greek and Roman theater on this site. In what ways was the theater in the classical world similar? In what ways did it differ?

2. Multiple Roles, a Few Actors. Athenian drama was scripted for two to three actors and a chorus of twelve to fifteen, all men. Yet many plays include more than two to three main parts. Consequently, each actor would have to play several different parts. Study two or three Greek plays, such as *Oedipus Tyrannos*, *Antigone*, or *Medea*. Which parts would have to be played by the same actor? How would the use of masks have helped the players act several parts within the same play?

Similar/Related Sites

1. *Robin Mitchell-Boyask's Greek Drama Course Materials*—http://www.temple.edu/classics/ dramadir.html—This Web site provides extensive study guides, summaries, charts, and background materials.

Skenotheke: Images of the Ancient Stage
http://www.usask.ca/antharch/cnea/skenotheke.

Site Summary. Sponsored by the Program in Classical and Near Eastern Archaeology at the University of Saskatchewan, *Skenotheke* is a good second resource on theater as it provides extensive materials that illustrate the topics discussed on the *Didaskalia* site. The site provides excellent representations of scenes (including several of comic actors) taken from Greek vases, sculpture, frescoes, and mosaics.

Navigating the Site. The site is a single page of links and consequently is easy to navigate.

Discussion Questions and Activities

1. Masks.

   a. The idea of actors' wearing masks is often alien to modern theater-goers, but masks served an integral function in Greek and Roman theater, in which actors played many roles. Compare comic masks to tragic masks. What are the differences?

   b. This site includes an extensively linked map of Mediterranean locations where Greek and Roman theaters have been found. Look at the mask images found in these places and compare them with masks from other locations. What are their similarities? Differences? What does this tell you about the people who created and observed theatrical performances?

Similar/Related Sites

1. *Introductions to Greek Theatre*—Created by Professor Roger Dunkle of Brooklyn College, this Web site provides an excellent introduction to Greek and Roman theatrical production and genres, including the following:

   a. *Classical Backgrounds of Western Culture*—http://depthome.brooklyn.cuny.edu/ classics/dunkle/studyguide/studygde.htm—This site provides study guides for various Greek and Roman texts.

   b. *Tragedy*—http://depthome.brooklyn.cuny.edu/classics/dunkle/tragedy/index.htm

   c. *Comedy*—http://depthome.brooklyn.cuny.edu/classics/dunkle/comedy/index.htm

2. *Influence of Greek Tragedy*—http://www.classics.cam.ac.uk/Faculty/trag-theory.html —For more advanced students and for teachers, this Web site, last revised in 1997 by Bruce Fraser, University of Cambridge, describes the theoretical basis and influence of tragedy.

Author-Specific Sites

Homer

The Chicago Homer
http://www.library.northwestern.edu/homer/

Site Summary. Edited by Ahuvia Kahane, classics, and Martin Mueller, English, at Northwestern University, *The Chicago Homer* provides online Homeric texts in English and Greek, with commentary, in an electronic format. Although of greatest use to a user who knows Greek, this site is also of value to other persistent users. Users who do not understand Greek can compile Greek concordances; also, the site can be used to illustrate the difficulties involved in translation.

Navigating the Site. These instructions assume a non-Greek-speaking user. From the main page, click *Enter*, then click the *Browse* tab. When prompted, choose a text, e.g., *The Iliad*, then fill in a Book and Line number, e.g., Book 1, Line 1. Then click "Retrieve." The selection will appear in Greek, along with English and German interlinear translations. The user can now read the English translation, or can study specific word usage in the text.

To study word usage, click one of the underlined English words. The Greek translation will appear on the right. Clicking on this translated word brings up a list of all the other occurrences of the word in the work, enabling a user to identify different meanings and uses of the same word. Similarly, the user can track instances when one English word is used to replace several different Greek words, for example, both *daimôn* and *thea* for *goddess.*

Discussion Questions and Activities

1. Choose a particular word that occurs frequently in English translations of *The Iliad*; for instance, "gods" or "goddesses." Identify the Greek words used in the original language. Then read the English passages and try to identify possible differences in context that might account for different uses. Check your conclusions with a good Greek/English dictionary.

Similar/Related Sites

1. *The Homeric Problem Page*—http://members.aol.com/ikoulchine/homer/homer.html— This page is devoted to presenting issues surrounding Homer's existence and identity.

2. *Ancient Greek Civilizations*—http://www.anthro.mankato.msus.edu/prehistory/aegean/index.shtml —This page includes the full text of the *Odyssey* and the *Iliad*, as well as resources for the study of Greek art and history.

Plato

Exploring Plato's Dialogues
http://plato.evansville.edu/

Plato and His Dialogues
http://plato-dialogues.org/

Site Summary. Created by Professor Anthony Beavers at the University of Evansville, *Exploring Plato's Dialogues* is a virtual library and learning environment for the exploration of *The Crito*, *The Phaedo*, *The Phaedrus*, *The Symposium*, and *The Republic*. The site also provides access to numerous online essays, including *The Life of Plato*, as well as bibliographical resources, essays, and links to resources elsewhere on the Internet. The *Search Tools* and *Discussion List* are no longer available on the site due to funding cuts in the University of Evansville's information technology budget. Despite these nonfunctional elements, however, *Exploring Plato's Dialogues* is still a first-rate resource.

Another excellent site, conceived by computer scientist Bernard Suzanne when he visited Professor Beavers, is *Plato and His Dialogues*. Although Suzanne's goal is to propose a particular method for arranging the dialogues, this Web site has much to offer both the casual visitor and the scholar as it provides links to a large number of translations, excellent maps of the classical world, and an extensive index of people and locations.

Navigating the Site. *Exploring Plato's Dialogues* is easy to navigate from the left-hand navigation bar, although some of the links on internal pages no longer function. *Plato and His Dialogues* is presented in pages dense with text, but a navigation bar appears at the top and bottom of each page.

Discussion Questions and Activities

1. *Exploring Plato's Dialogues*

   a. Begin with the overview of Plato's life. Why did Plato turn from politics to philosophy? What philosopher had the greatest influence on him? What happened to him? What famous school did Plato later establish? Who was his most famous pupil?

   b. Read one of Plato's dialogues, beginning with one of Benjamin Jowett's excellent introductions to *Phaedrus*, *Symposium*, or *Phaedo*. Then read one of the dialogues. How does Socrates teach his students? What are his key ideas?

2. *Plato and His Dialogues*

   a. Begin with the **Biography** and **Works** links, or search for a particular person or place using the **Index of Persons and Places** link.

Vergil

Virgil.org
http://www.virgil.org

Vergil's Homepage
http://vergil.classics.upenn.edu/home/

Site Summary. These two Web sites are dedicated to the study of Rome's preeminent poet, Publius Vergilius Maro, or Vergil. Created and maintained by David Wilson-Okamura, *Virgil.org* provides searchable, online translations of Vergil's pastoral *Eclogues* and *Georgics*, as well as his epic *The Aeneid*. Wilson-Okamura also provides numerous links to other Web sites. *Vergil's Homepage* is a collaborative project sponsored by the University of Pennsylvania and funded by the National Endowment for the Humanities, the Pew Charitable Trusts, and others. *Vergil's Homepage* provides the Latin text of Vergil's *Aeneid*, with each word glossed via hyperlink in several ways:

1. Either internally (to the site) or to the *Lewis and Short Latin Dictionary* on the *Perseus* site at Tufts University.

2. Internally to user commentary on the word or phrase

3. Internally to a concordance

Non-Latin speakers can work with a good translation (e.g., a volume from the Loeb Library of Classical Literature), using the line numbers to locate English/Latin equivalents, which can then be tracked through the concordance or the dictionary on this site.

Navigating the Sites. Navigate the *Virgil.org* site via its left-hand navigation bar. To navigate *Vergil's Homepage*, click on the **Text and Commentary** link located in the center of the page. Select the type of help desired on the upper left-hand side of the page, then enter the desired book and line number of *The Aeneid* on the right and click **Run Query**. Twenty lines of the poem, in Latin, will appear in the right-hand frame. If **Reading Assistance** is selected on the left, simply click on a word for an analysis of its function in the sentence. For a complete definition of that word, click on the word located on the right. You will be connected to the *Lewis and Short Latin Directory* on the *Perseus* site (see above), which provides a complete definition of the word as well as its uses in other classical works. If the **Concordance** is selected on the left, simply click on a word; all occurrences of the word will be retrieved.

Discussion Questions and Activities

1. The story of Dido and Aeneas in Book 4 of *The Aeneid* is among the most discussed in literature. Begin by selecting one of the translations of *The Aeneid* at *Virgil.org*; see the right-hand column for links. Read Book 4 of the *Aeneid*. Why do Dido and Aeneas fall in love? Why does Aeneas leave her? If Aeneas is the embodiment of Roman heroic values, what does this episode suggest about how Romans thought about love and duty?

2. After Dido and Aeneas fall in love, *fama* (usually translated as *Rumour*), personified, flies throughout the countryside, spreading the story. Use *Vergil's Homepage* to search for all occurrences of the word *fama* in the *Aeneid*. Identify its possible meanings. What does *fama* mean in this story? What does *fama* mean when it refers to Dido? What does it mean when it refers to Aeneas?

3. Visit *Vergil's Dido: A Multimedia Path* (below) to view the story of Dido and Aeneas as artists have imagined it.

Similar/Related Sites

1. *Vergil's Dido: A Multimedia Path*—http://cti.itc.virginia.edu/~mpm8b/dido/dido.html —This Web site provides artists' conceptions of the story of Dido and Aeneas from ancient times to the nineteenth century.

2. *Dryden's Aeneid*—http://www.ilt.columbia.edu/publications/virgil.html—This Web site provides an online edition of Dryden's translation of the Aeneid in iambic hexameter, most frequently reproduced on the Internet because it is not subject to copyright restrictions.

3. *Wired for Books*—http://www.wiredforbooks.org/aeneid/—Listen to Wilfried Stroh read Book IV of *The Aeneid* in Latin.

Horace

Horace's Villa
http://www.humnet.ucla.edu/horaces-villa/

Site Summary. Through plans, video clips, and descriptive narration, this Web site documents the excavation of the villa believed to have been built by the Roman poet Horace. The site provides a detailed glimpse, not just of the location where some of Horace's poetry was written, but also of how influential Romans lived. The key area of this site is the *Study Center*, which provides access to QuickTime video tours, extensive plans, images, and descriptions of the site's key features and uses. The site also provides access to Horace's odes, epistles, satires, and epodes that mention the villa, in the original Latin (some with recordings) and in English translation.

Navigating the Site. To view the site, you must have Netscape 4.03 or higher, Internet Explorer 5 or higher, and Apple's QuickTime 4.0 or higher. The site is easy to navigate. Begin from the index page (above); click **Enter** when ready to enter the site. On subsequent pages, a navigation bar at the bottom provides links to pages that provide an **Overview**, a **Study Center**, information on **New Excavations**, and a page **For Our Friends**. Each of these pages has its own set of navigation links at the bottom, and terms within each page are cross-linked with definitions. To gain access to Horace's poetry and prose, choose the *Study Center* link. Clicking on the *Villa Poems* link at the bottom of that page displays Ode 1.17; an additional set of links at the bottom of the Ode 1.17 page leads to the other odes, epistles, satires, and epodes.

Discussion Questions and Activities

1. Landscape and Nature in Roman Life. Study the plans and descriptions of Horace's villa. How are they different from or similar to the homes in your own geographical location? Judging by the layout of the villa, what is the relationship between exterior and interior space? How does the villa's plan reflect the kinds of activities valued by wealthy Roman citizens?

2. Pastoral. Horace's poetry is well known for its pastoral elements; that is, the elements that depict the rustic life of shepherds in a distant past, sometimes implicitly contrasted with life in the more complex, urban present. Pastorals often describe rural landscapes as conducive to reflection. What elements of the pastoral appear in Horace's "villa poetry"?

3. Satire. Contrasted with Juvenalian satire, Horatian satire is said to be gentle and humorous in its attempts to correct human error or vice. What human frailties are the target of Satire 2.7? How does Horace incorporate the pastoral into this satire? What is the position of Horace's villa within this satire?

Ovid

The Ovid Collection
http://etext.lib.virginia.edu/latin/ovid/

Site Summary. The visual qualities of Ovid's *Metamorphoses*, a twelve-book poem that retells stories of transformation from Greco-Roman mythology, have inspired outstanding work by many book illustrators. Sponsored as part of the e-text library at University of Virginia, this Web site offers online page images from important historical editions of Ovid's *Metamorphoses*. Included are versions in Latin, English, and German. Particularly useful to Renaissance scholars are translations by Posthius (1563), Golding (1567), Sandys (1632), Garth (seventeenth century), Brookes More, and Kline (contemporary).

Navigating the Site. The site is exceptionally difficult to navigate because of an unclear navigation scheme. To view specific illustrations, sometimes accompanied with complete English translations, follow these URLs directly to the page that indexes the translation:

English translations	
Posthius (1563)	http://etext.lib.virginia.edu/latin/ovid/posthius1-7.html
Golding (1567)	http://www.perseus.tufts.edu/cache/perscoll_Greco-Roman.html (This translation is believed by some scholars to have been consulted by Shakespeare.) (The University of Virginia site links to the Perseus site for this translation.)
Sandys (1632)	http://etext.lib.virginia.edu/latin/ovid/sandys/contents.htm (Images are mapped to the text; position your mouse over the mythological image of interest, then click your right mouse button.)
Garth, Dryden, et al. (1717)	http://etext.virginia.edu/latin/ovid/others.html#Garth1717fr http://etext.lib.virginia.edu/toc/modeng/public/OviEMet.html
Brookes More (1860)	http://www.perseus.tufts.edu/cache/perscoll_Greco-Roman.html (The University of Virginia site links to Perseus for this translation.)
Kline's linked concordance	http://etext.virginia.edu/latin/ovid/trans/Ovhome.htm#askline (Includes a guide to mythological characters/events in the book.)
Other Topics	
Parallel Ovid Cycles	http://etext.lib.virginia.edu/latin/ovid/ovid1563.html#cycles
Word/Phrase Search and Concordance	http://etext.lib.virginia.edu/latin/ovid/search.html
The Renaissance Reception of Ovid in Image and Text	http://etext.lib.virginia.edu/latin/ovid/abouttext.html

Discussion Questions and Activities

1. Backgrounds to Classical Literature. Read the story of Medea and Jason in *The Metamorphoses*. What details does this story provide that clarify the relationship between Medea and Jason in Euripides's play *Medea*?

2. Literary Allusions. Poetry to the present day makes reference to the story of Philomela, who was transformed into a nightingale. Read her story in *The Metamorphoses* for background to the use of one allusion in T. S. Eliot's *The Wasteland*.

3. Biblical Parallels. Compare the stories of creation and the flood in *The Metamorphoses* to the accounts in *Genesis*.

Similar/Related Sites

1. *The Classic Text*—http://www.uwm.edu/Library/special/exhibits/clastext/clshome.htm— This site, a special exhibit at the University of Wisconsin Golda Meir Library, provides a context within which to view the collaboration of artists and writers that produced the books in the University of Virginia's *Ovid Collection*. From the main page, locate the first set of links that appears after the introductory text, then click **Ovid**. The illustrations include some by Picasso.

2. *The Ovid Project: Metamorphosing the Metamorphoses*—http://www.uvm.edu/~hag/ ovid/index.html—This Web site offers online images of plates from the 1703 edition of Ovid's *Metamorphoses*, with engravings by Johannes Baur, as well as the 1640 translation into English by George Sandys. Also linked to this page are images from more than 250 slides of classical subjects, collected by Professor Ambrose at the University of Vermont.

3. *The Metamorphoses*—http://classics.mit.edu/Ovid/metam.html—Online version of the seventeenth-century translation of *The Metamorphoses* translated by Sir Samuel Garth, John Dryden, and others.

4. *The Funeral of King Midas*—http://www.museum.upenn.edu/new/research/Exp_Rese_ Disc/Mediterranean/Midas/intro.shtml

5. *Apuleius' Golden Ass*—http://www.jnanam.net/golden-ass/

CHAPTER 8

Europe: Before Print

Mega-Sites

On-line Reference Book for Medieval Studies
http://the-orb.net/

Site Summary. Founded in 1995 by medieval scholars and hosted by the College of Staten Island, City University of New York, The *On-line Reference Book for Medieval Studies* (ORB) lists online texts and reference materials from a wide variety of contributors. Authors retain rights to their own material, and the editorial board encourages proposals for submission. The site is exceptionally well edited; few links are broken, and all lead to highly useful resources, classified into six resource categories: an encyclopedia, a library, a reference section, teaching tools, a category of general resources, and links to off-site resources. The *Encyclopedia* provides a listing of core topics, which has been expanded since ORB was established, linked to resources written specifically for ORB or edited by ORB and maintained elsewhere. The *Library* includes ORB documents and links to resources on Paul Halsall's site (see Chapter 4) and in the Global Catholic Network Library. The *Reference Section* provides links to several major Internet resources, most discussed elsewhere in this book. The *Teaching* section provides a variety of resources on teaching about manuscripts, the Great Vowel Shift, medieval self-representation, and medieval history and geography; also provided are syllabi, study guides, sample exam questions, and tutorials, as well as tips for teaching with computer technology. A new section provides assessments of films about the medieval period.

Navigating the Site. The site is easy to navigate. All major resources are available through links on the main page. The site carries a disclaimer stating that because of its recent move to a new server, the search engine may not be operable.

Similar/Related Sites

1. *Labyrinth Library of Medieval Resources*—http://www.georgetown.edu/labyrinth/labyrinth-home.html—Founded in 1994, directed by Martin Irvine and Deborah Everhart, and hosted by Georgetown University, *Labyrinth* provides free access to resources pertaining to medieval studies and is one of the most widely mentioned sites for medieval studies. A recently updated page, located at http://labyrinth.georgetown.edu/, incorporates database technology, which allows users to construct sets of resources based upon their own search criteria. Unfortunately, although some of these new pages have been thoroughly updated, others have a number of dead links. Still, the site includes texts in translation and in the original languages from France, the Iberian peninsula, Italy, and Britain, in addition to extensive materials on Byzantine, Celtic, English, French, German, Iberian, Italian, and Scandinavian cultures. Resources are also provided for the study of

105

archaeology and cartography, arts and architecture, history, Latin, manuscripts (paleography and codicology), music, philosophy and theology, social history, religious history, and the sciences. Special topics include Arthurian studies; the Crusades; heraldry, arms, and chivalry; women; and Vikings, runes, and Norse culture. A small collection of scholarly texts and a small special section providing pedagogical materials for university and K–12 teachers are also available.

2. *Netserf.org*—http://www.netserf.org/—Created by Beau A. C. Harbin in 1995 and hosted by the Catholic University of America, *Netserf* provides access to an impressive variety of resources related to study of the medieval world. Recent upgrades to the site include application of database technology; future plans include resources that will allow users to save bookmarks and searches. The site currently provides access to 1,655 links pertaining to archaeology, architecture, art (including clip art for Web pages), Arthuriana, civilizations, culture, drama, history, law, literature, music, people, philosophy, religion, science and technology, and women. In addition, the "Research Center" provides access to scholarly resources. A unique feature is a section devoted to the medieval period in the media, which appears on the site as a column of links on the left-hand column of the main page.

CELT: Corpus of Electronic Texts—The Online Resource for Irish History, Literature, and Politics
http://www.ucc.ie/celt/index.html

Site Summary. The CELT project serves as a major resource for the study of Irish literary and historical culture (in Irish, Latin, Anglo-Norman French, and English), publishing historical, literary, and folklore texts in a form that can be used by a wide variety of readers and researchers, including academic scholars, teachers, students, and the general public. Where possible, English translations are also provided. The site was created and is maintained by researchers from University College, Cork, Ireland; it is funded by Professor Marianne McDonald through the American Ireland Funds, the Higher Education Authority Ireland, and University College, Cork. The site is also linked to the Cork Multi-Text Project in History, which currently provides published historical e-texts associated with the mid-nineteenth-century potato famine in Ireland and the 1916 uprising (see http://www.ucc.ie/ucc/depts/history/multitext.html).

Navigating the Site. The site is easy to navigate. A navigation bar across the top provides access to the site's key features and to index pages organized by language. To locate English translations, choose from among the ***Published***, ***Captured***, or ***Languages*** navigation links, then click on the link to ***Translated Texts***.

Discussion Questions and Activities

1. Saints' Lives. (See also the *Military Martyrs* Web site, listed under "Similar/Related Sites" below.) Extremely popular in the medieval period were the "saints' lives," highly similar retellings of the lives, miraculous experiences and often, the martyring of Catholic saints. Go to the **Published** page (http://celt.ucc.ie/publishd.html) and scroll down to the saints' lives provided on this site (these include *On the Life of Saint Patrick*, *Bethu Brigte*, *On the Life of Saint Brigit*, *On the Life of Saint Columba*, and *The Life of Columba*).

   a. Read the two accounts about Saint Bridget or the two accounts of Saint Columba. How do the two versions compare?

b. Read the stories of two or more saints and make a list of similarities. What elements of the form and plot are the same in several stories? What sorts of miracles are associated with each saint? Do they have a common structure? Based on your reading, begin to compile a list of features that might be common to most saints' lives.

c. Look at some of the illustrations of saints' lives and martyrs on *The Age of King Charles V* site (described below; see specific page at http://www.bnf.fr/enluminures/ themes/t_2/st_2_03/a203_003.htm). What aspects of their lives are emphasized?

2. Irish Literary Tradition. From the Published page, scroll down to the text of *Deirdre*. Read the opening scenes of the story. What kind of poetry is valued by the people at the banquet? What does the story of Deirdre's birth tell you about the beliefs of the Irish people at this time?

3. Epic Values in Early Irish Literature. The Irish national epic is the *Táin bó Cúalnge*, which includes tales about the Irish epic hero Cúchulain. Read the English translation of the *Táin bó Cúalnge*. What characteristics did this culture value in its heroes? Depending on your other reading, compare Cúchulain to such epic heroes as Beowulf, Achilles, and Odysseus.

Similar/Related Sites

1. *In Parenthesis*—http://www.yorku.ca/inpar/—Maintained by the University of York, Canada, this site provides access to e-texts, in PDF format, from a wide array of medieval world literatures (e.g., Canadian, Castilian, Catalan, Dutch, English, Ethiopian, French, German, Irish, Italian, Latin, Provençal, and Russian). A handful of texts from other periods are also provided, including texts in Chinese, Greek, Japanese, Malayan, Old Norse, Peruvian, and Sanskrit, that pertain to concepts and movements such as the Gothic and Orientalism. No background materials accompany most selections, but the selection is eclectic.

2. *Steve Taylor's Celtic Pages*—Although Steve Taylor is not a Celtic scholar, these pages reproduce previously published editions of two well-known Irish sagas in side-by-side English/Gaelic translations. Links to these editions are as follows:

a. *The Story of McDathós Pig*—http://vassun.vassar.edu/~sttaylor/MacDatho/

b. *Cattle-Raid of Cooley (from the* Táin Bó Cúalnge*)*—http://vassun.vassar.edu/~sttaylor/Cooley/index.html

3. **Erin and Alba** page from *Legends*—http://www.legends.dm.net/celt/index.html—*Erin & Alba*—This site provides links to materials and texts for the study of Irish Literature, specifically the *Mythological Cycle* (Tuatha Dé Danaan stories), the *Ulster Cycle* (including King Conchobar and Cúchulain), the *Fenian Cycle* (the stories of Fin MacCumhaill), and the *Historical Cycle* (pertaining to the kings of Ireland).

4. *Military Martyrs*—http://www.ucc.ie/milmart/—Created by David Woods, Lecturer in Classics at University College Cork, Ireland, this page provides translations of the stories of a number of martyred saints who were also military figures.

5. *Celtic Tales*—available at the International Children's Digital Library at http://www.icdlbooks.org/—This book might serve as an introduction to Celtic folklore for younger children (see the longer entry for the ICDL in Chapter 4).

The Age of Charles V (1338–1380)

http://www.bnf.fr/enluminures/aaccueil.htm

Site Summary. This site, hosted by La Bibliothèque Nationale de France, provides 1,000 illuminations from medieval manuscripts, cross-linked with a history of the life and rule of Charles V or English translations of the original manuscripts. The manuscripts include the following:

Fourteenth Century
  Grandes Chroniques de France
  The Catalan Atlas
  John of Berry's (Jean, duc de Berry's) Petites Heures
Fifteenth Century
  Jean Froissart, *Chronicles*
  Bartholomeus Anglicus, *On the Properties of Things*
  Gaston Phoebus, *Book of the Hunt*
  Breviary of Martin of Aragon

The Web site is well indexed, with a detailed history of Charles V's reign, cross-linked with manuscript images; a thematic index with manuscript pages illustrating each theme; and a manuscript list. Particularly useful is the thematic index, which provides access to excellent images depicting the following:

History
  Ceremonies
  Banquets
  Coronations
  Dedications
  Entrances and receptions
  Funerals
  Homages
  Messengers
Wars
  Battles: history of France
  Combats and Jousts
  Crusades
  Captures and pillages
  Surrenders
  Sieges
  Military exploits
Events
  Arrests and prisoners
  Assassinations
  Executions
  Jacquerie (Peasant Revolt)
  Paris Rebellion (1356/1358)
  Tortures and martyrdoms
Historical figures (many)
Other historical themes
  Historical and mythical Antiquity
  Byzantium and the Near East
  Muslims, (see also: Crusades)
  Paris

Religion
Bible
  Pentateuch
  Prophets
  David
  Other old Testament
  Christ
  Life of the Virgin

Liturgy and devotions

Hagiology (Saints' Lives)

Science and technology
  Agriculture and seasonal labors
  Astronomy and cosmography
  Geography
  Medicine
  Natural sciences

Sports and entertainment
  Hunting
  Banquets
  Jousts
  Music

Miscellaneous themes
  Allegories
  Author portraits
  Personifications
  Dreams and visions

Navigating the Site. Navigating the site is straightforward. From the main page, select *Introductory Texts, Themes*, or *Manuscripts*. Within the *Introductory Texts* sections, manuscript links are marked by a magnifying glass; links to illuminations are marked by a window pane. Textual links are also provided. Each illumination is accompanied by a caption; clicking on the caption produces an enlarged image and more information. Clicking on the image again produces an even larger image.

Discussion Questions and Activities

1. Cosmology and Geography. The *Catalan Atlas*, a fourteenth-century atlas of the universe created in Spain, provides insight into how people in Charles V's world saw and understood their universe.

   a. Medieval Cosmology. Under the thematic listing for *Science and Technology*, explore the *Astronomy and Cosmography* images. How did people at that time view the world? How does their view differ from our own? *Astrology* is listed here as a component of *Science and Technology*. How do people today view astrology as compared with science? Study the images provided on the *Astrology* page, particularly *Zodiacal Man* and illuminations of each sign of the zodiac. How did people believe the stars influenced people's lives? What other kinds of images are combined with representations of the zodiacal signs?

   b. Representing Other Cultures. Also under *Science and Technology*, explore the *Geography* links. View several of the maps. How are places in Europe depicted? What about places in Africa and Asia (be sure to check out the links to detail images that follow the links to large area maps)? Why, for instance, does the map of Europe depict primarily national flags and locations of cities? Look at the map of Asia, then view the detail images that follow the large-area-map links. Why does the map of Asia include large images of pearl divers (see detail map), a caravan on the silk road, Noah's ark, Alexander the Great and Satan against the Tartars, and funeral practices (look up the word "immolate")? Why do the People of Gog and Magog bear banners celebrating Satan? Who are the People of Ichthyophagi on the Map of China? Think about why people in fourteenth-century Spain would map Asia and Europe in these different manners. Use these insights to help you analyze the depictions of the Saracens, for example, in *The Song of Roland*.

2. Court Life. From the main page, choose "Manuscripts" and page through several of the images drawn from Froissart's *Chronicles* (see the reference under "Related Links," below, for the text of some of the *Chronicles*.) What kinds of activities were of interest or significant to people at court?

Similar/Related Sites

1. *Index of Cartographic Maps 400-1300 A.D.*—http://www.henry-davis.com/MAPS/ EMwebpages/EM1.html and http://www.henry-davis.com/MAPS/AncientWebPages/ Ancient1.html—This site provides more maps of the medieval world for analysis.

2. *Tales from Froissart*—http://www.nipissingu.ca/department/history/muhlberger/ froissart/tales.htm—Created by Professor Steve Muhlberger at Nipissing University, this page provides English translations from the French of Froissart's *Chronicles*, as published in an 1849 edition of a translation by Thomas Johnes (1805). Dr. Muhlberger has

included particularly those portions that relate to chivalric and military deeds. The page provides an introduction and several indexes that sort the tales by title and theme.

3. *The Chronicles of Froissart (1523–1525)*—http://etext.lib.virginia.edu/subjects/Literature-in-Translation.html—Part of the University of Virginia e-text repository, this site offers another translation of Froissart's *Chronicles*, translated by John Bourchier and Lord Berners, and published in 1910.

Saga and Epic

Online Medieval and Classical Library
http://sunsite.berkeley.edu/OMACL/

Site Summary. Created by Douglas B. Killings when he was a graduate student at Berkeley, this e-text site provides access to no-frills translations of several important early European works not available in reliable form elsewhere on the Internet. The following are frequently referenced on the Internet by medieval scholars:

1. Norse saga

   a. *Heimskringla: A History of the Norse Kings with Ynyngla's Saga* (Trans. Laing)

   b. *Laxdaela Saga* (Tr. Muriel Press)

   c. *The Life and Death of Cormac the Skald* (*Kormak Saga*) (Trans. W. G. Collingwood and J. Stefansson)

   d. *The Saga of Grettir the Strong* (*Grettir Saga*) (Trans. G. A. Hight)

   e. *The Story of Burnt Njal* (*Njal Saga*) (Trans. George DaSent)

   f. *The Story of Egil Skallagrimsson* (*Egil Saga*) (Trans. W.C. Green)

   g. *The Story of the Ere-Dwellers* (*Eyrbyggja Saga*) (Trans. William Morris and Eirikr Magnusson)

   h. *The Story of the Heath Slayings* (*Heitharviga Saga*) (Trans. William Morris and Eirikr Magnusson)

   i. *The Story of the Volsungs* (*Volsungasaga*) (Trans. William Morris and Eirikr Magnusson)

2. *Lay of the Cid* (Spanish national epic)

3. *Nibelungenlied* (~1200 C.E., German) (Trans. Daniel B. Shumway)

4. *The Song of Roland* (1100 C.E., French) (Trans. Charles Moncrief)

Navigating the Site. The site is easy to navigate. Click on the appropriate link to reach the text and the transcriber's and translator's notes.

Discussion Questions and Activities

1. Norse Saga. Although *Beowulf* is believed to have been written down by an Anglo-Saxon monk in Mercia (a portion of medieval Great Britain), its characters and subject matter reflect its origins in the traditions of Norse saga and the Germanic-pagan warrior tradition. Read one or more of the Norse sagas available at this site and compare them with *Beowulf.* What insight do the sagas offer into such themes in *Beowulf* as the warrior culture, the cycle of revenge, the concept of wergild (or blood price), and the lord–thane relationship of reciprocity?

2. The Crusades. The *Song of Roland* is an epic depicting the clashes between Christian Europe and Islam over possession of the Holy Land during the Crusades, told from a Christian perspective.

    a. What are the fundamental differences between the two sides, as depicted in the epic? What terms are used to describe the Saracens? The Christians? In what ways do these terms influence readers to see each side in particular ways? What insight does the poem offer into Middle Eastern issues today?

    b. Even if you cannot read a text in the original language, comparing translations of the same text can provide insights into the significance of a work in the time of the translator. Compare several translations of *The Song of Roland* (provided below under "Similar/Related Sites") . What elements appear to stem from the original (usually elements held in common)? What elements appear to have been interpolated by the translator (often interpretations imposed on the text by a later age)?

    c. Read more medieval representations of the reign of Charlemagne (see Vika Zafrin's site under "Similar/Related Sites") . What insights do these sites provide into the concerns of medieval peoples?

    d. Think about how Charlemagne and Roland compare with kings or heroes in earlier epics, such as *The Odyssey*, *The Aeneid*, and *Beowulf.* Would Roland be at home in these earlier epics? Charlemagne? What does Charlemagne's depiction suggest about the evolving role of kingship? What does Roland's depiction suggest about changing definitions of the heroic?

Similar/Related Sites

1. *Song of Roland* translations:

    a. *Moncrief's Translation*—http://sunsite.berkeley.edu/OMACL/Roland/

    b. *Hagan's Translation*—http://www.fordham.edu/halsall/basis/roland-ohag.html and http://www.bartleby.com/49/2/ (e-text based on Harvard Classics ed.)

2. *Legendary Texts of Charlemagne*—http://www.brown.edu/Departments/Italian_Studies/people/zafrin/sitemap.html—This Web site, created and maintained by Vika Zafrin, a recent M.A. graduate of Brown University's Department of Italian Studies, excerpts and translates eclectic materials from the *Song of Roland* (France), *Cân Rolant, Priest Konrad's Song of Roland, Karlamagnus Saga,* Celati's *Orlando Innamorato, Orlando Furioso*, and *The Inferno*.

Beowulf on Steorarume (Beowulf in Cyberspace)

http://www.heorot.dk/

Site Summary. Created by Benjamin Slade, a doctoral candidate at Johns Hopkins University, this Web site is described by many scholars as the best *Beowulf* Web site on the Internet. The site provides side-by-side translations of Beowulf from Anglo-Saxon into English, German, and Hindi; the translations are glossed with hypertext links, which appear in an adjacent frame. Although the site does not provide a "no-frames" version, and the "frames" version may be difficult to view on some smaller screens, the site provides an excellent tool for students and scholars alike. The site also provides access to related materials not as readily available in anthologies, including the *Finnsburh Fragment*, *Waldere*, *Deor*, *Woden's Nine Herb Charm*, *Charm Against a Sudden Stitch*, and Bede's account from *The Ecclesiastical History of the English People* of "Caedmon's Hymn," often referred to as the earliest known poem written in English (that is, Anglo-Saxon). Sound files of Anglo-Saxon scholars reading the shorter pieces are also provided. Finally, the site includes a number of essays about the *Beowulf* manuscript and story.

Navigating the Site. The site is easy to navigate but must be viewed in frames. All of the site's major resources for the study of Beowulf are linked to display in the left-hand frame.

Discussion Questions and Activities

1. Names. Read the notes associated with the names of several characters in *Beowulf*. What is the general "rule" for the relationship between names of individuals and tribes? What might Grendel's name have signified to an Anglo-Saxon audience? In the modern English translation provided on this site, click on the first occurrence of Grendel's name. In what other contexts is the word *Grendel* or *Grindel* used? Read the notes about other names, such as *Beowulf*, *Wealtheow* (Hrothgar's queen), and *Unferth* (the member of Hrothgar's retinue who taunts Beowulf prior to his battle with Grendel).

2. Anglo-Saxon Poetics. Anglo-Saxon audiences valued poetic devices that may seem unfamiliar to audiences today. An example is the extensive use of *kennings*, or compound metaphors that were used for variation. Look for kennings in *Beowulf*, such as "whale-road" and "peace-weaver," and in the *Finnsburh Fragment*, such as "war-wood" and "bone-helm." (For more kennings, see the *Jörmungrund* site below; click on the *kennings* link.) What do these figurative terms mean? For what objects are they used? What do they tell us about the preoccupations of Anglo-Saxon people?

3. Pagan or Christian? Read Benjamin Slade's essay about *Beowulf* as a pagan or Christian poem for insight into this controversy about *Beowulf*.

4. Values of a Warrior Culture. Read the Anglo-Saxon poem "The Wanderer" (below), and compare the concerns expressed by the narrator to those of the warriors in *Beowulf*. Especially consider the concerns expressed in the "lament of the last survivor," the speech in *Beowulf* delivered by the warrior guarding the hoard of treasure eventually possessed by the dragon. What values are expressed? What is the Wanderer's problem? What sort of life does he desire, and why is he unable to attain it? How does his perspective differ from those of people today?

Similar/Related Sites

1. *Jörmungrund*—http://www.hi.is/~eybjorn/—Isolated for hundreds of years from outside influence, Icelanders are unique in that their modern language has remained very similar to that of the original Scandinavian settlers of Iceland. As a consequence, modern Icelanders can understand Old Norse literature, whereas modern English readers must study Anglo-Saxon (Old English) as a foreign language. This Icelandic Web site focuses on early Norse literature, primarily Eddaic and Skaldic poetry, and its structural and linguistic features. The site is especially useful for its extensive classification and listing of kennings, as well as analysis of metrics and analogs. Some of the pages on this site are in Icelandic, but most provide Icelandic texts side-by-side with English translations. The site includes the following poetry: *Þórsdrápa* (a saga); *Svipdagsmál* (*The Lays of Svipdag*); *Hymiskviða* (*The Lay of Hymir*) (including images of the manuscript); *Hrafnagaldur Óðins*, and *Völsa Þáttur* (*Song of Völsi*).

2. *Anglo-Saxon Archaeology*—http://www.gla.ac.uk/Acad/Archaeology/resources/Anglo-Saxon/index.html—This Web site provides links to articles and images of archaeological sites and findings, such as the Sutton Hoo burial site, that provide glimpses into the lives and beliefs of people like those described in *Beowulf*.

3. *The Wanderer*—http://www.aimsdata.com/tim/anhaga/edition.htm—This Web site offers a translation of the Anglo-Saxon poem "The Wanderer," which offers additional perspective on the warrior culture described in *Beowulf*.

4. *Introduction to Anglo-Saxon Manuscripts*—http://www.fathom.com/course/10701049/index.html—This site provides an overview of the physical and cultural processes by which Anglo-Saxon manuscripts were created, maintained, and read.

Manuscripts and Visual Art

Medieval Manuscript Manual
http://www.ceu.hu/medstud/manual/MMM/

Site Summary. Created by faculty members at the Department of Medieval Studies at Central European University, Budapest, this excellent Web site provides a history of medieval manuscripts, describing book materials, layout and organization, typology, and illumination. Detailed descriptions of processes and how they changed over time are also provided. The text is also cross-linked with a scrolling glossary that appears in a window at the bottom of the page.

Navigating the Site. The Web site is easy to navigate. The main page offers a translation in English; alternative Hungarian, Italian, and Russian translations are also available. Navigate to informational pages via links located at the top of the page; select *How to Navigate* first to learn about the navigation symbols on other pages. Use your browser *Back* button to return to the main page, then choose *Table of Contents*; this page is also a site map. Click on the desired topic to begin. From this point on, pages are organized with two scrolling text sections: the main text in the first, and a glossary in the second. Textual navigation links appear on the left, whereas pictorial navigation symbols appear at the bottom; these permit movement through the site in a linear fashion, one page at a time.

Discussion Questions and Activities

1. What are illuminated manuscripts? Compare an illuminated page from this site to a page in a recently published book. What materials are used to produce the newer book? What materials were used in the illuminated manuscript that are rarely used today? How did book copyists create the colors that appear on the page (e.g., gold leaf, lapis for deep blues, etc)? Try creating your own "illuminated manuscript," integrating text and image.

2. Book History. Speculate on the effects of manual production on book distribution and ownership. How would this differ today?

3. Publishing Materials. Use the instructions on this site to make paper, paint, and writing/scoring utensils similar to those used in medieval Europe, but from the safer materials described here. Using the materials you create, construct an exhibit on manuscript creation demonstrating the processes.

4. Applying the Knowledge.

   a. Using the information gained from this site, visit the *Roman de la Rose* and *Aberdeen Bestiary* sites, described below. Based on your reading and the images on these sites, how might the images have been created?

   b. Go to the *Interpreting Ancient Manuscripts* site below and practice the art of textual criticism by reconciling variations of the same text, transcribed by different scribes. How do scholars decide which text to include in an anthology?

Similar/Related Sites

1. *Paging Through Medieval Lives*—http://www2.art.utah.edu/Paging_Through/index. html—This Web site, created by Professor Elizabeth Peterson to accompany a 1997–1998 exhibit at the Utah Museum of Fine Arts and a course in book history, offers an excellent introduction to both the details of book creation in medieval Europe and the rudiments of paleography (the study of manuscripts). The pages address the needs of both general and scholarly audiences; general comments about each page appear first, followed by details about the manuscript itself. Accompanying the images of Bibles, Korans, and other books are summaries, enlarged images, assessments of manuscript condition, commentaries on the techniques used to create the pages, and a description of each document's provenance, or subsequent history. The site requires a browser that will support frames.

2. *Interpreting Ancient Manuscripts*—http://www.earlham.edu/~seidti/iam/interp_mss.html —Created by Dr. Timothy Seid of Earlham College's School of Religion, this Web site provides an introduction to paleography, the study of ancient writing and manuscripts. In addition to engaging definitions of key terms and excellent page images that illustrate key points, this Web site provides an accessible exercise in textual criticism that permits users to practice the art of reconciling variations of the same text.

Roman de la Rose: Digital Surrogates of Three Manuscripts
http://rose.mse.jhu.edu/

Site Summary. Before the invention of the printing press, books were copied by hand and frequently embellished with elaborate images. The manuscript images on this site provide excellent representations of the ways in which page decoration and illustration could be integrated with text. A project of the Milton S. Eisenhower Library (The Johns Hopkins University) and the Pierpont Morgan Library, this site is hosted by The Johns Hopkins University to permit study of three illuminated manuscripts of *Roman de la Rose*, an important and influential thirteenth-century secular work written in Old French by Guillaume de Lorris and Jean de Meun. The site provides outstanding page images and additional pages that describe the history of the manuscript and summarize the narrative itself.

Navigating the Site. The site is well designed and easy to navigate. From the main page, click ***Continue***. Choices on the next page include an e-mail link to the site's coordinator to request the password and a link to a page describing ***Conditions of Use***. Clicking on the acceptance links leads to a site map; links to important resources appear in the left-hand column, and corresponding pages appear on the right. To use the manuscript, enter the username and password provided by the site coordinator. Several viewing choices are available: entire manuscripts, rubrics, miniatures, or bibliographic information. Images can be enlarged by clicking on the image or scaled by choosing a different zoom factor or image size.

Discussion Questions and Activities

1. Dream Visions. The *Roman de la Rose* is an allegorical representation of the experience of love that begins with a dream vision, a popular medieval genre that begins with the narrator falling asleep, usually over a book, after which the sleeper experiences an elaborate dream with allegorical significance (here, the dreamer visits a garden, peopled by abstractions such as idleness, mirth, and danger, and conveys the experience of love). How does the copyist/illustrator of the manuscript convey the narrative thematically through the illustrations?

2. Characterization and Allegory. In this dream, the narrator encounters several "characters" in the medieval sense; that is, they represent abstract qualities such as "envy" and "avarice," rather than "people." These are conveniently cataloged on the Web site. Students might be asked to explain how a given image conveys the quality it represents.

Similar/Related Sites

1. *Western Manuscripts to c. 1500, at the Bodleian Library*—http://www.bodley.ox.ac.uk/dept/scwmss/wmss/medieval/medieval.htm—This site provides page images of some of the same *Roman de la Rose* manuscripts, but at higher resolution. *Note:* Although of higher quality, these pages are extremely slow to load, even on a fast computer. View these pages in Internet Explorer 5.0 or above for best results.

2. *St. Albans Psalter*—http://www.abdn.ac.uk/stalbanspsalter/english/index.shtml—This site provides page images and commentary on the St. Albans Psalter, which is believed to have been created for a twelfth-century anchoress, Christina of Marykate, who, according to legend, abandoned a forced marriage for the church. (An anchoress lived an ascetic life in a cell attached to a church. A psalter is a book of psalms; this psalter includes calendrical information and beautiful illustrations of key moments in Christian history.) These high-quality page images are accompanied by translations and explanations that provide details of the iconography present in the images.

3. *Illuminated Manuscripts at Collect Britain*—http://www.collectbritain.co.uk/collections/illuminated/—This site provides 3,500 beautiful images of manuscripts from the eighth through the fifteenth centuries C.E. The images can be enlarged and viewed using a special zoom tool.

Book of Hours: Les Très Riches Heures du Duc de Berry

http://www.ibiblio.org/wm/rh/

Site Summary. A "book of hours" was a volume used by both Christian laypeople and clergy to guide them in their religious devotions throughout the liturgical day. This site, connected with the *WebMuseum, Paris* Web site, provides excellent images and commentary pertaining to this famous book of the liturgical hours, which was created by the Limbourg brothers for their patron, Jean de Berry. The accompanying pages also provide biographical backgrounds and insight into the materiality of fifteenth-century art.

Navigating the Site. The main page of the Web site provides links to four secondary pages, each devoted to a quarter of the year; these secondary pages feature thumbnail images and descriptive passages. Click on the thumbnails to enlarge the images. The main page also provides links to biographical and art history pages.

Discussion Questions and Activities

1. Iconography and Symbolism. Read about the images and their origins. What aspects of the images telegraph the social status of Jean de Berry?

2. Medieval Lives. Study the images themselves. What activities did people value in medieval France? What can you learn about the social structure by examining these illustrations?

Similar/Related Sites

1. *Jean du Berry's Petites Heures*—http://www.bnf.fr/enluminures/texte/manuscrit/aman9. htm—This site provides an example of another book of hours.

2. *Hill Monastic Manuscript Library*—http://www.hmml.org/vivarium/—Founded in 1965, the Hill Monastic Manuscript Library (HMML) is among the world's largest archives of medieval and Renaissance works. In addition to preserving its own works, the library is also engaged in a project to microfilm all surviving medieval and Renaissance manuscripts. This project has preserved approximately 25 million pages from volumes in European, Near Eastern, and North African libraries and archives. The site provides page images of several books of hours linked to its pages devoted to the *Bean, Bethune*, and *Gertrude Gavin Hill Collections.*

The Aberdeen Bestiary

http://www.abdn.ac.uk/bestiary/bestiary.hti

Site Summary. The Aberdeen Bestiary project provides full-page images, transcription of the twelfth-century Latin text, and an English translation. This text provides the opportunity to investigate interesting links among the disciplines of folklore, literature, art, and the history of science because it is based primarily on the fourth-century Greek *Physiologus*, a text with origins in Indian, Jewish, and Egyptian legends and in the natural history texts of Aristotle, Herodotus, Pliny, St. Paul, and Origen.

Navigating the Site. The site is easy to navigate. The main page provides a set of navigation links to an ***Introduction, History***, the ***Bestiary*** itself, a detailed description of the ***Codicology*** (how the book is constructed), and a ***Bibliography*** of sources for further research; these links are repeated across the top of each subsequent page. Select the ***Bestiary*** link to reach the page images. Links include an introduction to ***What Is a Bestiary***, a ***Commentary, Translation and***

Transcription page, the capability to *Search*, and perhaps most useful, a *Full Index*. Choose the *Full Index* link to locate pages pertaining to specific animals in the bestiary.

Discussion Questions and Activities

1. Characteristics of Animals

   a. Everything in the medieval universe was believed to have its place in a hierarchy that ranged from God at the top to the lowliest speck at the bottom. Animals, too, had places in the hierarchy. Read about the lion, which was considered at the top of a hierarchy of animals. What characteristics gave it this status?

   b. How were the behavior and characteristics of animals interpreted by medieval people? Why was the panther considered a type of Christ? Why are foxes depicted as crafty? Why does Dante, in his *Inferno*, have the sinful pilgrim Dante chased back into the forest of worldliness by a leopard, a lion, and a she-wolf? What does the dove symbolize, and why?

2. Creating a Medieval Book. To gain insight into how medieval books were made, choose the *Codicology* link.

   a. Creating a Quire. Medieval bookmakers used vellum, or split cowhide, to create durable books. Try creating a *quire* out of paper: fold a sheet of paper in half and in half again. Trim off the folds. Fold the quire in half. Quires would then be stacked to form a book.

   b. Ensuring Regularity. Read about how bookmakers used pinpricks and rules to ensure that written lines were straight within a page and regular from page to page.

   c. Planning for Illustration and Embellishment. How did medieval bookmakers ensure that their illustrations were properly placed and decorated? Read about *pouncing* and *embossing* on this page.

Similar/Related Sites

1. *Leaves of Gold: Treasures of Manuscript Illumination from the Philadelphia Collection*—http://www.leavesofgold.org/gallery/index.html—This page provides more images of medieval manuscripts, but also an excellent slide show describing how medieval manuscripts were made. To view the slide show, click the *Learning Center* link; to view illustrations of the manuscript collection, follow the exhibit links.

Bayeux Tapestry

http://www.hastings1066.com/

Site Summary. Despite grammatical errors and some factual ambiguities, this site provides beautiful, high-resolution photographs of the Bayeux tapestry, a 70-by-1.2-meter embroidered linen panel commemorating William the Conqueror's decisive victory over King Harald of Britain at the Battle of Hastings in 1066, the event that is generally considered to mark the end of the Anglo-Saxon period in England. The tapestry, which was probably commissioned by Bishop Odo, half-brother to William the Conqueror, is on display in Bayeux, France. The tapestry offers fascinating insight into how medieval Normans thought about their world.

Navigating the Site. The recommended method of viewing this site is as follows. From the main page, click on the link labeled "The Full Bayeux Tapestry" to gain access to thumbnails of the tapestry, divided into thirty-five segments. Clicking on a thumbnail provides an enlarged image and a translation of the Latin inscription.

Discussion Questions and Activities

1. Read the translations of the captions embroidered on the tapestry from start to finish to learn the story behind the Battle of Hastings. What elements of the story suggest that it is told from the French perspective rather than the British perspective?

2. Using the commentary from the Bayeux Tapestry Digital Edition (below), study the tapestry for what it suggests about how eleventh-century Northern European people viewed the world. Make a list of what you learn about their values, customs, and beliefs.

3. Study the motifs in the borders of the tapestry, especially representations of scenes from Aesop's fables. Speculate on why these scenes are present and how an eleventh-century medieval audience might have interpreted them. (See the Digital Edition and the lecture below in the related links for help.)

Similar/Related Sites

1. *Bayeux Tapestry*—http://www.ukans.edu/kansas/medieval/108/lectures/bayeux_tapestry. html—This site provides slides from a lecture pertaining to the Bayeux tapestry.

2. *Bayeux Tapestry Digital Edition*—http://www.essentialnormanconquest.com/bayeux/ startpc.dcr—This site provides adequate, scrollable images of the tapestry; excellent commentary can also be found below the tapestry. The commentary provides summaries of important and competing scholarly commentary on the tapestry.

Cultural Backgrounds

The Black Death in Europe

http://www.scholiast.org/history/blackdeath/index.html

Site Summary. Various forms of plague still exist today, but most can be cured by prescribing a course of antibiotics. In medieval Europe, the disease called the Black Death was devastating. Various estimates suggest that the population in Europe was reduced in two years by one-third to one-half; in major cities, the population was reduced by as much as two-thirds. This Web site provides an overview of various incidences of plague, maps depicting its spread, and statistics. Part of a larger site, *Scholiast.org*, this set of pages in particular maps the spread of bubonic plague in Europe from 1347 to 1350, the outbreak that claimed the life of Petrarch's Laura (the inspiration for his poetry) and which Boccaccio describes as the occasion for the storytelling in his *Decameron*.

Navigating the Site. The site is easy to navigate. From the main page, choose among the navigation links at the bottom of the page.

Discussion Questions and Activities

1. Choose the link **What Is the Black Death?** to read about the outbreaks. Then choose **Arrival: 1347** and page through the maps.

   a. Spread of the Disease. Note the geographical locations of the cities. Are most of the infected cities on the coast or inland? Speculate on how the disease was spread.

   b. Boccaccio's *Decameron*. Boccaccio wrote *The Decameron* between 1347 and 1353. Locate Italy on the map, then position the cursor over outbreak symbols to reveal the names of the cities. Using your cursor, identify when the disease first took hold in Florence, the city from which Boccaccio's narrators flee (Florence is *Firenze* in Italian). During what period would Boccaccio's characters have witnessed the breakdown of their society, chronicled in the *Decameron's* introduction? Compare the description of the plague from the *Decameron* to the eyewitness account provided below.

Similar/Related Sites

1. *The Plague in Renaissance Europe (1348)*—http://jefferson.village.virginia.edu/osheim/intro.html—This Web site provides three eyewitness accounts of the same plague outbreak as that referenced by Boccaccio in his *Decameron*.

Skip Knox's E-courses at Boise State University
The Crusades Virtual Course—with a Medieval Pilgrimage to Jerusalem
http://crusades.boisestate.edu/
History of Western Civilization
http://history.boisestate.edu/westciv/

Site Summary. Created by Dr. Skip Knox, an adjunct professor in the History Department at Boise State University, these accessible Web sites provide materials that support online and traditional Western civilization courses, including a specialized course on the Crusades from 1095 to 1291 C.E., discussed primarily from a Western perspective. One key aspect of the *Crusades* site is a "Virtual Pilgrimage"; although still in development, this feature is largely complete, providing both historical and contemporary images with commentary for most pilgrimage stops. The *Western Civilization* course provides extensive links to sites supporting study of periods from the ancient world through the early modern period. The courses are subdivided into a number of study eras. These in turn are linked to considerable commentary and a number of primary historical texts. Only the discussion boards are inaccessible to the public.

Navigating the Site. The site is easy to navigate. The main pages provide links to a *Visitor Center*, *Registration* for a virtual course, and the *Classroom*. The **Visitor Center** page provides access to information about the site, the professor, conditions of use, and a content index; the *Crusades* site provides a link to the *Virtual Pilgrimage* pages. The **Classroom** pages provide study units, each with extensive links to commentary and readings. Only the *Virtual Pilgrimage* could be easier to navigate; once the journey has begun, no escape links appear until the last page.

Discussion Questions and Activities

1. The *Virtual Pilgrimage*. Throughout the medieval, Renaissance, and Enlightenment periods, travel was both popular and arduous. Take the *Virtual Pilgrimage* on this site. It does an excellent job of demonstrating both points, especially for older students, who would be more able to digest the text and cityscape presentation.

2. Margery Kempe and Chaucer's *Prologue* to the *Wife of Bath's Tale*. Both Margery Kempe (actual person) and Chaucer's Wife of Bath (a fictional character) report having completed pilgrimages to Jerusalem. In *The Canterbury Tales*, the Wife of Bath is, herself, on a pilgrimage to Canterbury in the company of other pilgrims. Read one or both of these pilgrimage accounts (both are heavily anthologized). Based on your reading, identify elements of their journeys that correspond to this site's *Virtual Pilgrimage*.

Similar/Related Sites

1. *A History of the Crusades*—http://libtext.library.wisc.edu/HistCrusades/—This site, hosted by the University of Wisconsin, reproduces a comprehensive, six-volume history of the Crusades, published between 1969 and 1989, in searchable form. Produced under the guidance of general editor Kenneth Setton, these volumes provide numerous essays by respected historians. The search feature is particularly useful; for instance, the search terms *Roland* (*Song of Roland*), *Cid* (*Lay of the Cid*) , and *saga* produced a number of hits. This site would be particularly useful for teachers or older students who want access to an authoritative reference book on the Crusades.

Annenberg/CPB Learner.org
http://www.learner.org/exhibits/

Site Summary. This Web site, part of a larger Web site described in Chapter 4, provides a medieval exhibit of particular value to teachers of world literature: the *Middle Ages*. Medieval topics include feudal life, religion, homes, clothing, health, arts and entertainment, and town life. The pages also include interactive matching and role-playing features that allow users to engage more fully with the periods of the Annenberg/CPB's "Teacher's Lab."

Navigating the Site. The site is well designed and easy to navigate. From the main exhibits page, locate the *Middle Ages* in the left-hand navigation bar under "Exhibits." Click on the link. The **Middle Ages** page features an entry page; click on *Enter* to bring up the first page, **Feudal Life.** Subsequent pages can be navigated by clicking on the page links listed on the right-hand side of the page.

Discussion Questions and Activities

1. Middle Ages. Page through the *Middle Ages* site, which provides a good overview of living conditions, particularly for commoners. Gain insight into the period by working through the site's activities; for instance, identify clothing worn by men and women of various social classes and occupations and learn about medical practices by diagnosing and treating patients.

Similar/Related Sites

1. *Life in the Middle Ages*—http://www.kyrene.k12.az.us/schools/Brisas/sunda/ma/mahome.htm—This site was created to showcase the research of fourth- and fifth-grade students into life in the medieval period. Maintained by R. Sunda and sponsored by Kyrene de las Brisas Elementary School in Chandler, Arizona, this site is an outstanding example of the ways in which Web publishing can emphasize critical thinking and reinforce the validity of student work.

The Age of Chivalry

The Arador Armour Library
http://www.arador.com/

Site Summary. This outstanding site was created by Eric Slyter and provides access to extensive digital images of armor in museums; well-researched essays describing the functions, construction, and components of armor; and detailed, illustrated, downloadable manuals on how to create armor. Some of the projects described on this site would be suitable for high school students with access to a metal shop. The goal of the site is to correct, through access to actual museum images and scholarly research, much of the misinformation about armor promulgated by films and reenactment groups. In particular, the information on this site is useful in explaining the elements associated with the arming of the warrior in both medieval epic and romance, an important convention associated with the definition of genres.

Navigating the Site. The site is easy to navigate. Enter the site by clicking on the helmet image, located on the main page. All subsequent pages display a navigation bar on the left-hand side of the page; the page topic with supporting links appears on the right.

Discussion Questions and Activities

1. Gallery of Armour. Click the left-hand link to *Gallery of Armour* to view outstanding images of armor held by major museums throughout the world. Compare the images. How did armor evolve over time within a given geographical region? How did it differ by geographical region? Why?

2. Construction Techniques. What armor did knights wear, and how was it built? Begin with the link to *Techniques and Tutorials*. Read the introductory materials, then go to *Armour Articles and Essays*. Full-length essays and manuals in PDF format provide background materials on what knights wore and how it was constructed. If your school has a metal shop, check with the shop teacher about whether facilities exist to build one of the simpler articles of armor.

Similar/Related Sites

1. *Knighthood, Chivalry, and Tournament Resources*—http://www.chronique.com/—Created and maintained by Brian Price as a resource for the Society for Creative Anachronism, one of the largest reenactment groups in the United States, this site is widely cited as a useful resource for background materials on chivalric ideals and knighthood. In addition to an annotated bibliography of medieval works that describe chivalry, the site also provides background essays and primary texts, divided among pages that cover the topics of knighthood, chivalry, tournaments, fighting, arms, and history. The site also provides a glossary of terms that is cross-linked with the essays and introductory materials. This site is best viewed in Netscape Navigator.

2. *Code of Chivalry*—http://www.astro.umd.edu/~marshall/chivalry.html—This site provides a handful of codes, in addition to a collection of links to sites pertaining to chivalry.

Camelot Project

http://www.lib.rochester.edu/camelot/cphome.stm

Site Summary. Created in 1995 and sponsored by the University of Rochester Robbins Library, a branch of Rush Rhees Library, the *Camelot Project* is managed by Alan Lupack, curator of the Robbins Library, and is the product of a large staff of contributors. This Web site provides resources for the study of the broad range of Arthuriana (including *Tristan and Isolt*, located at http://www.lib.rochester.edu/camelot/trismenu.htm). The site also provides online student research projects (most excellent), e-texts of thematically related Arthurian works (e.g., those pertaining to Tom Thumb), bibliographies, interviews with contemporary authors who draw on Arthurian legend, and research sites, as well as indexes of Arthurian characters and symbols. Another significant portion of this site is accessible under the menu for *Other Scholarly Projects*. For example, the *TEAMS Middle English Texts* project publishes, online, a significant body of Middle English literature that provides insight into how medieval people thought about their world.

Navigating the Site. The site features a search engine, as well as a Main Menu, which lists Arthurian characters; each character page, in turn, is linked to medieval and modern narrative texts and images. Alternative organizations include indexes by author and artist.

Discussion Questions and Activities

1. Tom Thumb. From the University of Rochester Student Projects menu, select Susan Bauer's site on Tom Thumb variations. Compare some of them, noting when they were written. In what ways has this fairy tale and its association with Arthurian legend been adapted to fit the cultural settings of later times?

2. Medieval Women. How did medieval people understand the roles and actions of such women in Arthurian legend as Guinevere, Elaine, Igraine, and Vivien? Begin with Katherine Marsh's student project "Women of the Arthurian Legends." Then read several of the texts provided as part of the scholarly TEAMS project for insight into depictions of women in Arthurian Legend.

Similar/Related Sites

1. *Arthurian Resources*—http://www.arthuriana.co.uk/—Maintained by Thomas Green of Exeter College, this no-frills Web site provides excellent background commentary on Arthurian legend.

Specific Authors

International Marie de France Society

http://www.people.vcu.edu/~cmarecha/

Site Summary. This society, founded in 1992 by Chantal A. Maréchal of the Virginia Commonwealth University, is an organization for scholars and students that facilitates discussion of medieval lais, especially those of Marie de France (twelfth-century France). In addition to describing services for members and the society's journal, this Web site provides a comprehensive set of links to transcriptions and translations of Marie de France's lais and fabliaux, as well as bibliographical materials, links, and teaching resources.

Navigating the Site. The site is easy to navigate. The main page also serves as a site map. A navigation bar across the top provides links to features farther down in the page; the bulk of resources for non-members can be located by clicking on *Useful Links*, which transfers the user to another set of navigation links, organized in a table. Most of these links point to materials even farther down the same page. The link to *Resources Online*, however, leads to a separate Web page that provides a particularly rich source of teaching materials. See "Similar/Related Sites" (below) if links to the tale translations do not work. Viewing this site requires Adobe Acrobat 4.0 or above.

Discussion Questions and Activities

1. Introduction. Begin with Marie de France's "Introduction" to her *lais*. Why does she say she chose these particular stories for transcription? How did these stories differ from those transcribed and translated by earlier writers? Marie de France dedicates her work to a noble patron, probably Henry II of England. How does this dedication differ from dedications written in books today? What does this say about the publishing conventions of the medieval period and how they differed from publishing today?

2. Courtly Manners and Values.

    a. Knightly Virtue. Read about the chivalric ideal on Brian Price's *Knighthood, Chivalry, and Tournament* resources (above), or look up the term *chivalry* in the *New Advent Encyclopedia* (also known as the *Catholic Encyclopedia* and located at http://www.newadvent.org/cathen/). Then read Marie de France's ironic reference to those ideals in "Equitain" and "Lanval." How do the knights described in these lais fall short of the chivalric ideal? What does this suggest about the state of chivalry at the time these tales were in circulation?

    b. Courtly Love. Read excerpts from Andreas Capellanus's *De Amore* (see "Similar/Related Sites") . In what ways is the behavior of women in "Lanval," "Equitan," "Laustic," and "Chaitivel" clarified by this work? How might these stories have been understood by medieval audiences?

Similar/Related Sites

1. *Translations of Marie de France's Lais*—http://web.english.ufl.edu/exemplaria/intro. html—This page provides translations of "Equitan," "Le Fresne," "Bisclavret," "Lanval," "Yonec," "Laustic," "Chaitivel," and "Chevrefoil," by Judith Shoaf, University of Florida.

2. *Excerpts from Andreas Capellanus' De Amore* (*The Art of Courtly Love*)— http://www.courses.fas.harvard.edu/~chaucer/special/authors/andreas/de_amore.html—A reliable transcription of excerpts from Capellanus's treatise, this page sums up (perhaps ironically) the concept of courtly love implicit in many medieval courtly romances, including works by Marie de France, Chaucer, and the authors of other Arthurian romances.

Princeton Dante Project

http://etcweb.princeton.edu/dante/index.html

Site Summary. Created through funding from the W. Mellon Foundation, the Gladys Krieble Delmas Foundation, and the Edward T. Cone Foundation and hosted by Princeton University, this outstanding Web site project is a comprehensive site for the study of Dante Alighieri (1265–1321, Italy) and his works. Features of this site include side-by-side Italian/English translations of Dante's minor works; a hypertext, searchable edition of Paget Toybee's *A Dic-*

tionary of Proper Names and Notable Matters in the Works of Dante (Oxford University Press, 1968); lectures on allegory, the moral situation of the reader, Virgil, and Dante's life; canto summaries; and multimedia presentations of images, audio recordings in Italian and English, geographical maps, diagrams, and family trees of people mentioned in the *Commedia*. For those who want to know more, the site also provides a 100-page bibliography of works about the *Commedia*.

Navigating the Site. Before using this site for the first time, click on ***Register*** and provide the information requested on the registration form. Following registration and entry into the site, navigate through the main site map/navigation page. Each subsequent page includes a navigation bar with drop-down menus that can be used to gain access to the other main features of the site.

Discussion Questions and Activities

1. Reading the *Inferno*. How are readers meant to understand the tribulations faced by the souls in *The Inferno*, and why are the pilgrim Dante's sympathetic responses to them criticized by Beatrice and Virgil? Read Robert Hollander's "The Moral Situation of the Reader of Inferno" for insight into the dilemma of the reader encountering the *Inferno*. Then find instances in the *Inferno* that show the pilgrim Dante's evolution from a sinner sympathetic to the damned souls, to a redeemed pilgrim disdainful of their complaints.

2. Allegory. What exactly is *allegory* as Dante understood it, and from what tradition is it derived? Read Robert Hollander's excellent essay on medieval allegory for insight into how a medieval audience would have understood Dante's *Commedia*. What is the literal story of *The Inferno*? How does the literal story correspond to the allegorical meaning of the story as it is reflected in the life of the pilgrim Dante? How does this story in turn correspond to the life of a Christian in general? Of the progress of Christianity as a whole?

3. Symbols. Throughout the *Inferno*, animals appear who are symbolic of certain abstract ideas; for instance, Dante attempts to climb up out of the dark wood of worldliness, only to be chased back into it by a leopard, a she-wolf, and a lion. Go to the *Aberdeen Bestiary* (above), read about these animals, and speculate on what they signified to a medieval audience. Why are these animals particularly appropriate at this point in the pilgrim Dante's spiritual journey?

4. Crime and Punishment. Throughout the *Inferno*, Dante depicts a series of punishments that, from the perspective of Catholic theology and medieval cosmology, fit the crime. Why is it particularly fitting, for instance, that a Christian suicide be imprisoned in a tree? Why are seers, such as the blind prophet Tiresias, forced to spend eternity with their heads facing backward? Make a list of sins and punishments, explaining how each fits the crime, from a medieval perspective.

Similar/Related Sites

1. *Dante's "Clickable" Inferno*—http://www.carthage.edu/dept/english/dante/Title.html—This Web site, created by Charles Moore as a computer science project at Carthage College, is only marginally interactive, but it does provide the facility to compare side-by-side translations by Mandelbaum, Ciardi, and Pinsky of Cantos V and XXXIII of the *Inferno*, as well as a number of illustrations of these cantos and maps of *The Inferno* by renowned artists.

2. *Renaissance Dante in Print*—http://www.italnet.nd.edu/Dante/—Created by Theodore Cachey and Louis Jordan of University of Notre Dame, in collaboration with the Newberry Library and the University of Chicago, this site provides a fascinating look at the early book history of Dante's *Commedia*, documenting its publication from 1502 to 1629 C.E.

3. *Site for Dante Study*—http://www.arches.uga.edu/~redman/—Created by University of Georgia student David Felfoldi, this Web site provides resources for study as well as a well-designed graphic conception of *The Inferno*. Although not a scholarly site, the page is well designed and entertaining. The site also provides brief biographical information, a character list, brief essays related to Dante, and two conceptual maps of the *Inferno*. The site offers both high and low resolution graphic interfaces.

Decameron Web

http://www.brown.edu/Departments/Italian_Studies/dweb/dweb.shtml

Site Summary. Designed primarily for use by college and high school teachers and students, the *Decameron Web* is a comprehensive site for the study of Giovanni Boccaccio (1313–1375) and his most important work, described on the site as "a true encyclopedia of early modern life and a *summa* of late medieval culture." Created by the students of Professor Massimo Riva at Brown University, who edits the site with Professor Michael Papio (College of the Holy Cross), this Web site features the recognized Italian critical edition of *The Decameron*, Boccaccio's sources, two English translations (1620 and 1903), annotations and commentaries, bibliographies, critical and interpretive essays, and visual and audio materials. Future plans for the site include adding side-by-side Italian and English text of *The Decameron* and e-texts of Boccaccio's minor works. The **Pedagogy** link at the bottom of the page provides access to syllabi, lesson plans, and other materials for teachers. Other site features are included on the following links to pages:

1. **Search.** Offers simple and advanced Boolean searches.

2. **Brigata.** Describes each character and his or her tales.

3. **Plague.** Describes the impacts of the plague on Boccaccio and his contemporaries.

4. **Literature.** Discusses medieval attitudes about literature; relationships between Boccaccio and other literary figures; and pedagogical, narratological, and theoretical issues pertaining to *The Decameron*.

5. **Overviews of History, Society, Religion, and the Arts.** These sections provide brief overviews of how beliefs, events, and people influenced Boccaccio.

6. **Geographical and thematic maps.** Provides maps of *The Decameron's* world, contemporary antique maps, and tables that show the region in which each story takes place.

Teachers below college level should check the content of Boccaccio's stories before assigning them, as many are bawdy.

Navigating the Site. The site is easy to navigate. From the main page, select among the links provided in the left-hand navigation bar. Within each category, select among hypertext links within the right-hand frame. At this writing, some attempts to link to the English-language text of *The Decameron* yielded server errors; presumably, this is a temporary problem.

Discussion Questions and Activities

1. Plague. The outbreak of plague in the early fourteenth century provides the backdrop for *The Decameron* and serves as the reason the storytellers leave the city without the usual chaperones. How does the plague function in *The Decameron*? Compare the tone of the prologue with those of the stories. Why do the storytellers tell so many comic or bawdy stories at such a serious time? For specific stories that deal with the plague, choose the **Themes and Motifs** link from the left-hand navigation bar, then choose **The Plague** link that appears on the right-hand frame.

2. Pedagogy. Choose the **Pedagogy** link at the bottom of any page. Use the advice for teachers and students to plan classroom activities relating to *The Decameron*.

3. Themes. On each of the ten days of *The Decameron*, the narrators focus on a particular theme or set of themes. To identify these, choose **Syllabus** from the navigation bar at the bottom of any page, then choose the text link to **Online Activities**, located at the upper left-hand corner of the syllabus. The predominant theme represented in a given week corresponds to the tales listed on the syllabus.

Similar/Related Sites

1. See Web sites listed above that pertain to the spread and consequences of the plague in Europe.

2. *The Most Pleasant and Delectable Questions of Love*—http://etext.lib.virginia.edu/ toc/modeng/public/BocMost.html—This site, part of the University of Virginia's e-text archives, provides insight into beliefs about the nature of love held by medieval people in general and Boccaccio in particular.

CHAPTER 9

Early Modern to Contemporary Europe

Annenberg/CPB Learner.org
http://www.learner.org/exhibits/

Site Summary. See the overview description of this outstanding project in Chapter 4. This project provides resources of particular value to teachers of medieval and Renaissance world literature within the *Renaissance* exhibit. Renaissance topics include pages on exploration and trade; the printing press and humanism (**Printing and Thinking**); science, art, and music (**Symmetry, Shape, and Size**); and **Focus on Florence**, describing Florence, Italy as a model of Renaissance culture. The pages also include interactive matching and role-playing features that allow students to engage more fully with the periods.

Navigating the Site. The site is well designed and easy to navigate. From the main exhibits page, locate the *Renaissance* link in the left-hand navigation bar under "Exhibits." Click on the link. The **Renaissance** page provides links to various aspects of the Renaissance on the left-hand side of the page.

Discussion Questions and Activities

1. Renaissance. Page through the *Renaissance* site; activities are marked by a nautilus shell. Learn about the choices traders made by choosing the link to ***Exploration and Trade,*** then click on the nautilus shell to enter the spice trader role-playing activity. Learn about the mathematical concept of the "golden mean" by choosing the link to ***Symmetry, Shape, and Size.*** Click on the nautilus shell to learn about how Renaissance mathematicians uncovered the secrets of the seashell spiral.

Gutenberg Bible Digitization—British Library
http://www.bl.uk/treasures/gutenberg/homepage.html

Site Summary. In 1454–1455, Johannes Gutenberg revolutionized publishing when he invented a way to mechanize printing—making bookmaking less expensive and less labor-intensive and, ultimately, making possible greater access to and ownership of books. Sponsored by the British Library, this Web site provides complete digitized images of two copies of the *Gutenberg Bible*, the first major book printed. To illustrate choices made by printers, the exhibit includes the *King's Bible*, which was printed on paper and features elaborate decorative borders, and the *Grenville Bible*, which was printed on vellum and is relatively plain.

Navigating the Site. The site is easy to navigate, and despite the high resolution of the page images, the illustrations load quickly. From the main page, click on ***Background*** to bring up the information page, or choose ***The Texts*** link to view one or both bibles side by side. To view one of the books page by page, click on the ***prev*** and ***next*** arrows. To view an enlarged image of a given page, click on the image itself; the enlarged image will appear in a separate window.

Discussion Questions and Activities

1. The two versions of the Gutenberg Bible provided on this site are two copies of the same book, yet they are decorated very differently. Read the background information about how the texts were produced. What features of the books are similar? What features of their embellishment are different? Why?

2. Although these books are printed on a press, they look very much like earlier manuscripts and very different from books today. Why might these mechanically produced books be made to look like they were produced by hand? Are our ideas about the relative value of hand versus mechanically produced books different today?

Alciato's Book of Emblems

http://www.mun.ca/alciato/index.html

Site Summary. Emblem books are collections of engraved pictures that became popular in the fourteenth to seventeenth centuries; the pictures are often accompanied by moral sayings or proverbs that indicate what the pictures represent. At a time when symbolic interpretation was highly valued, emblematic images were objects of contemplation that could "read" for meaning. This site, created by William Barker, Mark Feltham, and Jean Guthrie, Department of English, Memorial University of Newfoundland, provides one such book containing 212 Latin emblem poems, engravings, proverbs, and commentary originally published by Andrea Alciato in 1531; the 1621 edition is used as the basis for the scanned images. The site also provides access to illustrations from several editions of the *Greek Anthology*, one of Alciato's sources. Also provided is a preliminary version of Whitney's *Choice of Emblemes* (1586), which draws upon Alciato's work.

Navigating the Site. The main page also serves as a site map, with links provided directly below the emblem depicting the Roman god Janus. The emblem poems can be viewed in Latin, in English, or in a format that provides side-by-side Latin/English comparison; commentary is also provided. Several options are available for navigating the site: Latin text only, English text only, Latin/English parallel texts, pages of thumbnails, a title list and search page, and a table of emblems. The site also provides a bibliography of secondary materials relating to emblem study.

Discussion Questions and Activities

1. Locate the emblems that represent virtues and vices in Alciato's time. What vices were frowned upon? What virtues were encouraged? Do ideas about these vices and virtues differ today? Think about the ways in which sins and sinners in Dante's *Commedia* are depicted. In what ways are these depictions *emblematic*? How does understanding the use of emblematic art help to explain the predicaments of the sinners in *The Inferno*? Check your ideas against representations in other emblem books, listed below under "Similar/Related Sites."

2. Locate the emblems that depict the goddess Fortuna and representations of Opportunity. Why does Opportunity have such a unique hairstyle (i.e., bald in the back, but with a long lock of hair in the front)? Compare these representations with the study of Occasion emblems at http://www.netnik.com/emblemata/inoccasionem.html. What do these representations say about the way people in medieval Europe viewed the workings of chance? Check your ideas against representations in other emblem books, listed below.

3. Locate the emblems that depict rulers (or princes). How were rulers viewed at this time? Check your ideas against representations in other emblem books, listed below.

Similar/Related Sites

1. *English Emblem Book Project*—http://emblem.libraries.psu.edu—Created and maintained by the Penn State University Libraries' Electronic Text Center, this project makes available scanned images of ten English emblem books.

2. *University of Glasgow Center for Emblem Studies*—http://www.emblems.arts.gla.ac.uk—This site provides scanned images of two emblem books, written in French, with no translation. The site also provides a page of useful links at http://www.ces.arts.gla.ac.uk/html/links.htm.

3. *The Abraham Cowley Text and Image Archive: Emblematica*—http://etext.virginia.edu/kinney/emblematica.html—Although not exhaustive, this site provides a further sampling of medieval emblems.

The Mariner's Museum—Age of Exploration Curriculum Guide
http://www.mariner.org/age/index.html

Site Summary. Sponsored by the Mariner's Museum in Newport News, Virginia, this Web site provides a survey of discovery and exploration from ancient times to Captain Cook's voyage to the South Pacific in 1768. Conveyed through timelines and menus of information cross-linked with images, video clips, biographies, maps, and commentary, the background and activities this site provides would complement any study of primary journal and travel writing, an increasingly important field of literary study.

Navigating the Site. The main page offers two paths: a timeline of travel and exploration and a menu, which is also a site map. The timeline is better suited for gaining a quick overview; more information is accessible through the menu. Click on a topic to bring up a new page; many pages are also cross-linked with brief biographies, maps of voyages, and images. Click on the images to view a version that is only slightly enlarged.

Discussion Questions and Activities

1. Click on the link to *Activities* to learn how to create a compass, an astrolabe, a quadrant, and a globe; how to identify navigational instruments and the parts of a ship; how navigators determined longitude and latitude; and how seamen endured the hardships of sea travel (hunger and diseases such as scurvy).

Similar/Related Sites

1. *1492 Exhibit*—http://www.ibiblio.org/expo/1492.exhibit/Intro.html—Originally created by Jeff Barry as an exhibition at the Library of Congress on the Spanish conquest of the Americas, this Web site is now hosted by IBIBLIO. The no-frills introductory page is deceiving; the site provides extensive commentary and excellent images that address both the European view and the syncretic responses of the native peoples, both to initial contact with Europeans during the fifteenth- and sixteenth-century conquest and to their subjugation under subsequent European rule. The Web site is divided into six major sections, which are listed on the main page. Two paths through the site are available. The user may choose to page through the entire site; to do this, click on the first major topic, then use the *Continue the Voyage* links that appear at the bottom of each subsequent page. Also available from the main page is an *Outline*, which leads to a comprehensive site map.

2. *Voyaging and Cross-Cultural Encounters in the Pacific 1760–1800*—http://
southseas.nla.gov.au/index.html—Created by the National Library of Australia, this Web
site provides page images and transcriptions of the journals and publications associated
with Captain James Cook's second voyage, a scientific expedition undertaken in the late
seventeenth century. Although the voyage's principal purpose was to observe the transit
of Venus from Tahiti in the South Pacific, the voyage is remarkable for its discoveries,
mapping, and revelations about native peoples and exotic places. This site provides the
opportunity for more advanced students to compare several versions of the same voyage
in the form of journals and official publications. In addition, the site is cross-linked with
excellent maps and charts, which in turn are marked with the dates of the corresponding
journal entries. Also available on this site are two accounts listed as "Indigenous Histories," which provide insight into the native practices described (and misunderstood) in official journals; both accounts are written or transcribed by European historians, although
they report having as their sources Tahitian natives. Although difficult to find, the engravings in Hawkesworth's compilation of journals from Cook's third voyage are available at http://southseas.nla.gov.au/journals/hv23/plates.html, linked to the contents page.

Early Canadiana Online
http://www.canadiana.org/

Site Summary. Begun in 1997 by the Canadian Institute for Historical Microreproductions, Early
Canadiana Online (ECO) is an outstanding online library of materials, published from the seventeenth through the early twentieth centuries, that pertain to the exploration and settlement of
Canada by Europeans. Although some of the materials relating to colonial, federal, and provin-
cial government publications, added since 2000, are available to ECO members only, the bulk
of earlier exploration, colonial, and settler materials, roughly 550,000 pages of material, remains accessible to the public. Also accessible to the public are another 20,000 pages of text
pertaining to the Hudson's Bay Company and 22,500 pages of text from the *Jesuit Relations*
(translated into English by Reuben Thwaites), which consists of the reports written by Jesuit
missionaries and other church officials to church authorities in Europe. Important collections
include 700 documents pertaining to *Canadian Women's History*, twenty volumes of the
Champlain Society Publications, 800 volumes of *English Canadian Literature*, a collection of
750 texts detailing the *History of French Canada* (French), and 900 documents classified as
Native Studies and providing both native and non-native perspectives on Canada's indigenous
populations. Available on the *Resource* page are links to projects on early Canadian history and
Exploration, the Fur Trade and Hudson's Bay Company, as well as evaluation reports pertain-
ing to their classroom use. Finally, also available on the *Resources* page is a set of *Online Lesson Plans* for students in grades seven to twelve; topics include "Internet research," "Essay
Writing," "Everyday Lives," "Native Americans," "Canadian Literature," "Women's History,"
"Travel and Exploration," and "Religion."

Navigating the Site. The site is well designed and easy to navigate. From the main page, choose
English (French is also available). Navigation tools appear in the left column; choose **Collections** to read about each collection. Both searching and browsing are supported from the
Search page; links to this page are available from most other pages of the site. To browse, you
may choose from title, author, subject, publisher, or date. The site is full-text searchable by keyword; Boolean searches are also supported. To view a document, click on the linked title; a list
of pages linked to scanned document images will appear. To view a page, click on the page
number. The page image can then be read as is, viewed in five different sizes, rotated, or refor-

matted as a PDF file for printing. A navigation bar permits movement forward or backward within the document.

Discussion Questions and Activities

1. Search on keywords to locate references to women, children, native peoples, and religious and missionary activities across the wide spectrum of the travel and exploration literature maintained on this site. For instance, searching on the term *women* brings up descriptions of women in a wide variety of cultures. Read some of these accounts. How did early travelers and explorers describe women in the cultures they encountered? Can they be described as objective? Or do the explorers and travelers describe them in European terms? Return to the search page and enter the terms *women* and *hardship* to bring up results that more narrowly describe the difficulties women faced on the frontier of settlement. How did women describe their experiences? What common themes are repeated in their descriptions of their lives? Finally, search on the terms *child* and *captivity*, restricting the results to those in which the two terms appear within fifty words of each other; this search yields over fifty works, many describing captivity narratives involving children. What elements recur in these narratives?

Similar/Related Sites

1. *Hakluyt's European Discoveries*—http://www.perseus.tufts.edu/—In addition to the classical materials described in Chapter 7, the *Perseus* site at Tufts University has also made available many of the extensive accounts of travel and exploration in Europe published under this title.

2. *Spain, the United States, and the American Frontier: Historias Paralelas*—http://international.loc.gov/intldl/eshtml/eshome.html—This site provides access to materials pertaining to the shared colonial histories of Spain and the United States through page images of Spanish- and English-language documents.

3. *Jesuit Relations and Allied Documents*—http://puffin.creighton.edu/jesuit/relations/—These documents are the source of much of what we know about early encounters between the native peoples of North America and European traders and missionaries, as well as many ensuing captivities. This Web site provides a transcription of the entire English translation of these documents by Reuben Thwaites.

Theodor de Bry's Engravings of Native American Life
http://www.csulb.edu/~gcampus/libarts/am-indian/woodcuts/

Site Summary. Scanned by Dr. Troy Johnson of California State University, Long Beach, as part of that university's Native American Studies site, this no-frills page provides access to excellent reproductions of Theodor DeBry's copper engravings and woodcuts of Native American life, which circulated widely in Europe, both separately and as part of Thomas Hariot's *A Briefe and True Report of the New Found Land of Virginia* (1590, Frankfurt). These engravings created some of the first impressions in the minds of Europeans of life in the Americas. For more detailed information about the provenance of the images, the user may want to refer to *Discovering the New World: Based on the Works of Theodore de Bry* (New York: Harper & Row, 1976).

Navigating the Site. The site is easy to navigate. From the main page, click on one of the **Collection** links. The resulting pages provide thumbnail images with titles; click on the title or the image to bring up the associated page, which provides a description of the image and another thumbnail. Click on the thumbnail to enlarge the image.

Discussion Questions and Activities

1. Page through the images, reading the accompanying commentaries. What aspects of Native American life caught the attention of early explorers? What kinds of activities are the focus of attention, and how do these compare with similar activities carried out by Europeans? Think about the possible European audiences for such engravings. How might the engravings and commentary have been received? What would have interested Europeans and why?

2. These engravings circulated alongside artistic renderings of people from many other cultures. Compare DeBry's engravings to the later engravings by artists who accompanied Captain James Cook to the South Pacific (linked to the contents page at http://southseas.nla.gov.au/journals/hv23/plates.html). What similarities and differences are apparent in the ways in which native peoples were depicted by European artists?

The Galileo Project

http://es.rice.edu/ES/humsoc/Galileo/

Site Summary. Created and maintained by the Rice University History Department and library, the *Galileo Project* provides extensive information not only about the life and discoveries of Galileo Galilei (1564–1642) but also about sixteenth-century science and religion. Separate pages provide Galileo's biography; the surviving 120-letter correspondence with his daughter, Virginia, a cloistered nun also known as Maria Celeste; detailed information about the contemporary scientific community and the church; and reference resources that include a glossary, maps, and timelines.

Navigating the Site. The site is extensively cross-linked and provides several paths for navigation. The main page is also a site map and provides a search engine. A second set of navigational links is provided from the **Galileo's Villa** page, which features a clickable map linked to other pages on the site.

Discussion Questions and Activities

1. What were Galileo's most important discoveries? Why did Galileo recant his discoveries, despite scientific evidence that he was correct?

2. Bertholt Brecht's modern play *Galileo* describes, through monologues and dialogues, the major controversies surrounding Galileo's conflict with the Roman Catholic Church and his eventual decision to deny the validity of his discoveries. What aspects of Brecht's play are explained by information on this Web site?

3. Read some of the letters from Galileo's correspondence with his daughter, Sister Maria Celeste (linked at http://galileo.rice.edu/fam/daughter.html). What concerns are expressed in these letters? What insights do they give you into the lives of Renaissance people?

Similar/Related Sites

1. *Institute and Museum of the History of Science, Online Multimedia Catalog—* http://brunelleschi.imss.fi.it/catalogo/—This outstanding site provides extensive online images and descriptions, in Italian and English, of the instruments and discoveries of Copernicus, Galileo, Brahe, etc.

Great Voyages: The History of Western Philosophy
http://oregonstate.edu/instruct/phl302/

Site Summary. The *Great Voyages* Web site was created to serve the needs of students enrolled in the 1600–1800 Western philosophy courses taught by Professor Bill Uzgalis of Oregon State University. The site provides excellent introductory resources for the study of the Renaissance humanists and Enlightenment philosophers. Among others, the site makes available materials that pertain to Machiavelli, More, Montaigne, Descartes, Hobbes, Locke, Berkeley, Hume, Pascal, Voltaire, Rousseau, Spinoza, Leibniz, Cavendish, and Wollstonecraft. Among the resources provided are timelines, study questions, biographical materials, full-text translations and transcriptions of principal works, and links to external sites.

Navigating the Site. From the main page, select *Next Page*. To reach major resources on the site, select *The Era.* From this page, *Stories and Themes* provides an overview of the period 1600–1800; *The Philosophers* provides access to the background sketches for each philosopher and, where available, full-text versions of their works. Returning to the main page, select *Next Page*, then *Reading* to reach study guides and questions for many of the readings.

Discussion Questions and Activities

1. For an overview of major changes in worldview from the medieval period to the Renaissance, read through the page on *Stories and Themes*. What point is Professor Uzgalis making about the map he provides on this page? What changes in perception and philosophy came about as stories of new people and continents trickled back to the known world?

2. Professor Uzgalis describes Montaigne's efforts in writing his *Essais* as a study of humanity through the study of himself. His chosen form of writing was the essay, a common form of writing today, but an innovation in the time of Montaigne. Read some of Montaigne's essays. Why is the essay form particularly appropriate to his subject matter? Why is it particularly appropriate for a humanist?

Similar/Related Sites

1. Humanism

   a. *Erasmus Text Project*—http://smith2.sewanee.edu/erasmus/—Although manifested in different ways, *Renaissance Christian humanism* began in fourteenth- to fifteenth-century Italy and spread throughout Europe, embracing a belief in individual perfectability through learning and reason. At the center of the northern European humanist circle that included Sir Thomas More, author of *Utopia*, was Dutch intellectual Desiderius Erasmus. This Web site was created by Chris Cudabac, a teacher of Latin and Greek at St. Timothy's/Hale School in Raleigh, North Carolina, to provide Web access to the editions of Erasmus's writings that have passed into the public domain. To date, Cudabac has added Web texts of *Colloquia* (1725 English translation), *Moriae Encomium* (Latin only), *The Praise of Folly* (1688 English translation), and a few others. Most of the works are available in multiple formats.

   b. *Sir Thomas More (1478–1535)*—http://osu.orst.edu/Dept/philosophy/club/utopia/utopian-visions/—Sponsored by the Department of Philosophy at Oregon State University, this site provides online texts of a lecture series, *Utopian Visions*, that explores the idea of *utopia* from Sir Thomas More's initiation of both the word and the genre in 1518.

c. *Montaigne's Essays*—http://etext.library.adelaide.edu.au/m/m76e/—This site also provides complete English translations of Montaigne's *Essays*.

2. *Philosophy Since the Enlightenment*—http://www.philosopher.org.uk/—This Web site provides synopses of the primary patterns of Western philosophical thought from Descartes to the present.

Cervantes Project

http://www.csdl.tamu.edu/cervantes/english/index.html

Site Summary. The Cervantes Project is directed by Eduardo Urbina and Richard Furuta of Texas A&M in collaboration with the Spanish National Library, the Centro de Estudios Cervantinos, the Center for the Study of Digital Libraries, and Dr. Fred Jehle of Indiana-Purdue University. The site's goal is to provide a comprehensive, multilingual site for the study of Miguel de Cervantes (1547–1616) and his writing through its work on the *Cervantes International Bibliography Online* (CIBO), the *Cervantes Digital Library* (CDL), and the *Cervantes Digital Archive of Images*. The CDL provides several versions of Cervantes's complete works in Spanish, English, and Italian; eventually, these will be cross-linked with the bibliography, images, and links. Most useful among the images are the portraits of Cervantes, many from frontispieces in editions of his work. For those wishing to perform further research, the site provides an outstanding bibliography of resources.

Navigating the Site. The main page provides links to the major subsections of this site.

Discussion Questions and Activities

1. Read the Cervantes biographies provided on this site, then read the detailed timeline for an account of some of the significant events in Cervantes's life. What experiences are likely to have served as resources as Cervantes wrote the satiric story of Don Quixote, a romantic knight arrant practicing chivalry in an unromantic world?

2. Read Chapter VIII of Don Quixote, Part I, which tells of Don Quixote's battle with the windmills, then explore the **Molinos de la Mancha** page, listed under "Similar/Related Sites," for images of windmills such as those Don Quixote might have encountered.

Similar/Related Sites

1. *Don Quixote de la Mancha*—http://quixote.mse.jhu.edu/—This site is a digitized exhibit of art and title pages of *Don Quixote* editions held by the George Peabody Library and curated by Harry Sieber, Johns Hopkins University. The site provides extensive commentary on all of the materials in the exhibit, accessible by selecting *Tour 2* from the site's main page.

2. *Molinos de la Mancha*—http://www.madridejos.net/molinog.htm—Although this site is written in Spanish, it provides graphics depicting windmills like those Don Quixote encounters on his adventures. Click on a graphic to enlarge it.

Golden Age Spanish Sonnets

http://sonnets.spanish.sbc.edu/

Site Summary. Inspired by the Italian writer Francesco Petrarca, or Petrarch (1304–1374), whose lyric poetry has influenced Western poets for hundreds of years, sixteenth- and seventeenth-century Spanish writers in particular embraced both the sonnet form and its conventions to express their thoughts about a wide variety of topics. This Web site, created by Professor

Alix Ingbar of Sweet Briar College, provides access to more than 100 translations of sonnets written by Spanish poets of the Golden Age.

Navigating the Site. The site is easy to navigate. From the main page, choose the ***Poems by Poet*** link from the left-hand column. Then click on one of the poet links that appears in the right-hand frame to view the poetry.

Discussion Questions and Activities

1. Imagery. Poetry of this era drew upon (and sometimes satirized) conventional descriptions of female beauty, sometimes referred to as *blazons*. How are women described in the poetry? Do these depictions in poetry written by men differ from depictions in poetry written by women? See especially Góngara's "Mientras por competir con tu cabello"; Hererra's "Trenzas que en la serena y limpia frente"; Medrano's (or Quevedo's) "Veré al tiempo tomar de ti, señora"; Quevedo's "Dificulta el retratar una grande hermosura"; and Vega's "De la belleza de su amada."

2. Metaphor: Rose. One of the most common metaphors used in poetry at this time was the rose, which stands in for a number of abstract ideas. Compare the uses of the rose as a metaphor in poetry of this time. For instance, how are roses used in Garcilaso de la Vega's sonnet "En tanto que de rosa y azucena"; Sor Juana Inez de la Cruz's "En que da moral censura a una rosa" and "Escoge antes el morir que exponerse a los ultrajes de la vejez"; Góngora's "Al sol porque salió estando con una dama y fue forzoso dejarla"; and Quevedo's "Dificulta el retratar una grande hermosura"?

3. Common Themes. Read several poems written in Golden Age Spain. What major themes are repeated? How do these thematic concerns compare with the concerns of people today? In particular, explore these sonnets for such common themes as death, love, loss, the passage of time, impermanence, and religious feeling. What commonalities can you find in the ways in which these themes are treated? What is unique about the ways poets treat these subjects? See especially the poetry of Francisco de Quevedo.

4. Allusions. Poets of Golden Age Spain consciously drew upon a wide range of classical literature to add richness to their poetry, frequently using allusions, or brief references to something outside the text of the poem itself. What references to mythical figures in classical literary tradition can you find in these poems? To classical modes of expression, such as pastoral (nostalgic references to shepherds and bucolic country life)? See especially the poetry of Lope de Vega.

5. Women. One of the major themes running throughout the poetry of Sor Juana Inez de la Cruz is women's limited access to knowledge and education. Read several of Sor Juana's poems, then investigate what the site dedicated to her poetry has to say about cultural attitudes toward educated women and the specific challenges facing women of Sor Juana's intellect (see "Similar/Related Sites" below).

Similar/Related Sites

1. *Anthology of Spanish Poetry*—http://users.ipfw.edu/jehle/poetry.htm—Selected by Dr. Fred Jehl of Purdue, this site provides e-texts of a number of Spanish poems, many with English translations. Also included are several pages on Spanish prosody.

2. *Sor Juana Inés de la Cruz (1648–1695)*—http://www.latin-american.cam.ac.uk/SorJuana/—This first rate site was created to accompany an "Introduction to Spanish Texts" course at the University of Cambridge. Included on the site is an excellent 1992

lecture by Geoffrey Kantaris, which lays out the major accomplishments of Sor Juana's life, as well as the thematic and figurative content of her works. The site also offers two video clips from a recent Spanish-language film about Sor Juana; these are very memory-intensive and feature illegible subtitles, but with the written commentary, the clips are very informative. The site links back to the main course page, where less well-developed materials are available on the work of other Spanish writers, including Cervantes, Lope de Vega, and Lorca. How do the challenges faced by women in Sor Juana's time differ from those encountered by women today? How are they similar?

Commedia

http://www.trinity.edu/org/comedia/index.html

Site Summary. This site is maintained by James T. Abraham, and Vern G. Williamsen of the Association for Hispanic Classical Theatre. In addition to a number of downloadable texts, the Web site also provides information about the organization and an extensive list of the organization's tape libraries, which can be checked out by the organization's members. Although most of the playscripts on the site are in Spanish, English-language translations of plays by Calderón, Mira de Amescua, Ruiz de Alarcón, Tirso de Molina, and Vega are also available on the site. A "Bibliography of Spanish Drama" in English translation is also provided, as are pages on Spanish prosody and grammar.

Navigating the Site. This no-frills site is easy to navigate, although the links are not always descriptive. Teaching and research materials, for instance, are located on the page labeled **A set of associated graphics, text, and bibliographic files**.

Discussion Questions and Activities

1. Both *Belshazzar's Feast*, by Pedro Calderón de la Barca, and the mid-fifteenth-century English morality play *Everyman* (a version is available online at http://www.fordham.edu/halsall/basis/everyman.html) use characters based on abstract ideas. For instance, both plays include the character Death. Compare the ways in which these two plays depict this character.

2. Compare the comedies of Antonio Mira de Amescua, Juan Ruiz de Alarcón, and Lope de Vega with those of Shakespeare. In what ways are they the same? In what ways do they differ? For instance, how do young lovers interact with one another in these comedies? How do they interact with and evade their elderly guardians? What rules govern marriage?

Voltaire Society of America

http://humanities.uchicago.edu/homes/VSA/

Site Summary. Created in 1996 and maintained by Jack Iverson of the ARTFL project at the University of Chicago, this site provides a range of primary English-language materials useful for teaching the works of François-Marie Arouet de Voltaire (1694–1778), especially *Candide*. Resources include letters; accounts of contemporary events; links to e-texts of Voltaire's work; and images related to book history, portraiture, and photographs of locations important in understanding Voltaire's life. Although this site has not been updated since 1999, most of its links are still intact and appropriate for use in high school and lower division undergraduate courses.

Navigating the Site. The site is easy to navigate. The first page is essentially a site map linked to a few other pages, devoted to the teaching of *Candide*, Voltaire's poetry, his correspondence, and images.

Discussion Questions and Activities

1. Resources Pertaining to *Candide*

   a. In Voltaire's *Candide*, the philosopher Pangloss espouses one aspect of the philosophy of Leibniz, that everything necessarily happens for the best in the best of all possible worlds. Voltaire's satire is expressed in part by having Pangloss and the other characters endure horrendous events and ordeals that suggest this philosophy is absurd. What did Voltaire himself think about Leibniz? From the main page, select the **Resources Pertaining to Candide** link, then the link to ***All is well*** for an entry from Voltaire's 1764 *Philosophical Dictionary*.

   b. A work from an earlier time sometimes gains relevance when parallel events inspire a later artist to update it. Click on the link to **Leonard Bernstein's musical comedy Candide**, then select the link to Leonard Bernstein's page on *Candide*. To what twentieth-century events did playwright Lillian Hellman link the events of Voltaire's *Candide*?

2. Letters from Voltaire. From the main page, select the link to **Letters from Voltaire**. Read some of the letters.

   a. What were some of the perils associated with writing satire?

   b. What were some of the issues that confronted people of Voltaire's time, and how did Voltaire feel about them?

3. Visitors to Ferney. From the main page, select the link to **Visitors to Ferney: A selection of Accounts.**

   a. Who visited Voltaire and why?

   b. What did Voltaire's visitors have to say about him and his attitudes? His importance? What were some typical reactions to encountering someone with Voltaire's reputation? See especially the contrasts between accounts written by his English visitors, for example, Boswell, Sharpe, Conyers, and Burney.

Similar/Related Sites

1. *A Treatise on Toleration*—http://www.wsu.edu:8080/~wldciv/world_civ_reader/world_civ_reader_2/voltaire.html—This site provides an excerpt from this essay by Voltaire.

2. *The Age of Enlightenment in the Paintings of France's National Museums*— http://www.culture.fr/lumiere/documents/files/imaginary_exhibition.html—This site provides a useful overview of the French Enlightenment, its art, its history, and its key figures, including Voltaire.

Russian Literature Pages at Northwestern University
Early Twentieth-Century Russian Drama
http://max.mmlc.northwestern.edu/~mdenner/Drama/index.html
From the Ends to the Beginning: A Bilingual Anthology of Russian Verse
http://max.mmlc.northwestern.edu/~mdenner/Demo/index.html

Site Summary. Sponsored by the Department of Russian and Slavic Languages at Northwestern University, these pages together offer an outstanding Web resource for students of Russian literature. This outstanding **Poetry** site is edited by Ilya Kutik and Andrew Wachtel of Northwestern

University, who suggest that "writers and readers of Russian poetry do not create or consume individual poems so much as they place those works in a living poetic fabric through a complex web of intertextual citation and reference." The editors have therefore attempted to show Russian poetry in its cultural context through multimedia presentations. Also included are an excellent introduction; 250 Russian texts facing English translations; over 75 archival recordings of poetry performed in Russian, many by the poets themselves (available as Real Audio, wav, or mp3 files); and detailed resource pages on 38 poets. Some of the poets included in this collection are Akhmatova, Ivanov, Mandelshtam, Lermontov, Pasternak, and Pushkin. The **Drama** site, developed by Michael Denner of Stetson University and hosted at Northwestern University, focuses on the Russian theater of Stanislavsky and Meyerhold, Chekhov, Mayakovsky and Bulgakov, Malevich and Tatlin, and Stravinsky and Shostakovich; the period covered is roughly from the 1890s to the 1930s. The site also provides resources pertaining to art and music, both of which were integral to the theater during this period of interdisciplinary activity. Included are outstanding materials, including biographies, set design and notes on staging, and images from early productions. Separate sections are accorded to designers, directors, and artistic movements and schools (realist painting, symbolism, the avant-garde, constructivism, and social realism) that influenced theatrical innovation. The **Resources** page provides links to additional information on all categories.

Navigating the Site. Both sites are well designed and easy to navigate. The main page of the **Drama** site provides a search engine and three sets of navigational links. Below the search engine is a descriptive roadmap to the primary features of the site. On the right is a set of links that lists the major subdivisions. Begin by reading about the ***Project*** and reading the FAQ at ***Answers***. Text links are available at the bottom of the page for those with earlier browsers. In addition, the site is extensively cross-linked. The main page of the *Poetry* site provides a site introduction by Andrew Wachtel. Read this, then click on an image or word to the left of the information box to move to a new section, or use the text links near the bottom of the page. A ***Home*** button is located at the top right of each subsequent page.

Discussion Questions and Activities

1. Drama. What kinds of planning go into the staging of a play? From the main page of the *Drama* site, choose the ***Plays*** link, then page through several of the plays.

    a. What kinds of planning are clear from the promptbooks that exist from an early staging of Chekhov's *The Seagull*?

    b. What artistic disciplines collaborated in the creation of the ballet *Petrushka*? As you page through this section, be sure to listen to the excerpt from Rachmaninoff's version of a folksong that was arranged by the Russian composer Igor Stravinsky for this ballet.

    c. From the main page, click on the link to ***Visual Arts***, then page through the major artistic movements affecting twentieth-century Russian drama. Next, page through the section dedicated to *Vladamir Mayakovsky: A Tragedy* and *Victory Over the Sun*. Watch the video clips provided. What artistic influences are readily apparent in the costume and set design for these plays? How do the themes of the plays connect with the focuses of the artistic movements?

2. Poetry

    a. Allusions. Allusions are brief references to events or texts outside the context of a poem itself. What allusions in Russian poetry point to external influences on poets?

For instance, read Prigov's "Reagan's Image in Soviet Literature," Akhmatova's "Lot's Wife," Mandelshtam's "Shubert on the Water" and "Impressionism," Tiutchev's "Cicero," Batiushkov's "Odysseus' Fate" and "Tasso Dying," and Tsvetaeva's "Dialogue Between Hamlet and His Conscience."

b. For insight into how these Russian poets viewed their craft, read Briusov's "To a Young Poet," Pushkin's "The Poet," Zhukovsky's "The Bard," Tsetaeva's "For My Poems, Written So Early . . ." and "Poets," Lermontov's "Death of the Poet," and Baratynsky's "The Last Poet." What challenges do the poets face? What is the purpose and inspiration for their poetry?

c. Poetry has long been used to commemorate events or people. Read Derzhavin's "On the Death of Prince Meshchersky" and Lomonosov's "An Ode in Memory of Her Majesty the Empress Anna Ivanovna on the Victory over the Turks and Tatars and the Taking of Khotin, 1739" for examples. What does Akhmatova have to say about this kind of poetry in her poem "I Have No Use for Odic Legions"? In view of this tradition, what can be said of Mayakovsky's poem "To His Beloved Self the Poet Dedicates These Lines"?

Similar/Related Sites

1. *Friends and Partners: Russian Literature page*—http://www.fplib.org/literature/index.html—Originally conceived by computer scientists Greg Cole (University of Tennessee) and Natasha Bulashova (Russian Academy of Science in Pushchino, Moscow) as a post-Cold War statement of unity, this Web site provides access to nearly 20,000 pieces of Russian literature. The site provides and links to a large collection of literature in Russian; however, it also provides English translations of some works by Tyutchev, Lermontov, Pushkin, Akhmatova, and Pasternak. The sources of the translations are not attributed, and users are advised to use the site with caution.

2. The following Russian literature sites are worth noting but are not authoritative; most have been created by fans of specific authors and should be used with caution.

a. *The Anton Chekhov Page (1860–1904)*—http://www.eldritchpress.org/ac/chekhov.html—Originally created by Yvan Russell, this Web site has been adopted and updated by Eric Eldritch, editor of an eclectic site of online e-texts and other literary resources. Although it has not been updated in some time and has a number of broken links, the site provides an excellent starting point for research on Chekhov's plays and short stories.

b. *Christiaan Stange's Dostoevsky Research Station*—http://www.kiosek.com/dostoevsky/—The *Dostoevsky Research Station* was created in 1996 and provides links (some broken) to artwork, critical essays, Web sites, e-texts, study guides, course materials, and other information pertaining to the study of Dostoevsky's works. The site has not been updated since 1999, and its plaintext works by Dostoevsky are not fully documented.

c. *Fyodor Mikhailovich Dostoevsky*—http://community.middlebury.edu/~beyer/courses/previous/ru351/dostoevsky/F.M.Dostoevsky.shtml—This site provides useful links created by faculty and students at Middlebury Community College. The links to e-texts are not fully documented, but the study guides may prove useful to some users.

d. *Leo Tolstoy*—http://www.ltolstoy.com/—This Web site provides a biography of Tolstoy, a timeline of his life, a genealogy chart, links to e-texts of forty-two works, reading tips, recommended editions, thirteen photographic portraits, images of Tolstoy's house and plantation, links to searches and a concordance, an illustrated version of *The Last Days of Leo Tolstoy*, and a comprehensive list of Tolstoy's creative and nonfiction works. Although the site's creator indicates he or she has a degree in Russian from Brigham Young University, little other background information is provided.

e. *Leo Tolstoy*—http://www.utoronto.ca/tolstoy/gallery/index.html—This site provides access to portraits of Tolstoy taken throughout his life.

f. *Last Days of Leo Tolstoy*—http://www.linguadex.com/tolstoy/—This site documents the memoir written by Vladimir Chertkov, who was present during Tolstoy's last days.

United States Holocaust Memorial Museum

http://www.ushmm.org/

Site Summary. Dedicated to memorializing and educating the public on the history and consequences of holocausts and genocide, the United States Holocaust Memorial Museum focuses much of this Web site on the Nazi Holocaust, although its materials on other holocausts also make it an outstanding introduction to holocaust studies in general. The site includes a holocaust encyclopedia (in progress); personal histories that detail eyewitness accounts; approximately 10,000 online images (with accompanying narratives) that comprise roughly one-eighth of the museum's holdings; and high-quality images of a large number of artifacts, most of which can be magnified for closer examination. Two areas of the site depict special projects: **Special Exhibitions** and **Special Focus**. **Special Exhibitions** include materials pertaining to the following:

1. Current events in Rwanda, Greece, Chechnya, and the Sudan

2. Nazi medical experiments and subsequent trials of the perpetrators

3. Anne Frank

4. A 1933 book-burning incident perpetrated by German university students

5. Nazi persecution of homosexuals

6. Accounts of Christian clergy and laypeople who assisted Jewish refugees

7. The 1933 Olympics in Germany

8. Accounts of ghetto life and pogroms against Jews living in them

9. Music, art, and poetry of the Nazi Holocaust

The **Special Focus** pages include materials on the following:

1. Liberation from concentration camps at the conclusion of World War II

2. Anti-Semitism

3. Women History and Black History Months

4. Contemporary films, such as *The Pianist* and *Shindler's List*

5. Persecution of specific groups, such as homosexuals and people with disabilities

Extensive archival materials accompany all of these special exhibits. The site also provides outstanding educational resources, especially well-designed materials teachers can use to guide their classroom practices and their introduction of this difficult material to students. These include a videotaped online seminar, online lesson plans (with student work), and application materials for the museum's generous teacher education program.

Navigating the Site. The site is attractively designed, although its complex layout and extensive links to supporting materials make it sometimes difficult to navigate. From the main page, use the left-hand navigation bar for access to major site features. Beyond this point, the pages appear to have differing designs. Take time and explore each one completely, but return to the main page frequently to ensure a thorough exploration of the site's many features. A more easily navigated ancillary site for students is accessible through the *Education* page.

Discussion Questions and Activities

1. Begin by exploring the site's extensive features. A good page to start with is the **Mapping the Holocaust** page. Where and when has genocide existed in the past? How did the Nazi Holocaust begin, and why was it allowed to proceed relatively unchecked?

2. Read about individual events of the Nazi Holocaust, viewing the accompanying photographs and video clips and transcripts of both historical and eyewitness accounts. Why is testimony and publication of eyewitness accounts so important to Holocaust survivors? How does the Web site further this goal?

3. Explore the education links on the site.

   a. If you are a teacher, select the *For Teachers* link on the main page under the category *Inside Education.* View the videotaped seminar on teaching the Nazi Holocaust. What are the central issues involved in helping students understand the significance and magnitude of the twelve-year period associated with the Nazi Holocaust? What strategies are offered to contextualize the events historically? To help students understand the events in human terms, rather than in statistical and geographic terms? Why is it so important to define and discuss particular terms with great precision and within complex historical contexts (e.g., terms such as *ghetto, concentration camp, race, resistance, perpetrator, rescuers, bystanders, victims*)? Why does the seminar emphasize the importance of studying eyewitness testimony as an integral part of any lesson plan on the Nazi Holocaust?

   b. If you are a student, click on the *For Students* link on the main page under "Inside Education," then select the link to *The Holocaust: A Learning Site for Students.* Finally, click on *Site Map.* The resulting page provides links to pages designed specifically for middle and high school students. These pages present many of the same materials as the larger museum site, but in a more accessible format.

Similar/Related Sites

1. *Remember.org*—http://www.remember.org—This Web site provides additional images, eyewitness accounts, and lesson plans for teaching and studying the Nazi Holocaust.

2. *Auschwitz-Birkenau Memorial and Museum*—http://www.auschwitz.org.pl/html/eng/start/index.php—The official Web site of the Auschwitz-Birkenau concentration camp museum, this Web site provides detailed images, plans, timelines, and historical information.

3. *The Nizkor Project*—http://www.nizkor.org/—This Web site provides information on the extermination camps of the Nazi Holocaust, as well as unethical Nazi medical research performed on concentration camp inmates.

4. *Simon Wiesenthal Center—Museum of Tolerance*—http://motlc.wiesenthal.com/— Sponsored by the Simon Wiesenthal Center, this well-designed Web site focuses on the plight of Jewish people in the Nazi Holocaust and provides additional research materials of use to students and teachers of the Nazi Holocaust. The **Multimedia Learning Center** page provide pages on the various groups involved (**Jews**, **Nazis**, **Resistance and Rescue**, **Righteous Among Nations**, the latter defined as those who assisted refugees) and historical topics (**World Response**, **Antisemitism and the Final Solution**, and **After the War**). Most of these pages in turn are subdivided into pages covering **Places**, **People**, **Organizations**, and **General Topics**. The site includes 10,000 photographs. The **Virtual Exhibits** page links to three exhibits. **Visas for Life** is dedicated to Chiune Sugihara and his efforts to rescue Jewish refugees. Two other exhibits are dedicated to the Warsaw ghetto: one to its history (**Dignity and Defiance**) and one to its inhabitants (**And I Still See Their Faces**). From the main page, the link to the **Special Collections** page provides access to nearly 14,000 documents.

5. *Jewish History Sourcebook*—http://www.fordham.edu/halsall/jewish/jewishsbook.html —Part of a larger resource discussed in Chapter 4, this page provides extensive links to materials on the history of Judaism and the Nazi Holocaust.

6. *Elie Wiesel page on EducETH*—http://www.educeth.ch/english/readinglist/wiesele/index. html—Created in 1995 as a collaborative site for educators by Hans Fischer and powered by the Swiss Federal Institute of Technology in Zurich, this Web site features a page dedicated to Elie Wiesel, Nazi Holocaust survivor and Nobel Prize winner. The ***Facts By*** and ***Facts About the Author*** link to pages providing extensive audio and video materials, as well as texts of Wiesel's speeches, interviews, and novel *Night*.

7. *German Propaganda*—http://www.calvin.edu/academic/cas/gpa/—This page provides an extensive archive of Nazi propaganda, useful in helping to establish the historical context of the Nazi Holocaust.

Franz Kafka

http://www.kafka.org/

Site Summary. Created in 1999 by Mauro Nervi, this outstanding site is an excellent place to begin study of Franz Kafka and his work, whether in English or in German. The site includes full-text versions of Kafka's published and unpublished works, including travel diaries, as well as a large number of scholarly articles and background materials. For readers of German, the site provides even more. Although the site does not provide Mr. Nervi's credentials, an article in the online resource *Wikipedia* indicates that he is a poet. Although many of the resources provided on the site do not include statements of the contributors' credentials, many others do. Consequently, users of this site should check translations against traditionally published print versions and investigate the credentials of contributors before citing them with confidence.

Navigating the Site. From the main page, navigate the Web site using the horizontal navigation bar across the top for major site features, or by using the left-hand navigation bar for access to materials pertaining to specific works by Kafka.

Discussion Questions and Activities

1. *Metamorphosis. The Metamorphosis* is perhaps Kafka's most famous work. Begin by reading the essay by Vladimir Nabokov, which provides an interpretive overview of the work. (To reach this essay, from the main page choose the link from the left-hand navigation bar to *The Metamorphosis*, then select the *Special Issue* link, then Nabokov's essay.) For ideas about teaching *The Metamorphosis* in a post-9/11 world, scroll down the main page to the "Articles, Essays, and Recommended Books" section, then select the link to the essay by Margaret Sönser Breen, which appears in the middle column.

Ibsen.Net
http://www.ibsen.net/

Site Summary. Ibsen.Net is the official Web site of the Norwegian Ibsen committee; its objective is to provide information about Ibsen and his legacy through "Ibsen Year 2006," which marks the 100th anniversary of Ibsen's death. The site provides a large number of links to e-texts in several languages (for a comprehensive list click on *Digitalised Ibsen Literature* on the left, and when the corresponding category appears in the center column, click on the desired text). Go to the *Ibsen Encyclopedia* for title pages, plot synopses, and links to e-texts for individual works. For production history, click on *Repertoire database,* then enter your search terms for a list of theaters and dates (for detailed production, performance, and cast information, click on the theater name). Choosing *Filmography* from the menu produces a list of films spanning 1911–1983. *Central Links* provides an astonishing array of outstanding Web resources in several languages.

Navigating the Site. The main page of this Web site is in Norwegian (http://www.ibsen.net); to reach the English-language version, click on the British flag in the upper left-hand corner of the main page. Each index page is laid out to look like a three-column newsletter with a masthead that provides links to major sections (Art, Library, Media, Museums, Research, School, Studies, Theatre, and Tourism). Special features of the site are listed on the left in a green box; click on one of the links to display the information in the wide center column. You may be able to expand a topic displayed in the center of the screen by clicking on "You are here." Note that on occasion, you may end up back in the Norwegian portion of the Web site. To get back, use the back button on your browser, or click on the British flag in the upper left-hand corner of the screen.

Discussion Questions and Activities

1. Translations. From the left-hand navigation bar, choose the link to *Digitalised Ibsen Literature*, then choose the *Read more here* link under "Texts Written by Ibsen." Choose a particular play with several English translations, locate a scene of particular interest, and compare the ways in which each translator has interpreted the same text. In particular, read William Archer's commentary on *A Doll's House*. In what ways do Archer's comments suggest *A Doll's House* might be updated for today's audiences?

2. Filmography. To locate film versions of Ibsen's play, choose the *Filmography* link from the left-hand navigation bar, then locate a play of particular interest. What film versions of *A Doll's House* have been made in English translation?

3. Production History. To study the production history of Ibsen's plays, choose the ***Repertoire database*** link from the left-hand navigation bar. On the resulting page, choose a play, then fill in the dates of interest, noting that this form field follows European date conventions, which place the day before the month. Then click ***Search.*** When was the first production of *A Doll's House* in the United States? After searching on the play *A Doll's House*, locate the 1880 production of the play at the Grand Opera House in Milwaukee, Wisconsin. What was the source of the translation used for this production?

CHAPTER 10

Non-European World Literatures

For other sites of potential interest, see also Chapter 5, "Religion and Folklore."

Transnational/Intercultural Projects

Nobel e-Museum

http://www.nobel.se/

Site Summary. This site is the ideal starting point for research on any Nobel prize winner. The official Web site of the Nobel foundation, this Web site was created to showcase the winners of the Nobel prize, provide a history of the selection criteria, and offer educational links. Author pages include a brief biography; transcripts, recordings, and/or videos of the author's Nobel lecture, banquet speech, and/or interview; excerpts from the author's work; images of the unique Nobel diploma awarded; the acceptance photo; and links to other resources. Interactive games include word searches on author's names; Nobel Radio, where the user can listen to the winners' acceptance speeches; and a role-playing game (RPG) in which the user visits the Nobel Village and meets authors while attempting to complete a novel. Also available are virtual tours of the Swedish Academy. Since 1991, the Nobel Prize committee has also sponsored symposia on topics in literature it believes have cultural or social significance, or are groundbreaking in nature.

Navigating the Site. From the main page, select ***Literature*** from the toolbar at the top of the page. Choose among links to ***Laureates, Articles***, and ***Educational*** topics. Choose ***Laureates*** to reach a timeline; click on the desired name to reach the records associated with a particular author. Choose ***Articles*** for general information or profiles of specific Nobel laureates. Choose ***Educational*** links to reach interactive games for children.

Discussion Questions and Activities

1. From the main page, select ***Literature*** from the top navigation bar, then choose ***Articles***. Choose Kjell Espmark's essay, "The Nobel Prize in Literature" for insight into the original charge of the committee and shifts in the way that charge has been interpreted over time. What criteria have been used since the prize's inception in 1901, and why have they changed?

2. Choose several laureates and read the brief excerpts from their work. What do the selected excerpts have in common?

3. Learn about Nobel laureates by playing the RPG.

The Modern Word

http://www.themodernword.com/themodword.cfm

Site Summary. Created and directed by Allen Ruch, with editorial assistance from several excellent scholars, this well-edited Web site offers an outstanding array of resources for the study of twentieth-century literature. In particular, the site offers access to reviews and publishers' notes on specific editions; book, film, and other performance reviews; critical essays; and interviews and other commentary by the writers themselves. The site includes most extensive coverage of Gabriel García Márquez (used as example below), Samuel Becket, Jorge Luis Borges, Umberto Eco, James Joyce, and Franz Kafka. Additional coverage is provided of authors Kobo Abé, Stanislaw Lem, Georges Perec, Raymond Queneau, Alain Robbe-Grillet, J. G. Ballard, John Banville, John Barth, Donald Barthelme, Anthony Burgess, Angela Carter, Philip K. Dick, William Gaddis, John Hawkes, Primo Levi, H. P. Lovecraft, Jeff Noon, Michael Ondaatje, Mervyn Peake, Thomas Pynchon, and Jeanette Winterson.

Navigating the Site. The site is superbly designed. The design elements for more complete resource areas (e.g., Márquez, Beckett, Borges, Eco, Joyce, and Kafka) are common from page to page, with different color schemes associated with different authors. For these authors, a relatively common set of linked buttons appear on the left (***News, Features, Biography, Works, Reviews, Interviews, Criticism, Quotes, Audio, Film, Theater, Music, Images, Influences, Papers, Articles, Communities, Centers, Bookstore, Links,*** and ***FAQs***). For other authors, a left-hand navigation bar appears listing all authors provided some coverage on the site; authors whose names appear in boldface have more comprehensive coverage that those whose names are not printed bold in bold type.

Discussion Questions and Activities

1. Jorge Luis Borges: *The Garden of the Forking Paths*—Twentieth-century writers like Borges influence and are influenced by a wide variety of works and media, including music, art, and film. Describe some of the works that influenced Borges. What genres in particular interested him? How does he modify or reinvent preexisting works, such as Miguel de Cervantes's *Don Quixote*, for contemporary audiences? (See especially the **Reviews** page, specifically Jordan McKay's review of *Collected Fictions* in the Austin Chronicle.)

   a. What reinterpretations of Borges's work are described on the site? (See especially the **Art, Music,** and **Film** pages.) What does this suggest about the need for students and teachers of literature to be aware of other art forms and of interdisciplinary influences on today's writers?

   b. In what ways do Borges's works participate in and comment on culture as a phenomenon jointly experienced by individuals in all fields of intellectual endeavor? Locate and read (on the **Reviews** page) Silvia G. Dapía's review in *Variaciones Borges 1996* of Floyd Merrell's book, *Unthinking Thinking: Jorge Luis Borges, Mathematics and the New Physics*, which explores how Borges's prose and essays can be seen, not as influenced by or influencing culture, but as participating in the same cultural milieu as twentieth-century mathematics, logic, physics, and philosophy of science scholars. How do this review and the book it describes challenge the traditional divisions among the liberal arts (e.g., literature, science, mathematics, art)? What implications does this have for the ways literature might be taught and studied in the future?

c. What do critics and scholars say about Borges and his works? Consult the **Criticism** page for an annotated bibliography of critical statements.

d. What contemporary authors influenced Borges? Which did Borges influence? Consult the articles provided on the **Influences** page to learn about connections among Borges, Melville, Joyce, Fuentes, García Márquez, Pynchon, and others.

Similar/Related Sites

1. *Audio Online: Recordings of UC Berkeley Speakers*—http://www.lib.berkeley.edu/ MRC/audiofiles.html—This Web site provides lengthy audio recordings of presentations at the University of California, Berkeley, by some of the most important writers and theorists of the twentieth century. Included are recordings of Umberto Eco, Michel Foucault, Carlos Fuentes, Malaysian poet Goh Poh Seng, and Czeslaw Milosz.

2. *Bohemian Ink*—http://www.levity.com/corduroy/—If this site were better maintained, it would rank as of significant informational value. Unfortunately, a number of its links are now broken; however, its value as a starting place for research on a number of important twentieth-century writers still makes it worth consulting. This eclectic site provides four main areas, each with its own descriptors. Of most value to teachers and students of world literature is the **Underworld** area, which is devoted to postmodern and postcolonial writers. This area of the site includes timelines and biographical materials for authors including Antonin Artaud, Samuel Beckett, Albert Camus, Umberto Eco, Hermann Hesse, Eugène Ionesco, Franz Kafka, Milan Kundera, Gabriel García Márquez, Salman Rushdie, Aleksandr Solzhenitsyn, and Louis Céline. The other three areas addressed by the site are **From Here to Modernity**, dedicated to poets of the Harlem Renaissance; the **Beatniks** area, devoted to American poetry produced by the Beat Movement and its successors; and the **Subterraneans** area, devoted to "writers of the undergrounds who have surfaced in certain circles and cliques but have yet to "break the major league skin."

3. *Jorge Luis Borges Center*—http://www.hum.au.dk/Institut/rom/borges/—Created in 1994 by the University of Aarhus, Denmark, and maintained by Professors Ivan Almeida and Cristina Parodi, this excellent Web site seeks to provide a comprehensive bibliographic resources and to publish, in *Veriaciones Borges*, a journal of outstanding international research on Borges studies. Although many of the articles and books published on the site are in Spanish, some full-text resources are published in English, making this a valuable set of resources for Borges studies in English.

4. *Pegasos*—http://www.kirjasto.sci.fi/—Mostly a biographical resource, this resource is widely cited on the Internet and provides lists of each author's major works.

The Academy of American Poets
http://www.poets.org/index.cfm

Site Summary. Founded in 1934, the Academy of American Poets promotes and sponsors the creation and dissemination of poetry in the United States through this Web site and such events as National Poetry Week. Despite its name, this Web site provides excellent background materials on international poets, including useful biographical materials, audio files of poetry (some read by the poets themselves), and excellent links to other Web sites. In particular, the site provides materials on Catullus, C. P. Cavafy, Anna Akhmatova, Yehuda Amichai, Guillaume Apollinaire, Hilaire Belloc, Siv Cedering, Miguel de Unamuno, David Diop, Jorge Guillén, Horace, Zbigniew Herbert, Miguel Hernández, Nazim Hikmet, Federico García Lorca, Osip

Mandelstam, Luis Palés Matos, Czeslaw Milosz, Eugenio Montale, Pablo Neruda, Michael Ondaatje, Jirí Orten, Ovid, José Emilio Pacheco, Boris Pasternak, Octavio Paz, Fernando Pêssoa, Rainer Maria Rilke, Sappho, Wislawa Szymborska, Paul Valéry, César Vallejo, Derek Walcott, Adam Zagajewski, Claribel Alegría, and Paul Celan. Also valuable on the site is an interactive feature, **My Notebooks**, which permits users to maintain files of poetry and make notes. Finally, a special area of the Web site, available via links *For Teachers* from the main page, provides access to the **Online Poetry Classroom** and to poetry curriculum units.

Navigating the Site. The site is well designed. The navigation toolbar on the left-hand side of the page links to resources that permit users to view poetry in large type and to locate poetry by author, title, and first line. The link to the *Listening Booth* provides access to a wide selection of audio files.

Discussion Questions and Activities

1. Online Poetry Classroom

    a. From the **Online Poetry Classroom** page, choose the link to *How to Teach*, then click on *Curriculum Units and Lesson Plans.* Locate the lesson plan entitled "Poetry in Translation." Read the learning objectives for this assignment and apply the questions raised to the selection of poetry provided from this Web site.

    b. How does one lead a poetry discussion, especially with little experience reading poetry? Also under *How to Teach* is an excellent article by Jack Collum, "Tips on Leading Poetry Sessions."

2. Thematic Connections: War Poetry. The series of events leading to, encompassing, and following numerous armed conflicts, including two world wars, were experienced by a number of European poets represented on the site. Read both the background information and the poetry published on the pages dedicated to Czeslaw Milosz, Paul Celan, Yehuda Amichai, Denise Levertov, Naomi Shihab Nye, and Wislawa Szymborska. How do these poets describe armed conflict and the decision makers responsible? How do they describe the aftermath of armed conflict?

3. Thematic Connections: Aftermath of Colonialism. Many of the most influential writers today live in cultures that continue to be affected by their countries' colonial past. Frequently, such writers write about feelings of alienation and isolation and a sense of being torn between differing systems of expression. Read the background information and the poetry published on the pages dedicated to Aimé Césaire, Vijay Seshadri, Reetika Vazirani, and Derek Walcott. How does the poetry of these writers display concerns that arise from their participation in a postcolonial world?

Similar/Related Sites

1. *Voices from the Gaps*—http://voices.cla.umn.edu/—This Web site provides background and a sampling from the writing of American women of color, but the site also includes writers such as Anita Desai, whose parents were German and Indian and who spoke no English until she entered school. Many of the writers on this site are excellent examples of how contemporary writers frequently straddle traditional boundaries, such as language and nationality.

2. *The Electronic Labyrinth (Non-linear Tradition in Literature)*—http://www.iath.virginia. edu/elab/elab.html—This site provides an introduction to contemporary literature and

hypertext; it includes materials about Italo Calvino, Robbe-Grillet, Cortázar, and Pavic, as well as useful pages about novels, realist novels, postmodern novels, etc.

3. *Poetry International*—http://www.poetryinternational.org/

Contemporary Postcolonial and Postimperial Literature in English
http://www.scholars.nus.edu.sg/landow/post/

Site Summary. This outstanding Web site, created and maintained by Professor George Landow of Brown University, is the ideal starting place for research on postcolonial and postimperial literatures of the nineteenth, twentieth, and twenty-first centuries. Begun as a course Web site in 1985, Professor Landow lists as contributors many of his students, as well as a number of internationally based independent scholars, students, and faculty.

Navigating the Site. The site is easy to use. The main page provides a grid of clickable tiles. To move to a particular geographical region, click its tile. A navigation grid for the region will appear with clickable tiles for categories that include ***Authors, Economics, Geography, History, Politics, Science & Technology, Visual Arts, Religion, Post-Colonial Theory, Nations, Theme & Subject, Bibliography***, and links for specific countries in the region. Individual entries in turn are cross-linked with other pages. Note that the site is in a perpetual state of development; author pages, for instance, feature links based on a template used for all authors; consequently, segments not yet written appear as broken links.

Discussion Questions and Activities

1. Chinua Achebe's *Things Fall Apart*

   a. Using the search tool from the main page, search on the term *Omoregie* to locate F-K Omoregie's online essay, "Rodney, Cabral and Ngugi as Guides to African Postcolonial Literature." Read the essay. According to Omoregie, how did colonial education and missionary activities impact indigenous populations? How did these institutions contribute to the subsequent disillusionment of educated Africans with the aftermath of colonization? Apply the ideas described in the essay to Achebe's *Things Fall Apart*. How does this essay clarify Achebe's description of the relationship between the missionaries and the people of Okonkwo's village?

   b. In *Things Fall Apart*, Okonkwo, the protagonist, kills himself when he cannot adapt to changes brought about by British colonial rule. Achebe romanticizes neither traditional Ibo society nor the encroaching Christian missionaries and British colonial authorities, who disrupt tribal traditions, religion, and family relationships. What are the key conflicts between pre- and postcolonial life in Okonkwo's village (neither featured as idyllic)? Compare your ideas with those in Omoregie's essay.

   c. Use the search tool to locate Karen Hauser's article about Ibo funeral ceremonies. What does the concept of "shameful death" explain about the treatment of twins in *Things Fall Apart*?

2. Wole Soyinka's *Ake*

   a. Read about the ritual practice of scarification, such as that described in Soyinka's *Ake*. How can such practices be understood within the context of African visual arts and Yoruba ideas about aesthetics, or the study of beauty?

Similar/Related Sites

1. *Postcolonial Studies at Emory*—http://www.emory.edu/ENGLISH/Bahri/—This Web site provides excellent background information on authors, theorists, and key terms in postcolonial study. Because the site's creator, Deepika Bahri, intends that the site complement other sites, however, it does not duplicate subjects covered extensively elsewhere and so does not claim to be comprehensive.

2. *Colonial and Postcolonial Literary Dialogues*—http://www.wmich.edu/dialogues/index.html—Created by Allen Carey Webb and hosted by Western Michigan University, this Web site adopts a thematic approach to exploring the way in which a wide range of colonial and postcolonial literary texts can be read as in dialogue with one another. The site includes excerpts from a number of texts, as well as extensive, accessible commentary and analysis.

3. *Caribbean Poetry: Barbados*—http://www.courses.vcu.edu/ENG-snh/Caribbean/Barbados/index.html—This Web site provides useful background material for the study of postcolonial poetry from the Caribbean.

4. *Postcolonial Writers on EducETH*—http://www.educeth.ch/english/readinglist/achebec/index.html—Created in 1995 as a collaborative site for educators by Hans Fischer and powered by the Swiss Federal Institute of Technology in Zurich, this Web site features a page dedicated to Chinua Achebe, author of *Things Fall Apart*. The **Facts By** and **Facts About the Author** link to pages providing extensive audio and video materials, as well as texts of Achebe's novel, interviews, and speeches. The site also provides a page on South African writer J. M. Coetzee, located at http://www.educeth.ch/english/readinglist/coetzeejm/index.html.

5. *Night Waves: Landmarks Broadcast on Joseph Conrad's Heart of Darkness*—http://www.bbc.co.uk/radio3/speechanddrama/landmarks.shtml—Audio file of a BBC broadcast about Conrad's *Heart of Darkness*, with commentary by experts and narration from the work.

Sites of Regional Interest

Africa

See Chapter 6 for writing in early African cultures. See Chapter 8 for sites on early Egyptian culture.

Cultures and Literatures of Africa Links
http://www.cocc.edu/cagatucci/classes/hum211/index.htm

Site Summary. Created by Professor Cora Agatucci for her humanities courses at Central Oregon Community College, this Web site is simply one of the best sites on the Web for teachers of African literature. The site provides links to materials on African storytelling; teaching materials for works such as *Things Fall Apart* and *Nervous Conditions*; extensive timelines for African history, oral culture, literature, and film; an African "literary map" that highlights several important African writers, stories, and their geographical settings; online lectures; coursepacks; and an extensive set of links. The site is constantly under revision and bears watching as Professor Agatucci adds even more resources.

Navigating the Site. The site is accessible from the main page either through links from the course schedules or through navigational links located at the bottom of the page (choose among *African Timelines: History, Orature, Literature, & Film*; *African Storytelling*; *Chinua Achebe, Things Fall Apart*; and *Tsitsi Dangarembga, Nervous Conditions*). Links to several other topics—*African Studies & History*; *Arts & Cultures*; *Diaspora*; *Music*; *Orature & Literature*; and *Women*—are available on the page by selecting *African Links*.

Discussion Questions and Activities

1. African History. Begin by exploring the outstanding *African Timelines* resources. For instance, how did the slave trade come about, and what literature was written documenting its rise, progress, and fall? *Part III: African Slave Trade and European Imperialism* provides outstanding resources documenting the history of the slave trade, as well as information on oral culture and slave narratives, especially that of Olaudah Equiano. *Part IV: Anti-colonialism and Reconstruction* provides links to resources that explain literature and other texts from the postcolonial period of African history.

Similar/Related Sites

1. *African Yoruba and Akan Art*—http://www.fa.indiana.edu/~conner/africart/home.html —Sponsored by the Art History Department and the Fine Arts Consortium at Indiana University and curated by the Lakeview Museum of Arts and Sciences in Peoria, Illinois, this Web site provides excellent images and commentary that demonstrate the intricate connections between African Yoruba and Akan art and folklore. Although the site now has a number of broken links and images, it is still valuable in showing that all African cultural expression is interconnected. Essentially a site dedicated to an exhibit of African Yoruba and Akan art, this site provides an accessible history of Africa's central-western coastal nations and its mythology, and is useful for teaching the work of Wole Soyinka.

2. *African Philosophy Resource*—http://pegasus.cc.ucf.edu/~janzb/afphil/—Created by Bruce Janz of the University of Central Florida, this site operates as a gateway to other resources on African culture, but the site also provides access to a significant number of textual resources. Particularly of interest to older students, teachers, and librarians are the archived essays that discuss perspectives within African studies today, especially such concepts as Afrocentrism, which suggests the need to study all African literatures, including African American literature, as part of a larger African-centered phenomenon.

3. General reference sites

    a. *World of African Literatures*—http://www.arts.uwa.edu.au/AFLIT/FEMEChomeEN. html#English—This site provides French and English versions of most materials, as well as a slide show to guide readers through the site. The site provides mostly reference materials.

    b. *Africana Collection*—http://web.uflib.ufl.edu/cm/africana/literature.htm—Although it functions primarily as a catalog of the University of Florida's collection of African materials, this site provides links to biographies, brief samples of poetry, and bibliographic citations for a several modern African writers.

    c. *Center for Electronic Resources in African Studies*—http://sdrc.lib.uiowa. edu/ceras/—Maintained by the University of Iowa, this site provides another list of possible resources for research in African literatures.

4. Reference sites about specific geographical areas

a. *Anglophone and Lusophone African Women Writers*—http://www.ex.ac.uk/~ajsimoes/ aflit/—Primarily a biographical and bibliographical reference, this site also provides limited texts written in English.

b. *The Maghrebi Studies Group*—http://www.maghrebi-studies.org/—Sponsored by the Maghrebi Studies Group, originally created by graduate students in the Translation Program and the Comparative Literature Department at Binghamton University (SUNY), this site provides brief biographies of modern African writers from Tunisia, Morocco, and Algeria, with lists of works available in English translation. The site is currently undergoing substantial revision to improve its value to researchers.

The Story of Africa (BBC)
http://www.bbc.co.uk/worldservice/africa/features/storyofafrica/

Site Summary. This Web site accompanies two BBC radio broadcasts on African history, conceived, written, and edited by reporter Bola Olufunwa to relate "the history of the continent from an African perspective"; that is, focusing on Africa in terms of the priorities of its people, rather than based on Western perspectives of African achievements. In addition to outstanding cultural and historical materials pertaining to the African continent, the site provides the opportunity to listen to fifteen hours of full-length radio broadcasts. The broadcasts themselves, created by Olufunwa during 2001–2002, provide the perspectives of leading African studies historians, as well as separate overviews of African history.

Navigating the Site. The site is easy to navigate. From the main page, choose the historical period of interest. Subsequent pages are divided into three vertical columns. The left-hand column provides access to other historical periods. The center column provides an overview of the historical period selected, as well as access to the radio broadcasts. The right-hand column provides access to more in-depth coverage of the period. Although not all of the external links work, the links that do work and the valuable information on the site itself more than compensate for any inconvenience.

Discussion Questions and Activities

1. Who writes history? Read the **Living History** pages. According to the Web site's author, what cultural features are most likely to appear in a traditional history of Africa written in a Western country? How might history be conceived differently by people in Africa?

2. The Rosetta Stone. Why was the Rosetta Stone so important to Egyptologists? Go to the **Nile Valley** page, then go to the **Rosetta Stone** page to find out.

3. The Atlantic Slave Trade. To understand early slave narratives, such as those of Olaudah Equiano and Mary Prince, it is important to understand the many manifestations of slavery in Africa and how the transatlantic slave trade was established. Go to the **Slavery** page and read about historical slavery in Africa. See especially the page on the **Atlantic Slave Trade**. What kinds of slavery existed in Africa before Europeans intervened in the early sixteenth century? How did the institution of slavery change, and what was the effect on the cultures of Africa and on the people subjected to Western slavery? For further classroom study of slavery, consider pairing this site with the online book *The Amazing Adventures of Equiano* at International Children's Digital Library at http://www. icdlbooks.org/ (see entry in Chapter 4). At the same site, see also the story *Bildad Kaggia* for an African account of colonial rule and its aftermath in Kenya.

4. African Folklore. At the *Explore Africa* site (below), begin with the lesson plan on *African Arts and Music*, Learning Activity Six, "A Dramatic Tale." Follow the links to the two stories about the Yoruban trickster figure, Anansi. Follow the directions in the lesson plan and choose one of the tales and plan a dramatic production, planning appropriate costumes and set designs. For additional Anansi stories, see the *Jamaica Anansi Stories* archive on the *Sacred Text Archive* at http://www.sacred-texts.com/afr/jas/index.htm. Select a story and adapt the lesson plan accordingly.

Similar/Related Sites

1. *Explore Africa*—http://www.pbs.org/wnet/africa/—Designed primarily for students in grades K–12, this Web site was designed as the companion site for the PBS series. The link **Explore the Regions** leads to a series of pages pertaining specifically to the Sahara, Sahel, Ethiopian Highlands, Savanna, Swahili Coast, Rainforest, Great Lakes, and Southern Africa; these can be explored using a clickable map tool that leads to narratives about the lives of African children, video and audio files, and fact sheets. The **Africa Challenge** link, suited for older students, leads to a fast-paced quiz that covers facts about historical and present-day Africa. The **Photoscope** link leads to photo essays about AIDS, conflict, urban issues, environmental issues, and women in Africa today. **Africa for Kids**, for younger children, leads to a page that includes a photo essay about a young Nigerian boy, an interactive thumb piano, audio and text files of a Swahili folk tale, and a page of mask patterns that is accompanied by a video. The **Teacher Tools** link leads to a series of lesson plans and a teacher's guide. All of the lesson plans are interdisciplinary and include a language arts component.

2. *Africa Focus Database*—http://africafocus.library.wisc.edu/—Created March 1, 2000, and sponsored by the African Studies program at University of Wisconsin-Madison, this Web site provides access to 3,000 slides, 500 photographs, and 50 hours of sound files from across Africa.

3. *Southeast Nigerian Art and Culture*—http://www.siu.edu/~anthro/mccall/jones/—This Web site provides photographic images of the arts and cultures of Ibibio-, Igbo-, Ijo-, and Ogoni-speaking people and would be particularly useful in the study of Chinua Achebe's work. The site also provides images of life in and artifacts of a typical Igbo village.

Asia

See Chapter 5 for sites on Asian religions and belief systems, including Buddhism, Shinto, and Taoism.

Asia for Educators—Literature Pages

http://afe.easia.columbia.edu/

Note: This site can be used in conjunction with the *Electronic Text Center* site, described below.

Site Summary. Still under construction, this outstanding site sponsored by Columbia University provides an extraordinary collection of audio, visual, and textual materials pertaining to Asian studies. Of particular note to librarians, teachers, and students of literature, accessible through the **Time period** navigational menus, are the following resources available on this site:

Literary Resource	Navigation
Shinto Creation Myths	Choose *Time period: 4000 BCE-1000 BCE,* then Links under *Japan: Religion.*
Introduction to Chinese Literature	Choose *Time period: 1000 BCE-300 CE,* then *Introduction to Chinese Literature* under Han Dynasty
Tang Poetry (Wang Wei, Li Bo, and Du Fu); The Chinese Scholar-Official	Choose *Time period: 300-1000 CE,* then under *Tang Poetry Multimedia Unit*
Literature of Classical Japan; The *Manyôshû and Kokinshû Poetry Collections; The Tale of Genji* (also a Multimedia Unit)	Choose *Time period: 300-1000 CE,* then *Society/Literature: Classical Japan*
Literature of Medieval Japan: Tale of Heike (Buddhist), Essays, Japanese Noh Drama	Choose *Time Period: 1000-1500,* then *Literature* (under *Medieval Japan*).
Saikaku (comic novelist); Chikamatsu (dramatist); Bashô (travel narrative and haiku poetry), Bunraku (puppet theatre)	Choose *Time Period: 1450-1770,* then *Literature* (under *Tokugawa/Edo Period*).
Lu Xun, Pearl Buck, Mao Zedong, Autobiography Teaching Guides, Hao Ran (Revolution)	Choose *Time Period: 20th Century,* then *Literature* (under *Republic of China* sections) (For *Autobiography,* see also links under *Topics: Literature: China>Autobiography*).

Navigating the Site. The site is easy to navigate; see above for navigation to literature resources through the timeline. The site is best viewed using Microsoft Explorer 5+ or Netscape Navigator 6+. From the main page, choose the *Literature* link; the topics listed above are accessible through the drop-down menus that appear. To gain full use of this site, explore the following navigational options, organized in drop-down menus to materials sorted by Topic, Type, Time period, or Interdisciplinary topic. Subject areas include art, language, literature, religion and philosophy, geography, population, society and culture, economy and trade, foreign policy and defense, government and politics, inventions/ideas, and history. A few of the sections under *View by file type* are under construction, but substantial materials are available under links to *Key points & central themes, Multimedia units, Timelines, Primary sources*, and *Resource lists.* In addition, cross-disciplinary pages include teaching guides on *Asia in Western and World History, Masterworks of Asian Literature in Comparative Perspective* (organized by nation and genre), and *Asia: Case Studies in the Social Sciences*, as well as featured lesson plans on *The Mongols in World History, The Song Dynasty in China*, and *The Tale of Genji.*

Discussion Questions and Activities

1. Featured Units. Explore the units currently featured; these are located across the bottom of the main page. For instance, the featured units available as of June 2004 included *The*

Mongols in World History; follow the cultural links to information on the Mongols' writing system and primary literature. Another featured unit, *Contemporary Japan*, includes video representations of animé and manga animation. These units change periodically; earlier units can be found by following the hierarchy of links available from the main menu.

2. Tang Poetry. From the subject menu, follow these links to reach a series of pages explaining this important classical Chinese poetic form: **Literature>China: Teaching Units>Classical Literature.**

3. Tale of Genji. *Tale of Genji* was written by Murasaki Shikibu, a lady in waiting in the imperial court during the Heijan period. From the subject menu, follow these links to reach a series of pages and activities/questions about this classical Japanese work: **Literature>Japan: Teaching Units>Classical Japan.**

Similar/Related Sites

1. *AskAsia.org*—http://www.askasia.org/—The Asia Society, founded in 1956 by John D. Rockefeller III, maintains this Web site as a K–12 teaching resource. The Asia society seeks to increase understanding and dialogue between the people of the United States and Asia. Although *AskAsia* is the primary learning resources site for K–12 educators, click on the link labeled **Who We Are** to gain access to six allied Web sites that also provide excellent teaching materials. The *AskAsia* Web site provides extensive resources for teachers, students, and school leaders, including outstanding interdisciplinary lesson plans and links that address both historical and contemporary pedagogical concerns. The **Readings** link from the **Instructional Resources** page provides access to excellent readings pertaining to Asian belief systems, traditional Chinese writing, and the Japanese family. The **Readings** page also offers a detailed lesson plan, "Using Chinese Literature in Translation." The site is easy to navigate. From the main page, locate the navigation bar on the right. Choose either the **Teachers** or Students link, then explore the resources available.

2. *Paul Halsall's Chinese Cultural Studies Materials*

   a. Texts—http://acc6.its.brooklyn.cuny.edu/~phalsall/texts.html—This page provides excerpts from a large number of Chinese texts used by Halsall in his teaching.

3. *Images*—http://acc6.its.brooklyn.cuny.edu/~phalsall/images.html—This page provides links to images, including maps, archaeological artifacts, art, divinities, historical sites, technologies, customs, and stereotypes to accompany Halsall's course at CUNY.

4. Although the following eclectic sites are not set up explicitly for educational purposes, they provide a number of resources that may be helpful in understanding Chinese culture and its influence on literature.

   a. *China the Beautiful, Main Room*—http://www.chinapage.com/china-rm.html

   b. *The China Experience*—http://www.chinavista.com/experience/index.html

The Electronic Text Center—Chinese Texts
http://etext.virginia.edu/
Note: This site may be used in conjunction with the *Asia for Educators* site, described above.

Site Summary. This Web site, established in 1992 by the University of Virginia Library, features 10,000 SGML-coded e-texts and 164,000 images that are accessible to the public. Many other texts are also available on CD-ROM and free of charge in various formats for use with Microsoft Readers and Palm Pilot e-book readers. The site reports that high school students comprise its largest community of users. The Web site is authoritative and provides complete bibliographic and transcription information on the information page that precedes each work. Two sections of this Web site that address Chinese literature are of particular interest to an English-speaking audience.

1. ***Chinese Text Initiative: 300 Tang Poems (Chinese).*** This area of the *Chinese Text Initiative* provides Chinese text as well as Witter Bynner's translations of 310 poems from the Tang period of Chinese history (618–907 B.C.E.), plus an additional ten translations by Arthur Wright from Chinese into English. The site is located at http://etext.lib.virginia.edu/chinese/frame.htm.

2. ***Traditions of Exemplary Chinese Women.*** This new, growing collection, located at http://jefferson.village.virginia.edu/xwomen/intro.html, is dedicated to the study of the *Lienü zhuan* (*Traditions of Exemplary Women*), written by Liu Xiang (77–6 B.C.E.). This site, based on the earliest known Chinese statement about women's education, provides resources such as essays, timelines, maps, themes, and lesson plans pertaining to Chinese and English texts of the following materials:

Core Texts

- Lienü zhuan, *Biographies of Exemplary Women*

Source Texts

- Shi Jing, *Book of Odes*

- Liji, *Book of Rites*

- Mengzi, *Mencius*

- *Biographies of Buddhist Nuns*

In addition to these texts, the site lists additional resources that will be added later.

Navigating the Site. Because no consistent set of navigational links appears on all pages of this Web site, the easiest way to negotiate the University of Virginia's e-text sites is to use the URL of the specific collection (see above).

Discussion Questions and Activities

1. Tang Poetry. Read about the conventions of Tang poetry at http://www.mc.maricopa.edu/dept/d10/asb/asb_china/links/poetry.html, then read several of the Tang poems provided in the *Chinese Text Initiative* site. What evidence of the folk roots of Tang poetry can you locate? Of realistic detail? What concerns do the authors of the poetry express?

2. Traditions of Exemplary Chinese Women. As of this writing, this site was under construction, primarily with the "source texts" in place. To read about two themes pertaining to expectations of women, click ***Themes*** on the circular image map, then follow the resulting links to one of the available themes (at this writing, **childbirth** or **virtues**), then follow the ensuing links.

Similar/Related Sites

1. *Traditional Songs and Stories of the Hua Miao of South West China*—http://www. archives.ecs.soton.ac.uk/miao/songs/index.html—Hosted by the Department of Electronics and Computer Science at the University of Southampton and maintained by Dr. Steven Rake, this Web site hosts the translation and transcription work of a family of Christian missionaries in China.

2. *Ballad of Mulan*—http://www.chinapage.org/mulan.html—This page provides an English translation and a Chinese calligraphic version of the Ballad of Mulan, the basis for the loosely similar Disney film.

National Bunraku Theatre—Osaka

http://osaka.yomiuri.co.jp/bunraku/english/index.htm

Site Summary. This outstanding site is the official site of the Japanese national theater, dedicated to Bunraku puppetry, in Osaka, Japan. The site features extensive photographs of scenes from well-known Bunraku stories, a history of the art form and of the puppets themselves, and detailed information on the puppeteers' costuming and puppet construction.

Navigating the Site. The site is most easily navigated from the frames page. Select a link from the left-hand navigation bar, then navigate the resulting pages using the links that appear on the right.

Discussion Questions and Activities

1. Narrator and Shamisen. What is the role of the narrator and the shamisen in Bunraku puppetry?

2. Puppets and Puppeteers. How are the puppets designed and assembled? What do the traditional head designs signify to theater audiences?

Similar/Related Sites

1. *Puppetry Home Page*—http://www.sagecraft.com/puppetry/traditions/index.html—This Web site provides links to a wide variety of Web sites that document puppetry traditions from around the world.

The Kabuki Story 2001

http://www.lightbrigade.demon.co.uk/index.htm

Site Summary. This project, created for Great Britain's Japan Festival in 2001, was intended to support school programs and was supervised by the London Symphony Orchestra in collaboration with the British Museum and the Scottish Chamber Orchestra. The site was intended to enable school students to explore Edo period Japan through Kabuki theater. Designed to support cross-curricular innovation, the site provides pages on drama, dance, music, literature, language, art, history, religion, and geography. Pages that address historical and social contexts and provide detailed information on Kabuki theater itself are cross-linked with a glossary of terms. The site provides outstanding activities, including exercises for rhythmic development, instruction in the formation of melodies, practice in narrative singing, and assistance with dance construction. The glossary and activities are cross-linked with separate pages that provide images and sound files that illustrate concepts and demonstrate musical instruments.

Navigating the Site. The site is easy to navigate. The site's primary pages are linked from the main page. Words in these pages are linked to the glossary, which links in turn to supporting materials, such as illustrative sounds, scales, and images of musical instruments.

Discussion Questions and Activities

1. History and Social Context. Use the resources on this site to gain an understanding of how Kabuki theater evolved as an art form before moving on to its performance aspects.

2. Production Elements. Follow the **Anatomy of Kabuki** link to learn about such elements as the story, musical elements, dramatic content, dance, costume, makeup, theater design, and relationship between actor and audience.

3. Creative Activities. The activities provided on these pages are an excellent starting point for learning about the underlying elements of Japanese traditional theater. Begin with the rhythm, music, and dance exercises on this Web site, then practice narrative singing, and finally compose a *nagauta* using a familiar story (here the balcony scene in *Romeo and Juliet).*

Similar/Related Sites

1. *Kabuki for Everyone*—http://www.fix.co.jp/kabuki/kabuki.html—This Web site provides photographs of contemporary Kabuki artist Ichimura Manjiro, a Kabuki *onnagata,* or male actor specializing in female Kabuki roles.

2. *Jeff Blair's Kabuki Page*—http://www.aichi-gakuin.ac.jp/~jeffreyb/kabuki.html—This Web site provides plot summaries for a number of Kabuki plays, a detailed timeline, and information on present and past seasons of the Misonoza Theatre in Japan.

The Electronic Text Center—Japanese Texts
Nō Plays
http://etext.lib.virginia.edu/japanese/noh/index.html

Site Summary. This Web site, part of a larger site sponsored since 1992 by the University of Virginia Library, hosts the **Japanese Text Initiative: Nō Plays,** a highly stylized medieval dramatic form that integrates dance, acting, music, and poetry in a drama that includes characters such as gods and supernatural beings, warriors, women, mad figures, and topical characters. This Web site provides an unparalleled Web collection of Nō plays, many with reputable English translations by Royall Tyler, Ezra Pound, and Arthur Whaley. The English and Japanese texts are displayed in English and Japanese in parallel frames.

Navigating the site. Because no consistent set of navigational links appears on all pages of the *Electronic Text Center* Web site, the easiest way to navigate the collections is to use the URL of the specific collection.

Discussion Questions and Activities

1. From the **Nō Plays** main page, read the "Notes on the English Translation." Next, choose the play *Hagoromo,* and then choose the corresponding link to *Japanese and English in Parallel Frames.* Compare the translations by Royall Tyler (1978), Arthur Whaley (1922), and Ezra Pound (1916). How similar are the translations? Characterize some of the key differences. What reasons might the translators have had for making these particular choices?

2. From the *Nō Plays* index page, choose *Technical Terms for Nō Plays,* and study Tyler's notes on staging the plays. Choose a play and stage an informal approximation of the play. What elements of the play are clarified through performance? Which need further research?

3. Read *Aoi No Uye*, a dramatization of a portion of *Tale of Genji* written by Lady Murasaki Shikibu. What folkloristic elements appear in this play? Of Buddhism (for background on Buddhism, see Chapter 5)? Now read *Aya No Tsuzumi* or Zeami Motokiyo's *Kagekiyo*. What elements of folklore appear in this play? Elements relating to Buddhism?

4. What is the place of art, music, dance, and poetry in Nō drama?

Similar/Related Sites

1. *History of the Noh Theater*—http://web-japan.org/museum/noh/noh.html—This page provides an overview of Nō drama, with labeled photographs that diagram the stage.

2. *Noh Dancing*—http://linus.socs.uts.edu.au/~don/pubs/noh.html—Created by Don Herbison-Evans at University of Sidney, this page describes the choreography and masks used in staging No drama.

3. *Noh Masks*—http://www.mis.atr.co.jp/~mlyons/Noh/noh_mask.html —This page shows how the construction of Nō masks allows them to display different expressions depending on the angle of the mask.

4. *Noh-Kyogen Plays*—http://www.iijnet.or.jp/NOH-KYOGEN/english/english.html— This site provides an introduction to Japanese Nō drama, an historical outline, a detailed stage diagram with a keyed legend, photographs of musical instruments with audio files, and costume and mask images.

5. *Noh Project Topics from ArtsEdge*—http://artsedge.kennedy-center.org/content/3418/3418_noh_guide.pdf—This document provides a list of projects pertaining to Nō theater that can be used in the K–12 classroom.

6. *Sano-Noh-Theater Site*—http://shofu.pref.ishikawa.jp/shofu/geinou_e/nougaku/index_e.html —This Web site provides additional information about Nō theater, with excellent images documenting performances at the Sano-Noh Theater.

The Electronic Text Center—Japanese Poetry

Ogura Hyakunin Isshu, or, 100 poems by 100 poets
http://etext.lib.virginia.edu/japanese/hyakunin/index.html
Selected Tanka poetry from Kokinshu
http://etext.lib.virginia.edu/japanese/kokinshu/Cook/CookKok.html/
Selected Haiku and Tanka of Masaoka Shiki
http://etext.lib.virginia.edu/japanese/shiki/beichman/BeiShik.utf8.html
Japanese Haiku Topical Dictionary
http://etext.lib.virginia.edu/japanese/haiku/saijiki/

Site Summary. Most of the Japanese pages on the *Japanese Text Initiative* site are not translated into English; however, several translations of tanka and haiku poetry are worth noting.

The **Ogura Hyakunin Isshu** pages reproduce text and translations of the *Ogura Hyakunin Isshu*, an anthology of 100 tanka poems that is believed to have been created by Fujiwara no Sadaie (Teika) and perhaps his son Fujiwara no Tameie. The poems are arranged chronologically from the seventh through the thirteenth centuries. As indicated in the online introduction to the collection, waka or tanka poems consist of five lines that total thirty-one syllables (arranged 5, 7, 5, 7, 7). In addition to a well-written introduction, the site offers an updated English translation; the Macaulay translation upon which the newer translation was based; a romanized

Japanese text, text in Japanese characters; and an entertaining "Note on the English translation," which explains the rationale for the updated translation and provides seven parallel translations of the same poem to demonstrate the challenges of translating tanka poetry.

Other tanka poetry, *Selected Tanka Poetry from Kokinshû, is provided on a separate set of pages (see URL above), along with commentary by the translator, Lewis Cook.*

Tanka poetry was the dominant poetic form in Japan until haiku became popular in the seventeenth century. The **Masaoka Shiki** page shows this transition, providing translations of selected tanka and haiku poetry, translated by Janine Beichman.

Although largely in Japanese, the pages on **The Haiku Topical Dictionary** site provides seasonal images with English descriptions. To gain access to the images, from the URL provided above, choose the *Images* link, then choose the *image* link below the photograph of interest.

Discussion Questions and Activities

1. Translation.

   a. On the **Ogura Hyakunin Isshu** site, read the "Note on the English translation." The Web site editors provide a parody of a Greek tragedy translation by A. E. Housman. What is Housman's point in this parody? At what is he poking fun?

   b. On the same page, a word-for-word translation is provided of the anthology's thirty-fifth poem, written by Ki no Tsurayuki. What are the barriers to understanding posed by this translation? What does it suggest about the task of the translator? What does it suggest about language? Nine other translations of the same Japanese passage follow. How do they differ? Why?

2. Japanese Poetry and the Haiku Topical Dictionary. Japanese haiku focuses more on presenting intense sensory perceptions of natural phenomena than on complex metaphors or metric devices. What themes and topics come up repeatedly in the Japanese poetry provided on these sites? Make your own list of Japanese poetry that describes such natural phenomena as the heavens, daily life, the earth, animals, and plants (all listed on the introductory page to the topical dictionary). Compare several poems written on a single topic. What elements do the descriptions have in common? What are the differences? Identify the features valued by Japanese poets in their poetry. (See "Similar/Related Sites" below for an overview.)

3. Text and Art. Each of the poems provided in the *Ogura Hyakunin Isshu* is accompanied by a wood-block print, which appeared in an 1867 edition, printed for women. View the text and prints in parallel frames; to view the wood-block print, click on the poem's number. How do the thematic elements of the block prints compare with those of the poetry?

4. Writing Poetry. What are the challenges of writing poetry in Japanese forms? Try the activities that follow to find out.

   a. Tanka. Read the introduction to *Ogura Hyakunin Isshu* for the rules governing tanka poetry. Try writing one yourself.

   b. Haiku. Next, try writing a haiku poem (seventeen syllables total, divided into three lines, with syllables divided 5-7-5).

c. Haikai, or linked poetry. Finally, simulate the seventeenth-century practice of writing poetry communally. (For the cultural history of this practice in Japanese literary culture, see Professor Oxnam's **Matsuo Bashô** pages at http://www.columbia. edu/itc/eacp/asiasite/topics/index.html?topic=Haiku+subtopic=Intro, located on the **Asian Topics** Web site described above.) This activity can be completed with teams (or with more advanced students working in pairs). The first team or individual creates a haiku (three lines, seventeen syllables, divided 5-7-5) and passes the haiku to the second team. The second team adds two lines of seven syllables each to the haiku (the result is a *haikai*) and passes it to another team. The new team begins a new haikai with the two lines added by the second team, and then adds to these three more lines (5-7-5). The next team begins a haikai with the three additional lines, writes two lines (7-7), and so on.

Similar/Related Sites

1. Tanka (waka) poetry

   a. *The Flowering of Japanese Literature*—http://www.wsu.edu:8080/~dee/ ANCJAPAN/ LIT.HTM—Part of the World Civilizations Web site described in Chapter 4, this page provides an excellent overview of the Tokugawa period and the basic assumptions underlying poetic practices.

2. Haiku poetry

   a. *Haiku of Kobayashi Issa*—http://webusers.xula.edu/dlanoue/issa/—Created by Professor David G. Lanoue, this site provides a translation database of 3,500 haiku by Kobayashi Issa (1763–1827), considered a master of the form. Dr. Lanoue also provides online versions of several of his published essays on haiku (see his **About me** page).

   b. *History of Haiku from Mushimegane*—http://www.big.or.jp/~loupe/links/ehisto/ ehisinx.shtml—Written by Ryo Rotsuya, these pages are part of his Web site *Mushimegane*, a literary magazine dedicated primarily to publishing new haiku poetry. The Web site provides a helpful overview of the innovations and practices of historically significant haiku poets and translations of their poetry, including the following:

Bashô Matsuo (1644–1694)	Sekitei Hara (1889–1951)
Buson Yosa (1716–1783)	Hisajo Sugita (1890–1946)
Shiki Masaoka (1867–1902)	Suju Takano (1893–1976)
Kyoshi Takahama (1874–1959)	Kakio Tomizawa (1902–1962)
Ippekiro Nakatsuka (1887–1946)	Koi Nagata (1900–1997)

   c. *Aha! Poetry's Haiku Page*—http://www.ahapoetry.com/haiku.htm—This page provides a series of essays about haiku, both as written traditionally in Japan and as it can be written by English speakers today. The essays by Jane Reichold are especially good; see in particular her essay on progressively building haiku skills. Also, Keiko Imaoka's essay on English haiku provides variations that may be found more suitable for English-speaking poets.

d. *World of Haiku*—http://edsitement.neh.gov/view_lesson_plan.asp?ID=305—Part of the EDSitement project, this Web site provides lesson plans and educational objectives pertaining to the teaching of haiku poetry.

Women's Early Music/Art/Poetry

http://www.womensearlyart.net/reference/poets.html

Site Summary. This eclectic site is part of a larger site dedicated to women in the arts; this portion of it offers a large collection of Japanese women's poetry, music, and art; background context; bibliographies; and assessments of translations in print. The photographs and reproductions of Japanese art that accompany the poetry are stunning. The pages on individual authors and artists are extensively cross-linked with resources and translations located on other Web sites.

Navigating the Site. From this page, which is a chronologically organized site map, navigation is easy, although the directional navigational arrows on connecting pages are inconsistent and sometimes counterintuitive. For easiest navigation, use the *Back* button on your browser.

Discussion Questions and Activities

1. Poetry and Art. Japanese poetry and art are closely linked. Analyze a poem and identify how the figurative language it includes captures the essence of the object or phenomenon described.

Similar/Related Sites

1. *Universes in Collision: Men and Women in 19th-century Japanese Prints*—http://viva. lib.virginia.edu/dic/bayly/docs/top.html—This Web site accompanied a 1997 art exhibit at the Bayly Art Museum depicting men and women in conflict. Prints are accompanied by thematically linked poetry. Although viewing the virtual exhibit requires special software, the commentary can be viewed using a standard browser, as can the exhibited art and poetry (view it wall by wall).

Teaching (and Learning) About Japan

http://www.csuohio.edu/history/japan/index.html

Site Summary. Created by Professor Lee Makela of Cleveland State University, this comprehensive Web site provides insight into Japanese culture, with special attention to the ways in which visual literacy shapes Japanese thought. Particularly valuable is Professor Makela's visual literacy exercise, which demonstrates how Japanese block prints depict both Japanese life and attitudes toward surroundings. This exercise is extremely useful in understanding the preoccupations expressed in Japanese poetry. Makela's presentation, *Beyond Stone and Moss: The Japanese Garden in Its Cultural Context*, provides outstanding guidance on interpreting the Japanese garden, which emulated and served as an inspiration for poetry and a location in which Nō plays were performed and poetry contests were held. The *Aspects of Popular Culture* page, which features an image from Hayao Miyazaki's film *My Neighbor Totoro*, provides links to pages that explore contemporary Japanese animé and manga, an artform growing in popularity worldwide. The *Traditional Theatre* page provides overviews of dance forms such as Gagaku, theater forms such as Nō and Kabuki, and traditional puppetry such as Bunraku.

Navigating the Site. Begin by paging through the main features of the site. From the main page, choose each of the three linked images at the bottom. Next, page through the site's overview pages by choosing *Forward* at the bottom of each page. Finally, return to the index page and select the links to the materials of greatest interest. Broken links can be circumvented by clicking on the *Page Index* link and then selecting the next page in the sequence.

Discussion Questions and Activities

1. Visual Literacy Exercise. Page through the *Visual Literacy Exercise* to gain insight into the thematic material treated in Japanese art, but also in Japanese literature. What preoccupations do you note? Which images are displayed in many images?

2. Nature and Gardening. Page through the *Japanese Garden* pages to gain a conceptual knowledge of the interrelationship among art, landscape gardening, and literature. What elements of a Japanese garden appear to be reflected as well in Japanese poetry?

Similar/Related Sites

1. *Virtual Museum of the Japanese Arts*—http://web-japan.org/museum/perform.html —This comprehensive site provides overviews and photographs of Japanese fine arts, performing arts, martial arts, crafts, and pastimes. The **Performing Arts** pages include discussions and photographs of Nō and Kyogen drama, Kabuki theater, Bunraku puppet theater, and Japanese traditional vocal music and dance. The Kabuki portion of this site is particularly rich in images.

The Animé Café
http://www.abcb.com/index.htm

Site Summary. This Web site, created in 1997 and edited by Akio Nagatomi and Jane Nagatomi, is an excellent introduction to animé, or Japanese film animation, extremely popular today among children and adults worldwide. The site also provides materials on manga, Japanese print animation. Although not all areas of the site are completely current, the site is regularly maintained. Particularly useful features include the **Café Reviews** page, which provides rating criteria and reviews of feature films, television series, and manga through 2002, sorted by title and genre. The **Parent's Guide** page provides synopses and astute analyses of films, indicating recommended age restrictions and details concerning potentially objectionable or difficult content. The **Encyclopedia** page explains concepts and Japanese terms associated with animé. The **Café Trivia** page provides 359 trivia questions to challenge animé fans. The **Café Latte** page provides a humorous take on animé as a genre with "The Laws of Animé" and "All I've Ever Learned, I've Learned from Anime." The **Café Espresso** page provides reviews, essays, interviews, and general information. Finally, the **Forum** page is a bulletin board with a number of different threads and recent posts.

Navigating the Site. The site is well designed and easy to navigate. Use the navigation links on the left to reach the site's main features. On second-level pages, the same navigation links appear on the left, while pages that further subdivide the topic appear on the right.

Discussion Questions and Activities

1. Start with "A Beginner's Guide to Animé" (select the link to *Café Espresso*, then locate the link to this page under "Guides"). What kinds of animé exist? In what ways do animé plots differ from the plots of American films?

2. How does animé depict roles of men and women? How might these reflect the values of Japanese culture? Read Eri Izawa's essay on "Gender Relations in Manga and Anime" for an accessible view of this topic. How might these ideas be adapted to explain the popularity of Japanese animé in contemporary American culture?

3. On the **Café Latte** page, locate the link to the satiric **Laws of Animé** page. View a few episodes of an animé television series (a number are listed in the "Beginner's Guide," or tune into the Cartoon Network on cable television for an hour or so). How accurate are the "Laws of Animé" in describing some of the characteristics of the genre?

4. Review Manfred Jahn's guidelines for film analysis on his Web site *Poems, Plays, and Prose: A Guide to the Theory of Literary Genres* (see Chapter 3). Then watch a recent Hayao Miyazaki film. What techniques of traditional filmmaking does Miyazaki use in his animated features? What additional criteria must be considered when analyzing an animated versus a traditional film?

Similar/Related Sites

1. *Rei's Anime and Manga Page*—http://web.mit.edu/rei/www/Anime.html—Maintained by Massachusetts Institute of Technology affiliate Eri Izawa, this Web site provides a large number of essays, most written by Eri Izawa, providing excellent background materials to a number of animé films.

2. *Hayao Miyazaki Web*—http://www.nausicaa.net/miyazaki/. This Web site provides a large number of fact sheets and FAQs pertaining specifically to Miyazaki's films and career.

3. *Librarian's Guide to Animé*—http://www.koyagi.com/Libguide.html—Created by a librarian for librarians, this Web site offers excellent definitions and resources for satisfying patron requests and locating additional information about animé.

4. *The Animé Turnpike*—http://www.anipike.com—Widely cited as an indispensable resource for information on animé, this site is unabashedly commercial and somewhat difficult to use. Nevertheless, it provides insight into the extent to which animé has become firmly embedded in the cultural landscape of the industrialized world.

Latin America

For materials on ancient Mesoamerican glyphs, writing, and códices, see Chapter 6.

Guaman Poma de Ayala's *El Primer Nueva Corónica y Buen Gobierno*
http://www.kb.dk/elib/mss/poma/index-en.htm

Site Summary. Sponsored by the Royal Library in Denmark, this Web site provides online images of Guaman Poma de Ayala's *New Chronicle and Good Government*. This remarkable document is a 1,200-page letter, with almost 400 drawings, written roughly fifty years after the Spanish Conquest by a native Inca to King Philip III of Spain. The goal of Poma's letter was to persuade the King of Spain to modify the frequently brutal manner in which Spain ruled its conquered territories. Although the document languished for centuries in a Danish archive, its recent explication by comparative literature professor Mary Louise Pratt has established its importance in postcolonial studies as an outstanding example of how colonized peoples create new forms of expression by combining earlier traditional materials with the newly introduced materials and writing technologies of the colonizer. Although the document is written in a combination of Spanish and Quechua (the language of the Incas), the drawings in the book provide a fascinating and unique representation of Incan life under Spanish rule, from the perspective of the conquered.

Navigating the Site. The site is easy to navigate. From the main page for this document, click the *Title Page* link. Navigational links on the left permit the user to page through the document or to move directly to a specific page. Page images appear in the frame on the right. An additional set of navigation links appears at the bottom. For non-Spanish speakers, the most useful links include *Table of Drawings, Essay*, and *Links*.

Discussion Questions and Activities

1. Begin by reading some of the available background materials relating to Poma's work.

    a. Begin with the *Essay* link, which appears at the bottom of the page; this link brings up a background essay written by Yale University Professor Rolena Adorno.

    b. Indispensable for interpreting Guaman Poma de Ayala's images and their iconography is Mary Louise Pratt's essay, "Arts of the Contact Zone," which is available at http://web.nwe.ufl.edu/~stripp/2504/pratt.html and in *Profession* 1991, a publication of the MLA. Pratt's essay explains how Poma's images attempt to combine the words and images of his Spanish conquerors with symbols from his own culture. (For an alternative view, see Tom Cummins's article, which is accessible on the *Links* page.) Read Pratt's essay and locate the corresponding images in Poma's work. Then compare the images Pratt "reads" with other images in the book. How does Poma use the images of both cultures to make his point?

2. Many of Poma's images portray the savage conditions under which conquered peoples lived during the colonial period in South America. Locate images that depict the lives of Incan people under Spanish rule.

Similar/Related Sites

1. For another illustrated view of the results of the Spanish Conquest in South America, see the following site that reproduces images of deBry's illustrations of Bartolomé de las Casas's *Brevísima relación de la destrucción de las Indias*, or *Brief Relation of the Destruction of the Indies*

    a. *Colonization and Print in the Americas*—http://www.library.upenn.edu/exhibits/rbm/kislak/viewers/debrylc3.html

2. *Myths and Dreams: Exploring the Cultural Legacies of Florida and the Caribbean*—http://www.jayikislakfoundation.org/millennium-exhibit/author1.htm—This site provides essays about pre- and postcolonial cultures of Florida and the Caribbean. In particular, the site provides a number of essays about the region's religious, ethnic, and racial composition.

Other Latin American Sites

Few Web sites that consider contemporary Latin American poetry and are translated into English have been stable over the past four years; however, here is a small collection devoted to the work of specific writers. Although many are not of sufficient depth to be considered for separate entries, considered together they may be of use to students and teachers seeking information on the work of these important writers.

Pablo Neruda (1904–1973, Chile)—http://sunsite.dcc.uchile.cl/chile/misc/odas.html

Isabel Allende (1942–, Chile)—http://www.isabelallende.com/

Near (Middle) East

For early writing of the Near(Middle) East, see Chapter 5 for sites that address writing associated with Judaism, Christianity, and Islam. For materials associated with early Sumerian and Egyptian writing, see Chapter 6.

The Electronic Literature Foundation
The Arabian Nights
The Rubaiyat of Omar Khayyam
http://www.arabiannights.org/

Site Summary. Sponsored by the Electronic Literature Foundation, this Web site provides complete translations two classics of Near Eastern literature. It provides an excellent user interface; translations and commentary by Lang and Burton; and a scholarly essay, written by Daniel Beaumont of University of Rochester, which details the origins of the works. The first work is the classic *Alf Layla Wa Layla*, translated as *A Thousand Nights and a Night*, a collection of Indian, Arabic, and Persian folk tales narrated by the fictional Princess Scheherazade, whose story serves as the framing narrative. This work is known variously to English-speaking audiences, in translation, as *The Arabian Nights*. Included on this site are translations by Andrew Lang and Sir Richard Burton, still among the most respected translations into English. The second work presented on this site is *The Rubaiyat of Omar Khayyam*, presented here in five editions, all translated by Edward Fitzgerald. Written as separate poems in a lesser stanzaic form known as the *rubai* (epigrammatic quatrains), Fitzgerald's famous translation connects the work of other poets with verses written as independent poems by Omar Khayyam, a poet better known in his own culture as an astronomer and scientist.

Navigating the Site. The site is easy to navigate. Use the navigational toolbar on the left to select a translation, a particular tale, and the number of lines to display.

Discussion Questions and Activities

1. *The Arabian Nights*

    a. Begin with the introductory article by Professor Beaumont (on the navigation bar in the left frame, click the ***Article*** link). What are the earliest known sources of the stories that make up *The Arabian Nights*? From what versions do our current translations derive? What are its antecedents? Why do we have more than one version of the work?

    b. Read the beginning of the framing narrative. Why does the Sultan marry and kill a new wife every day? Why does Scheherazade marry the sultan? What narrative strategy does she use to keep the sultan from killing her?

    c. Read the remainder of the framing narrative and a number of the stories. What roles are played by women? What social positions do they occupy? If they do not possess overt authority, what strategies do they use to negotiate the situations presented in the stories?

d. Identify characters who represent religion, magic, and the supernatural in the stories. What role do religion and magic appear to play in the cultures represented by the stories?

e. For younger students, see an online storybook version of *The Arabian Nights* at the International Children's Digital Library at http://www.icdlbooks.org/ (see entry in Chapter 4).

2. *The Rubaiyat of Omar Khayyam*

a. Omar Khayyam has been variously described as a Sufi poet (see *Rumi.org.uk* below) and as a pleasure-seeking skeptic. What elements of each can you detect in *The Rubaiyat of Omar Khayyam?*

b. *The Rubaiyat of Omar Khayyam* has been described as embodying the carpe diem motif (translated from Latin as "seize the day") . What elements in the poem support this description?

Similar/Related Sites

1. *The Arabian Nights*—http://www.library.cornell.edu/colldev/mideast/arabnit.htm— This Web site offers another rendition of Sir Richard Burton's *Arabian Nights* translation.

2. *Arab Gateway—Literature Page*—http://www.al-bab.com/arab/literature/lit.htm— Although this site now has many broken links, it includes some useful pages describing Arabic art, music, language, and literature, as well as poetry translations. The literature pages also include background material on Arabic literary history, major writers, and links to advice about teaching Arab literature.

3. *The Epic of Kings (Ferdowsi/Firdausi)*—http://etext.library.adelaide.edu.au/f/f52ek/ —This University of Adelaide Web site provides Helen Zimmern's full-text translation, from Persian, of this compilation of heroic literature, folk tales, and poetry.

4. *Turkish Legends and Poetry*—http://www.fordham.edu/halsall/source/turkishpoetry1. html—This page provides an historical analysis of the Persian and Arabic influences on Turkish poetry, as well as a number of English translations of poetry. Particularly well represented is the gazel and the rubai.

5. *The Book of Dede Korkut*—http://sircasaray.turkiye.org/anadolu/myth/dede.html—Part of the Turkish mythology area of *Sircasaray*, this page provides access to the Turkish national epic, *The Book of Dede Korkut*.

6. *Popular Arab Literature of the Jews*—http://www.uwm.edu/~corre/judeo-arabic2.html —Maintained by Alan Corre, professor emeritus at the University of Wisconsin, Milwaukee, this page offers translations of literature written and/or studied by Jews living in Arab territories over the past 2000 years.

Middle Eastern Mystical (Sufi) Poetry

Rumi.org.uk
http://rumi.org.uk/

Site Summary. Edited by Nihat Tsolak, this Web site is by far the most complete site on Middle Eastern Sufi poetry, particularly the poetry of thirteenth-century writer Rumi. The site includes translations by volunteer contributors into a number of languages, as well as resources for studying Rumi's poetry; the English translations are largely quoted from previously published books. The site also provides a biography; a description of Sufism; background information on Islam; and biographies and translations of poetry written by other Sufi poets, including Hafiz, Kabir, Yunus Emre, Mulla Nasrudin, and Idris Shah. The site also offers a large number of excellent quality recordings of meditational music associated with Sufism.

Navigating the Site. The site is easy to navigate. From the main page, consult the list of navigational links on the left-hand side of the main page, then choose a language.

Discussion Questions and Activities

1. Like the biblical *Song of Solomon*, Sufi poetry refers to the Sufi's relationship to the supreme being as akin to that between an individual and his or her beloved. Read the *Divani Shams* of Rumi and compare them to the *Song of Solomon*. What similarities are apparent?

2. Compare The *Rubaiyat of Rumi* with *The Rubaiyat of Omar Khayyam*, a work more widely known among Western audiences. What structural characteristics and themes do they have in common?

Similar/Related Sites

1. *Love and Yearning: Mystical and Moral Themes in Persian Poetry and Painting* —http://www.asia.si.edu/exhibitions/online/loveyearning/—This Web site is the online companion site for an exhibition of works from the Freer Gallery of Art and the Arthur M. Sackler Gallery of the Smithsonian Institution and from the Textile Museum. The site provides beautiful page images of illuminated poetry, background music, written commentary, and voice-over narration. Viewing the site requires Flash 6 or above.

2. Rumi. The following sites provide additional poetry written by Rumi.

    a. *Rumionfire*—http://www.rumionfire.com/—This site, maintained by Shahriar Shahriari, provides Shahriari's translations of Rumi's *Divan-e-Shams, Mathnavi*, and other miscellaneous poetry. Although this is an attractive sites, the translations were not evaluated and should be used with care.

    b. *Dar-al-Masnavi*—http://www.dar-al-masnavi.org/—This site provides full-text translations of Rumi's poetry, as well as background information.

3. Hafiz. The following sites provide a sampling of the poetry written by Hafiz, a fourteenth-century Iranian Sufi poet.

    Life & Love Poetry—http://www.hafizonlove.com/—This site, maintained by Shahriar Shahriari, provides Shahriari's translations of Hafiz's *Ghazaliyat, Rubaiyat*, and other miscellaneous poetry. Although this is an attractive site, the translations were not evaluated and should be used with care.

    Iran-Online's Hafiz page—http://www.iranonline.com/literature/index-hafez.html— This page is provided by the Iran Online, sponsored by Manou & Associates, a partnership of Iranian computing and marketing professionals. The page provides translations of a few poems by Hafiz, a brief biography, and an overview of Hafiz's contribution to Sufi thought.

    Hafiz—http://www.intratext.com/X/ENG0211.HTM —This full-text translation by Gertrude Lowthian Bell (1898) is part of the Intratext Digital Library.

4. *Sa'di—The Gulistan of Sa'di*—http://www. intratext.com/X/ENG0160.HTM—This full-text translation by Sir Edwin Arnold (1899) is part of the Intratext Digital Library.

5. *Ferdowsi (Ferdausi)—The Epic of Kings*—Known as the Persian national epic, a no-frills version this work, translated by Helen Zimmern (1883), is available as part of the *Sacred Text Archive* (see Chapter 5).

Other Near (Middle) Eastern Sites

Few Web sites that consider contemporary Near Eastern poetry and are translated into English have been stable over the past four years; however, here is a small collection that may suggest the variety of perspectives currently available on the Internet. Although many are not of sufficient depth to be considered for separate entries, considered together they may be of use to students and teachers seeking to gain insight into the concerns of Near Eastern peoples today.

Writer's Corner

http://www.art-arena.com/literature.htm

This Web site provides English translations of short stories, poetry, and excerpts from books by Near Eastern writers Mahmud Kianush and Pari Mansouri. Particularly interesting on this site are depictions of terrorism in some of Pari Mansouri's short stories.

Zan=Women

http://www.zan.org/antholo.html

This Web site exists to provide a forum for literature and essays written by Iranian women, many living outside Iran. The site claims to be open to Iranian women of all persuasions and publishes work expressing the concerns of women living in Iran today. Begin by reading some of the essays online at *Zan=Women*, then read some of the women's poetry. What issues appear to concern the women whose writing is published on the site? How are they similar to or different from the issues that concern women elsewhere? Next, on the *Writer's Corner* site, read some of the poetry and short stories that deal with terrorism and attempt to represent the concerns of people living with and experiencing terrorism. (For example, see Pari Mansouri's short story "The Glass Marbles" and any of the many poems listed on the World Poetry page.) What are some of the effects on people, both in the United States and in the Near East, of living with terrorism?

Contemporary Turkish Literature in Translation

http://www.turkish-lit.boun.edu.tr/

Turkish Poetry in Translation

http://www.cs.rpi.edu/~sibel/poetry/

These Web sites provide English-language biographies and translations of poetry written by Turkish poets Gulten Akin, Akgün Akova, Melih Cevdet Anday, Ahmad Arif, Osdemir Asaf, Ece Ayhan, Cuneyt Ayral, Ataol Behramoglu, Ilhan Berk, Edip Cansever, Fazil Husnu Daglarca, Ahmet Muhip Diranas, Metin Cengiz, Tevfik Fikret, Nazim Hikmet, Izzet Goldeli, Turkan Ildeniz, Attila Ilhan, Ozdemir Ince, Orhan Veli Kanik, Cahit Kulebi, Ozkan Mert, Ayten Mutlu, Behcet Necatigil, Kaan Ozbayrak, Oktay Rifat, Cemal Sureya, and Ulku Tamer.

South Asia

For textual materials pertaining to Buddhism, Hinduism, and Islam, see Chapter 5.

The Ramayana Project

http://www.maxwell.syr.edu/southasiacenter/Ramayana/index.asp

Site Summary. The product of two academic institutes focusing on *The Ramayana* under the leadership of Syracuse University's Dr. Susan Wadley, this outstanding site provides an excellent starting point for teachers of all levels. The site is hosted by Syracuse University through funding by the National Endowment for the Humanities and the American Forum for Global Education. The site features several versions of the epic *Ramayana*, one illustrated for younger students, a second providing the outline of the story and identifying its characters, and a third providing a longer summary of the epic. In addition, the site offers images of the *Ramayana* as conceived by artists and in performance; an explanatory page outlining the moral dilemmas presented in the *Ramayana*, a page describing oral tradition and variations of the story, a page introducing some of the basic concepts of Hinduism for a Western audience, a page offering excellent ancillary links and resources to aid teachers in bringing the *Ramayana* to their students, and page images from Bengali scrolls.

Navigating the Site. The primary site features are available from the links on the main page.

Discussion Questions and Activities

1. Epic. *The Ramayana* is the national epic of India and tells the story of Prince Rama. Compare Prince Rama's actions and dilemmas with those of other epic heroes, such as Beowulf (*Beowulf*), Achilles (*The Iliad*), Odysseus (*The Odyssey*), and Aeneas *(The Aeneid)*. In what ways are these heroes similar and different? Their choices and actions? What differences can be ascribed to the cultures in which these epic heroes maneuver?

2. Dharma. One of the primary didactic purposes of *The Ramayana* is its insistence that, regardless of the dilemmas facing them, characters should remain true to their *dharma*, a complex concept that embodies a worldview in which characters strive to act correctly according to expectations surrounding the roles into which they are born. Prince Rama is the heir apparent. Part of his *dharma* reflects this role, yet this role is in conflict with other equally (if not more) important roles as husband and son. Princess Sita similarly must negotiate conflicting demands to live according to her *dharma*. The same is true of other characters. Read *The Ramayana* and identify expectations placed on the characters based on their various positions and roles. What are the *dharmas* of Prince Rama and Princess Sita, and how successful are they in fulfilling them? What characters represent failure to live according to their *dharmas*? Compare these expectations with those levied on other epic characters. (One particularly productive exercise might be to compare Princess Sita with female characters in *Beowulf*, such as Hrothgar's wife Wealtheow.)

Similar/Related Sites

1. *Ask Asia Materials*—http://www.askasia.org/teachers/Instructional_Resources/Lesson_Plans/India/LP_india_5.htm—This page provides a lesson plan that describes how the *Ramayana* instructs its audience to find and live according to their dharma, or according to the moral codes and with the appropriate spiritual discipline, as described in sacred Hindu teaching. The lesson plan links to a comic book version of the *Ramayana*, located at http://www.askasia.org/adult_free_ zone/virtual_gallery/exhibitions/index.htm.

2. *Bhaghavad-Gita- (Sanskrit, 1st c. B.C.E.)*—http://www.wsu.edu:8080/~dee/ANCINDIA/GITA.HTM—Part of the larger "Western Civilizations" course created online at Washington State University, this site provides a partial translation of the Bhaghavad-Gita.

3. *Manas—India and Its Neighbor*—http://www.sscnet.ucla.edu/southasia/—This Web site provides general information pertaining to the culture, politics, and religions of India.

4. *Hindi: The Language of Songs*—http://www.cs.colostate.edu/~malaiya/hindiint.html—This Web site provides extensive links and pages on Hindi cinema, literature, songs, and history, in English translation, with background information on artists, and a number of sound files.

Other South Asian Sites

The Complete Site on Mahatma Gandhi
http://www.mkgandhi.org/

This Web site publishes online the entire corpus of written works attributed to the extraordinarily important Indian figure Mahatma Gandhi, including his letters, interviews, essays, etc. About a key figure in the humanities as a proponent of nonviolent resistance, this Web site of primary written materials is extremely important. Begin by tracing the evolution of Gandhi's key concept, *satyagraha*. Use the search engine to locate references to *satyagraha* in Gandhi's works. What ideas does this concept seem to embody? How did it evolve as an idea over time?

Index

Site Index

About the Author

ROXANNE KENT-DRURY is an Associate Professor in the Literature and Language Department at Northern Kentucky University, where she teaches courses in early world literature, seventeenth- and eighteenth-century transatlantic and British literature, and the literature of early exploration and travel. She is also a frequent reviewer for Addison-Wesley-Longman, most recently on its cultural studies-based anthologies of British and world literature. Her publications include articles on exploration and travel, eighteenth-century drama and performance, and professional writing. Most recently, she co-authored a book essay with Gordon Sayre, *"Robinson Crusoe's* Parodic Intertextuality,"* for the Modern Language Association's *Teaching Robinson Crusoe*, forthcoming in March 2005.